T

OF SOMALIA

THE INVENTION
OF SOMALIA

EDITED BY
ALI JIMALE AHMED

The Red Sea Press, Inc.
Publishers & Distributors of Third World Books

P.O. Box 1892

P.O. Box 48

Trenton, NJ 08607

Asmara, ERITREA

The Red Sea Press, Inc.
11-D Princess Rd.
Lawrenceville, NJ 08648

First Printing 1995

Book & Cover design: Jonathan Gullery

Library of Congress Cataloging-in-Publication Data

The invention of Somalia / edited by Ali Jimale Ahmed
      p. cm.
    Includes bibliographical references (p.)
    ISBN 0-932415-98-9. - - ISBN 0-932415-99-7 (pbk.)
     1. Somalia- -Politics and government. 2. Somalia- -Ethnic relations. 3. Clans- -Somalia. I. Ahmed, Ali Jimale.
DT403.25.I58   1995
967.7305 - - dc20
                                     94-37232
                                      CIP

This book is composed in New Baskerville and ITC Kabel Ultra.

CONTENTS

To all Somalis who, despite overwhelming odds and a pervasive sense of pessimism, still believe in the "optimism of the will"

PREFACE

Upon one body
Double heads opposing chop-
Stick beaks in order,
Peck peck pecking off to death
One bird:both heads and body.
— *Translated by Sam Houston Brock, qtd. in Donald Keene,*
Anthology of Japanese Literature

Siyaad Barre's ouster from power not only unleashed an internecine fighting among Somali clans, but also revealed the "hidden" class character of urban areas like Mogadishu. Yet, while different clan-based militias were fighting in the streets of the capital, youngsters belonging to the same warring clans organized themselves under the rubric of *mooryaan*. The term is from classical Somali and refers to the have-nots or to a group of people who are robbed of their property. The city's lumpen -shoe shine boys, pickpockets, displaced rural kids high on arabic gum (cola formica), in short, street urchins, formed the bulk of the *Mooryaan*. The term, therefore, is not as Maxamed D. Afrax explains, "a new Somali word invented to refer to the armed thugs who indulge in murder and extortion."[1] Nor does the origin of the word have any etymological affinity with marijuana, as suggested to this writer by many Somali informants. (Interestingly enough, no one has suggested that *mooryaan* might perhaps have something in common with the Nilotic word *morane.* The two words may shed light on the relationship and complexities of African initiation forms as they pertain to circumcision, age-group, and the overall processes through which boys become men.)

However, in the general scheme of things, the misdefinition of a word like *mooryaan*, one could argue, has a nugatory impact on the over all devastations and deprivations wrought on Somalia by the civil war. On the other hand, such misdefinition has deep implications for the civil war as it sheds some light on the Somalist scholar's inability to have discerned the formation and gathering of war clouds on the horizon. Most Somalists have relied heavily on what Roland Barthes had called the "monitorial mode" of history. In other words, pioneer scholars on Somalia based their writings on information gathered from politically conscious informers. Of course, a scholar's own analysis of the data remolds the information made available to him/her by informers. However, we must remember that such information at the disposal of the scholar is not impartial. The absence of impartiality, in and of itself, is no fault of the scholar's. After all, different informers give out different pieces of information. A scholar's writing, however, becomes counterproductive, I believe, if he/she becomes complacent with a single version of any reported event. Such complacency could become a travesty of scholarship when other scholars only glean information from past texts. It is here that Afrax's definition of *Mooryaan* poses the threat of becoming its own institutionalized quotation for future scholars.

In other words, as the sociopolitical reality of the war fades from the horizon of human memory, so too will the class content of a word like *mooryaan*. Future generations will be cheated out of the real reasons young armed thugs indulged in murder and extortion in the distant past of the 1990s. They would not know, for example, that these armed thugs were for a long time denizens on the margins who, when the time came, started to exact a vendetta on their compatriots on the greener side of the fence. In a poem by this writer published in 1981 in the English Weekly *Heegan*, a homeless woman with three kids on the curb-side of Croce del Sud (a fancy part of pre-war Mogadishu) vows that her kids will one day avenge her humiliation. The *Mooryaan* thugs could perhaps represent generically the protagonist's embittered kids. It is also here that the *Mooryaan* kids have something in common with the *Boheme* in Walter Benjamin's *Charles Baudelaire: A Lyric Poet in the Era of High Capitalism*. They both trace their origin to "[t]he brutal, starved, envious, wild Cain."[2] (Incidently, Cain's name reminds one of the scriptural genesis of the pastoral/peasant dichotomy—another dimension of the Somali civil war.) The *Mooryaan* are now living out their rancor in the era of high anarchic season midwifed, as always, by kleptocratic goons.

But there is also a more practical reason for using Afrax as the straw man. As one of the most astute critics of Somali sociopolitical and literary scene, Afrax's misdefinition of *mooryaan* reveals the locus of the Somali predicament. Definitions formulated by experts contribute to our conceptions of a defined word's outside referent. Somalia as a textual construction by scholars and explorers has turned out to be different from the "real" thing. From Burton to Lewis and beyond, the Somali has ritually become associated with a multiplicity of externally and home-grown duplicitous phrases (tropes): pastoral democracy, oratorical excellence, poetical ingenuity, static clan structures and various forms of androcentric metaphors. These phrases have over the years acquired official status. It was no wonder therefore that the civil war took many people by surprise.

Available scholarship on Somalia has hitherto revealed its inability to explain, much less anticipate, the purulent discharge which has followed Siyaad Barre's ouster. The reasons, as mentioned above, are many, but one deserves special analysis as it shows the locus of the problem. In their attempt to understand clan and clan politics in the Somali scene, scholars have formulated two diametrically opposed views of the same system. On the one hand, there are those who diminish its role to that of a social club where clan—as a concept—transcends the travesties perpetrated in its name. In this sense, clan is *Tol*-that which binds, literally that which sews together. Implicit in this view is the notion that clan represents a primordial identity, or, as Edward Said would put it, "the first intelligibility" of a group. The proponents of this concept believe that the acquisition of other forms of intelligibility through means outside the clan system will make it possible for some to see clanism for what it is. For the contributors of this volume—while accepting the major premise of this logic— however, things are not that easy. It is difficult to just slip through its horns. One has to deal with it realistically. Ahmed Samatar's new edited book is a step towards the right direction.

Opposed to the thinking of the first group is that which tells us of the inevitability of living with the pernicious side of the clan system. Clan, in this school of thought, is depicted as if it were static. This thinking ignores the dialectical nature of reality in which the social/political relations which nurture the kin corporate system are continually challenged by new realities. Both schools of thought have, for the most part, utilized the official narrative. Yet, the narrative that has eluded both sides is the unofficial one, the one which is now being written in blood. It is here that Basil Davidson deserves our gratitude for having mustered the courage to reexamine the trail Africanist scholarship, especially historiographical, had traveled in the last 3 or 4 decades. *The Black Man's Burden:Africa and the Curse of the Nation State* is an appropriate elegy to the now disregarded and bankrupt [read official] narrative of Africa's ruling elites. The book must also be read as a challenge to Africanist scholars to reinvent themselves and hone their tools of research as old roads taken thus far have come to an epistemological cul-de-sac. Ironically Davidson's book invokes the spirit of John Killens' *Black Man's Burden* written some 30 years ago as a pedagogical response to an epistemological dead end. A father in Killens' book tells his bewildered son that stories "about various life-and-death struggles between a man and lion...will always end like that [i.e.,the man beating the lion] until the lion learns how to write."[3] The lion's version of what had happened in history has, in Somalia and beyond, for a long time, belonged to an underground narrative.

This volume is important for two reasons. First, we agree with Holcomb's and Ibssa's assertions in *The Invention of Ethiopia* that "no available treatment of the history of [Somalia] dealt adequately with the factors that shaped [Somalia], that is, factors that generated the political and economic relations still found there and which account for the conflict currently raging within [Somalia]."[4] The essays in this volume deconstruct the Somali myth in order to analyze the factors which had contributed to the construction of the old Somalia. Secondly, this volume is important in that it attempts to re-imagine a Somali community which, as Renan argued, ought to "forget its past before it can begin to reconstitute itself."[5]

The essays in the volume were all solicited. With the exception of the essays by Christopher Ehret and Ali Jimale Ahmed, all of the articles in this volume were read as part of the "Invention of Somalia" seminars (at the ASA in Seattle 1992 and in Boston 1993 and also at the Somali Studies Association in Worcester 1993). My gratitude goes to all the contributors of the Seminars. It was the first time that such a distinguished group of scholars gathered to dissect the Somali past with the express aim of separating the seed from the chaff. No editor could have asked for a better group to work with. On behalf of the contributors, I would like to thank the audiences we have had in those three cities. Needless to say that their spirited and engaging discussions helped us to refine our thinking. To mention only a few would be counterproductive.

Amina Shariff and Omar Enow—two promising young scholars—deserve a special mention. Both scholars read their papers at the SSA in Worcester. Unfortunately, their contributions were by then late to include in the proceedings. However since the last chapter on the invention of Somalia has yet to be written (this volume is only a modest beginning), I am certain that Amina's and Enow's contributions would find space in future volumes.

To Kassahun Checole, our publisher, who, from the very beginning believed in this project, goes my sincere gratitude. Thanks also to Ginny Hill of the Red Sea Press for being such a wonderful editor to work with. Also at the Press, my gratitude goes to Pam and Martin for going out of their way to accommodate my incessant queries. I am grateful to Taddesse Adera with whom I have co-edited a volume on Ethiopian literature (while another book on the literatures of the Horn is on its way) for his friendship; to Hussein Adam, Ahmed Samatar, John Johnson, Edmond Keller, Giorgio Banti, Annarita Puglielli, Shinjiro Kobayashi, Said Samatar, Charles Geshekter, Yonas Admassu, Razak Ahmed and Maxamed D. Afrax for their undying support.

I would also like to thank my colleagues at Queens College and at the Graduate Center of the City University of New York for their suggestions and/or moral support: David Kleinbard, Clare Carroll, Chuck Martin, Burton Pike, Joel Lidov, Susan Spectorsky, Ammiel Alcalay, Tadessa Araya, Isabella Bertelotti, Tesfaye Asfaw, Hratch Zadoian, Ray Erickson, Ofuatey-Kodjoe, Jose Kozer, Gopal Sukhu, Carolyn Ruprecht, George Priestly, June Bobb, Tony O'brien and Barbara Bowen.

Finally, I am extremely grateful to Natalie Pinto for her many contributions in the preparation for the book. Also, a word of thanks to my brother Ahmed Jimale for being such a wonderful person to compare notes with.

As a quick reading of some of the essays in the volume will reveal, many prominent writers on Somali matters are, in the spirit of honest scholarship, taken to task. It is our belief that this volume will engender discussion on relevant topics that are, in the final analysis, germane to the reconstruction of a new Somalia.

Notes

1. Maxamed D. Afrax, "The Mirror of Culture: Somali Dissolution Seen Through Oral Expression," in Ahmed I. Samatar, ed. *The Somali Challenge:From Catastrophe to Renewal?* (Boulder,Colo.:Lynn Rienner Publishers,1994), p.251, fn.13.
2. Walter Benjamin, *Charles Baudelaire:A Lyric Poet in the Era of High Capitalism* (London: Verso,1983), p.25.
3. John Killens, *Black Man's Burden* (New York:Dial,1965),p.46.
4. Bonnie K.Holcomb and Sisai Ibssa, *The Invention of Ethiopia* (Trenton,N.J.: The Red Sea Press,1990), p.xiii.
5. Ali Jimale Ahmed and Irving Leonard Markovitz, "African Literature and Social Science in the Teaching of World Studies," *The Social Studies* 84,2 (March/April 1993):80.

Note on Somali Orthography
Whenever Somali orthography is used as in a Somali author's
name or book title, the following phonetic sounds need be
mentioned: X which is h; dh = d; c= 'a

The absence of agreed upon correct spelling in English of
Somali names necessitates the need for consistency to stan-
dardize the spelling of some Somali names used in this volume.

Variant spellings	Version Used
Abgal	Abgaal
Af Elai	Af Eelaay
Afgoye	Afgooye
Ajuran/Ajuraan	Ajuuraan
Bakol	Bakool
Banadir	Benadir
Brava/Barawa	Baraawe
Bardere/Bardhere	Baardheere
Juba/Giuba	Jubba
Bur	Buur
Darood	Daarood
Dikri	Dhikri
Gaaljeel	Gaaljecel
Hargeisa	Hargeysa
Hawiya	Hawiye
Huddur/Xudur/Hudur	Hoddur
Isaq/Isak	Isaaq
Luq	Luuq
Mijertein/Mijurteen	Majeerteen
Mogadiscio/ Muqdishu	Mogadishu
Samale	Samaale
Shangani	Shangaani
Shaikh/Sheekh	Sheikh
Siad/Siyad	Siyaad
Oman	Uman
Zaylac/Zeila	Zeila'

ISLAM IN SOMALI HISTORY: FACT AND FICTION

⚭

Mohamed Haji Mukhtar

The Bedouins are not concerned with laws, or with deterring people from misdeeds or with protecting some against others. They care only for the property that they might take away from people through looting and imposts. When they have obtained that, they have no interest in anything further. . . .

— Ibn Khaldun

It is evident that Somalia maintained commercial and cultural contacts with the ancient world, particularly with Egyptians, Southern Arabians, and other West Asian societies. Pre-Islamic Arabia and Persia established a very active trade in Somalia.[1]

Islam found its way to Somalia from the religion's very beginning. In fact, many Somalis claim — undoubtedly with some exaggeration — that their ancestors were converted to Islam before Islam even reached Medina, Islam's first capital city. Somalia has enjoyed a unique role in the history of Islamic Africa: As the only country in the whole continent whose population is virtually all Muslim,[2] all Somali Muslims follow the Shafi'i Suni school of thought.

One might expect, therefore, that in Somalia the effort to build a unified, harmonious nation would be more successful than in other African nations in which religious and sectarian differences hamper social integration. Furthermore, there is a strong belief that Somalia's ancestors descended from the household of the prophet Muhammad, so that all Somalis belong to the Hashimite stock of the Qurayshi clan. Again, this would seem to be another factor bound to boost Somalia's sense of common nationhood, unlike the other African nations, in which tribalism and clanism remain major obstacles to unity.

However, events in the past few decades, after independence and unification in 1960, raise some intriguing questions: Why did Somalia fail to build a unified nation? How can one explain the massacres and atrocities committed by a so-called government against its own people? What is there in Islam to foster murder, rape, and the starving to death of one's Muslim brethren? Yet these questions are not the focus of this paper, which rather emphasizes the issue of the development of Islam as a political force and a civilization in the history of Somalia. Using the methods of the sociology of religion, we will deal with questions related to ethos and patterns of societal life in Somalia's Islam.

Islam is professed to be both *Din* (religion) and *Dawla* (state). Islam is presented as an all-encompassing system of beliefs and ideas in which the realms of ethics and politics are intimately related to a system of supreme, all-embracing morality. Although theoretically all the resources of Islamic culture were open to Somalian Muslims, not all were available, because of the means and ways by and in which Islam spread to Somalia.

Despite the centrality of Islam in Somali life, very little is known about the manner and forms of its diffusion in the countryside, partly because Somalia remained an oral society whose languages were never put into a written form.[3] Moreover, scholars (Somalists) have not exhausted and explored sources on Somali history and culture in a comprehensive way.[4]

Early sources confirm a south Arabian presence along the Somali coast. Somali-Arab connections of the pre-Islamic period were manifested primarily in trade relations, although some historians believe that constant Arab visits and migrations cultivated strong cultural ties with the Somali people, including marriges.[5] It was, however, with the rise of Islam in Arabia during the 7th century A.D. that the Arab impact became pronounced. This was natural. Islam is a universal religion that strongly urges its adherents to spread and preach Islam all over the world, which requires travel and migration.

Concerning the early Arab Muslim migrations to Somalia, there are three possible scenarios to consider: *fath* ("conquest"), *hijrah* ("voluntary or forced migraton"), and *tijarah* ("trade and commerce"). Concerning the first scenario, "conquest," it is necessary to understand the nature and causes of Islamic conquest. The early adherents of Islam were looking for political stability and the betterment of their economic situation. They were surrounded by powerful empires that threatened their existence. Therefore, the early waves of Islamic "conquests" were defensive, purely reactive efforts at warding off perceived threats. However, Somalians, unlike the Persians, the Romans, or even the Arab chieftains, neither posed a threat to the Muslim community in Arabia nor offered any economic potential to be exploited. So Somalia as a whole cannot properly be regarded as part of an aggressive Islamic conquest.

Nevertheless, Arab sources indicate that parts of Somalia fell into the hands of Umayyad conquerors during the Caliphate of Abdulmalik Ibn Marwan (685–705). The Caliph sent a Muslim army led by Syrian General Musa Ibn Umar al-Khath'ami to conquer both Mogadishu and the neighboring East African city-state of Kilwa.[6] The directives given to Musa Ibn Umar were identical to those given to any other Muslim conqueror: to secure the taxation of *al-Kharaj*, to teach the Qura'n, and to safeguard the security of the country and assure its loyalty to the Islamic state in Damascus.[7] *Kitab al-Zunuj* confirms that the Umayyads controlled parts of Somalia until their downfall.

During the early stages of the Abbasid Caliphate, Somalia showed loyalty to the new administration. Yahya Ibn 'Umar al-'Anzi, the messenger of the second Abbasid Caliph Abu

Ja'far al-Mansur, reported that the Sultan of Mogadishu and the people of his country were "on their oath to the Caliphate and paid the taxes regularly." However, in the year 189 A.H., during the Caliphate of Harun al-Rashid, Mogadishu rebelled against Baghdad and refused to pay taxes to the Abbasids. Although al-Rashid sent a punitive mission to the region and managed to restore Abbasid sovereignty, the Sultanate of Mogadishu remained in constant rebellion.[8]

Thus it is clear that while the Muslims did not conquer the whole Somali peninsula, they did claim authority over significant parts of southern Somalia, known to the Arabs as *Bilad al-Zinj* (the land of the blacks), which extends from Mogadishu to Kilwa in East Africa. This region provided the Arabs adequate economic resources. Moreover, the region was politically volatile, as it was a refuge and safe haven for the disputing claimants to the Islamic throne in Medina, Damascus, and Baghdad.

Islam commends migration, one of the most effective factors in the spread of Islam throughout the world. The early Muslim migrants to Somalia, mainly from Yemen, Hadramaut, Uman, and Persia, were initially motivated by the desire to bridge Islam overseas; but since the economic and climatic conditions of the migrant's homeland were poor and harsh, they were also motivated by the desire to strike it rich in a land of opportunity. Furthermore, the emergence of Islam itself in Mecca, and the establishment of the Islamic state in Medina, generated tremendous tension between the followers of Islam and the pagan Arabs. Hence, newly converted Muslims victimized by severe persecution were advised by the Prophet Muhammad to migrate.[9]

It is also necessary to remember that the Muslims, immediately after the death of the prophet Muhammad, waged wars among themselves, particularly after the Umani tribes refused to pay the *Zakat* tribute and opposed the Caliphate, the new Islamic administration that succeeded the Prophet. These wars are known as the *Hurub al-Riddah*, the "apostasy wars." In the aftermath of these devastating wars, the Umanis were not only defeated militarily; they were totally excluded from participating in the creation of the "glory of Islam" that was part and parcel of "the Islamic conquests"; they were also severely persecuted by the Islamic Caliphate. Thus, there is good reason to believe that the earliest wave of Muslim immigrants to the Somali coast occurred as early as the period of Abu Bakar, the first Caliph of Islam.[10]

The Muslim migration grew tremendously from the rise of Islam to the tenth century A.D. According to authoritative Arab sources, there were eight major waves of Arab and Persian settlements in Somalia.[11] Inscriptions on some tombstones found along the coastal regions of Southern Somalia are vivid evidence of the presence of Islam in Somalia during the first few centuries of the Islamic era. Sharif 'Aidarus in his book, *Bughyat al-Amal,* offers ample evidence to show the arrival of many Arab tribes in Mogadishu, such as the Makhzumis.[12]

Medieval Muslim writers, as well as Benadiri oral tradition and genealogical claims, report the presence of Persian Muslims on the Benadir coast. In Mogadishu, inside the *Mihrab* niche of the Arba' Rukun Mosque, there is an inscription showing the name of the person who founded the mosque and the date of construction (Khusrow Ibn Muhammad al-Shirazi, in the year 667 A.H./ 1268–69 A.D.).[13] One of the ancient quarters of Mogadishu became not only predominantly populated by the Persians, but was also given a Persian name, *Shingani,* a Nishapurian place name in Farsi.[14] The *Shanshiya* tribe in present-day Somalia derives its name from a very prosperous district in Iran. The *Shanshiya* tribe today inhabits the coast as well as the interior of the Benadir region. The term *Benadir* itself, meaning "city" or "center," is of Persian origin.

To understand more about the Persian presence in Somalia, one must emphasize the Shi'i elements in contemporary Somali Islam. Somalis follow the Sunni school of law; however, unlike the rest of the Sunni Muslims, they regard the household of the Prophet Muhammad with special honor, particularly the fourth Caliph 'Ali and his wife Fatima, the daughter of the Prophet. In fact, the veneration of Fatima developed into a cult. Southern Somali women hold regular memorial ceremonies chanting poems on her deeds "Abaay Sitidey" or "Abaay Nabiyey," the latter referring to Fatima as the Prophet of womenfolk. The *Asharafs* of Somalia, who claim they are descendants of Fatima and 'Ali, are also credited with saintly attributes or quasidivine power — *Barakah* — with which they are automatically endowed at birth and never fail to exercise; no matter how irreverent or irreligious their lifestyle may be, they are considered saintly because of their innate *Barakah*.

Arab historians of the time described southern Somalia as predominantly Sunni Muslim. Ibn Sa'id al-Maghribi (d.1286) declared that by his time the majority of Somalis had become Muslims, particularly those of the coastal region of Benadir. He calls Mogadishu the city of Islam, *Dar al-Islam*.[15]

Al-Idrisi (1100-1166), in his *Nuzhat,* described the commercial coastal centers of southern Somalia — Marka, Barawa, and Mogadishu. In addition, he reported the rise of inland trade between the coastal centers and the hinterland, such as the caravan routes originating from Sarman, Luuq, Bardhera, Buur Hakaba just to mention some. He also reported the existence of Hawiya villages and settlements off the coast of southern Somalia. With regard to Mogadishu, he mentioned that it was a significant port in the region, and one of its various roles was that of a link between the east and west trading centers for Indian Ocean products.[16]

Commercial and religious activities in the southern Somali regions were conducted both by Somalis and by the Muslim migrant communities in their early stages, but eventually those activities were dominated by the Somalis. Al-Hamawi (d.1229), in his *Mu'jam,* describes Somalis as black to distinguish them from the migrant Asian communities. Mogadishu, he writes, "was predominantly populated by foreigners and not blacks."[17] According to al-Hamawi, Somalis provided for the inter-regional trade considerable quantities of ivory and hides of what he called "strange animals," such as giraffes, rhinoceroses, and leopards "not found elsewhere in the world."[18]

Ibn Battuta's eyewitness report provides clear evidence of an Arab presence and Islamic activities on the Benadir coast. The titles used by the rulers of Mogadishu and their assistants were either Arabic (e.g., *Sheikh,* head of a state; *Qadi,* judge; *Amir,* military leader) or Persian (e.g., *Wazir,* political assistant). From Ibn Battuta's account, we learn about the tremendous development of the Islamic judicial system, government, and educational institutions in the Somali sultanates of the Benadir coast, where a judiciary council — including the *Qadi,* the *Wazir,* the private secretary of the Sultan, and four of the chief *Amirs* — sat weekly to hear the complaints of the public. "Questions of religious law are decided by the *Qadi;* others are judged by the council. If a case required the views of the Sultan, it was put in writing for him. He sends back an immediate reply, written on the back of the paper, as his discretion may decide. This has always been the custom among these people."[19] He reported also that Somali Muslim centers placed great importance on education. Students from faraway places were provided lodging and food similar to what was provided at student hostels, such as the *Riwaqs* of al-Azhar and Porticos of Damascus, Baghdad, Medina, and Mecca. Ibn Battuta himself was lodged in the students' dorm in Mogadishu.

In the northern Somali coast, though more adjacent to the center of Islamic activity, the situation was quite different. Unlike southern Somali society, most of the present northern Somali clans claim to be the descendants of Arab ancestors.[20] However, it is hard to find evidence to support any Arabic or Islamic legacies; the Arab presence in the region seems to have been small and insignificant. Medieval Arab writers referred mostly to two centers, *Zeila'* and *Berbera*. Both al-Mas'udi and al-Hamawi described the two cities as non-Arab cities.[21] Indeed, al-Hamawi reported that the population of Zeila' were black.[22] It is very important to note that contemporary (9th–10th centuries A.D.) Arab geographers had difficulties defining the identity of Zeila'. Some of them considered it an Abyssinian port, whereas others referred to it as part of *Bilad al-Zinj,* the land of blacks.[23]

Despite the Somali belief that Islam was introduced in the northern region of Somalia as early as the time of the Prophet Muhammad, we lack evidence to support the claim. In al-Mas'udi's and al-Idrisi's account, Zeila' was an Abyssinian Christian city, and the adherents of Islam in it were few and were considered tribute-paying communities (*Dhimmis*) to the Abyssinians.[24] Al-Hamawi, describing the Benadir coast as made up of a chain of Muslim city states, wrote about the pagan customs of northern Somali groups, only lightly touched by Islam. He mentioned, for instance, that the *'adah* custom of bridegrooms cutting off male sexual organs of fellow villagers and displaying them as signs of virility to prospective brides (which is totally against Islamic values and teaching) was practiced there.[25]

Four factors illustrate the non-appeal of the northern region of Somaliland for Muslim migration. First is the region's proximity to the headquarters of the Islamic State. Fugitive Muslim migrants, concerned about their future security, would not risk settling in neighboring areas such as Somaliland. They drew this lesson from the first Muslim migration to Abyssinia, in which pagan Meccans sent to Abyssinia a punitive mission led by 'Amr Ibn al-'As to claim the repatriation of those expatriates. Secondly, there were few urban centers to attract Muslim migrants. Even today, northern Somalian nomadism would not have been conducive to the development of such an infrastructure. The nomadic life remained the predominant culture in the region throughout its history. The nomads roved behind their flocks, looking for pasture and water, and conducting their affairs through tribal customary law (*Heer*). Islamic culture is generally urban, but Somalia had relatively few towns and cities. Thus, where no town existed, Islam could not penetrate. Thirdly, the lack of natural harbors and the frequent violent cyclones made the journey to that part of Africa very dangerous. The ancient Egyptian story "The Shipwrecked Sailor" illustrates how wild the winds were along the Somali coast.[26] Al-Mas'udi on one of his travels to East Africa reported the sea storms, particularly toward the approaches of Cape Guardafui: "The people who cruise on this sea are 'Umani Arab tribes; when they get into the middle of the passage and find themselves between waves of the kind which lift them up and lower them, they sing the following rhyme at their work:

Berbera and Jafuni [Hafun] mad are thy waves
Jafuni and Berbera see their waves.[27]

The fourth reason why migrants were not attracted to the northern region of Somaliland was the lack of viable economic resources. Somalia, with the exception of the inter-river regions, consists largely of dry savannah plains. The rainfall is inadequate, as one goes north of the Shabelle River. It is also hot throughout the year, though seasonal winds have a moderating effect in localized mountain areas. Away from the well sites and rain basins, the land appears to lack human habitation. Frequent droughts and famine became part and parcel of Somali pastoral life.[28] This harsh environment, therefore, is not conducive to attract any foreign migration, even the Arab Muslims. The Arabs were migrating from a similar environment to that of Somaliland and were looking to enhance their economic life, as well as better and more pleasant climatic conditions. Thus, the northern Somalis' claim that they are "more Arab" remains enigmatic, perhaps more accurately "puzzling," according to Dr. Hersi, who concluded: "The groups who claim descent from Arab ancestors had the least signs of Arab habitation in the whole of the Somali coast."[29]

Apart from flocks of hardy goats and sheep and herds of camels, northern Somaliland offered no other viable economic resources.[30] Most available historic sources of the time refer often to Zeila' as a port for exporting Abyssinian goods and products and hides and skins and, perhaps, ostrich feathers and gums indigenous to Somaliland.[31] Terms such as "through" and "from" Zeila' are used by the medieval writers to indicate goods indigenous to Somaliland as distinct from goods originating elsewhere. According to al-Hamawi, "ivory, rhinoceros horns, giraffes, and leopard skins were mainly

exported *through* Zeila'."[32] Al-Istakhri noticed hides and leopard skins were exported *"from* Zeila."[33] Al-Biruni writes that
pearls were also Zeila' exports.[34]

The situation for the Benadiri ports and hinterland was
quite different. Diversified economic resources, from exotic
wildlife and marine resources to agriculture products, attracted the interest of Muslim migrants. According to al-Hamawi,
Mogadishu exported "ivory, aromatic woods, ambergris, and
hides of [animals not found elsewhere in the world]."[35] The
Benadir ports are the only coastal cities in East Africa to have
as their immediate hinterland a fertile riverine plain. On the
banks of the Shabelle and Jubba rivers, urban centers were
established in antiquity. The riverine regions were favored by
higher rainfall than the rest of the Somali peninsula. As a
result, the *Reewin*[36] clans who live there have long been agropastoralists.[37]

The hinterland towns and cities established a commercial
network linking the ports to the markets of East Africa,
Abyssinia, and as far as ports in the north. Among the most
important inland market towns were *Luq* and *Bardhere* on the
Jubba River; *Sarman, Baydhowa* (Baidoa), and Bur Hakaba in
the central interriver plain; and *Awdhegle* and *Afgoye* on the
lower Shabelle River. Then goods from the interior were
exported as far as Southeast Asia. Ibn Battuta, in his *Rihla,*
reported that he saw in the Maldive Islands "musk, livestock
and other goods exported from Mogadishu."[38] Chinese
medieval writings provide sufficient sources showing the trade
relation between China and the Benadir ports. Chinese merchants were mainly interested in ivory, ostrich feathers, tortoise shells, rhinoceros horns, giraffe hides, leopard skins,
gums, and aromatic products from Benadir.[39]

Furthermore, the Benadir region developed its own man-
ufacturing industries in which for centuries the local crafts-
men produced a unique cloth known as *Kar Guri* in the
hinterland and *toob Benadiri* on the coast. This cloth was not
only for local use but also exported to Southern Arabia and
Egypt.[40] Evidence of maize and grain grinding stones manu-
factured in Merca, one of the Benadir ports, survives today

in the interriver region. The techniques of oil grinding (via animal power) is also practiced widely along the Shabelle Valley. Thus it is fair to conclude that Islam found a more fertile ground in the southern regions of Somalia than in the north.

Islamicization and Arabization

What Islamic elements these migrant groups brought to Somalia, and what their legacy is in today's Somalia, will be our focus in the remainder of this study. Two major issues must be examined in this regard: Islamicization vs. Arabization and Islamic affiliation vs. tribal loyalty.

Islamicization and Arabization were twin processes in the spread of Islam beyond the Arabian Peninsula. Arabs, indeed, succeeded in Islamicizing as well as Arabizing certain areas of what is now known as the Islamic world, such as the north African region. Whereas, in certain other areas, the Arabs succeeded only in Islamicizing, as is the case with the rest of Islamic Africa, Central Asia, India, and Southeast Asia. However, Islam in Somalia was introduced not just by the Arabs; Southwest Asians participated substantially in the process, and eventually in Somalia's role in spreading Islam into its interior, as well as into neighboring African societies. It is necessary, therefore, to examine the sociopolitical conditions of the peninsula before the arrival of Islam.

Both archaeological excavations and non-Somali sources reveal the existence of urban centers in the Southern Somali Peninsula with forms of political structures superseding clan chiefdoms. The *Periplus of the Erythraean Sea* named the towns of *Serapion* and *Nicon* which Schoff identified with Mogadishu and Barawa, respectively.[41] However, the *Periplus*, in another section, describes the northern part of the Peninsula as made up of politically fragmented communities having no central authority except for perhaps what the ancient Egyptians referred to as a Puntite Kingdom.[42] Dr. Hersi and other modern Egyptian historians referred to the seat of the Puntite Kingdom as a place located near 'Alula at the eastern tip of the Horn.[43] However, it is intriguing that the name of the

Puntite King is Baraho,[44] a common name among the Hawiya clan that today predominantly inhabits the central regions of the Peninsula. It is possible that the Hawiya clan extended to that part of the Horn or that the seat of the Puntite Kingdom was located further south of *Ras Hafun*.

Modern archaeological excavations have identified several historic sites along the coast of the Peninsula. Most of them were located on the southern coast.[45] Early Arabic inscriptions on tombs, religious sites, and royal houses are common in the cities along the Benadir coast.[46] Indeed, the Italian and French as well as German colonial records, often ignored by Somali scholarship, indicate the existence of ancient towns and markets along the Jubba and Shabelle valleys.[47] It was in these areas, where the bulk of Muslim migrants found safe haven, that Islamicization ocurred.

It is important to remember that the immigrants themselves were coming from diverse social and political backgrounds. In certain areas of the south, the immigrants (Arabs, Persians, Indians, and other southwest Asians) came from different racial backgrounds. This reflects on their activities with regard to the Islamicization process. The earliest waves of Arab migration go back to the runaways of the *Riddah* apostasy wars, mainly of Umani groups. The leaders of the group were reported to be from the *Julanda* tribe, and they settled in places along what Muslim geographers of the time call the *Zanj* coast, later known as the Benadir Coast.[48] They were pushed to the hinterland by a Shi'ite group, the Zaidis, running away from the Umayyad persecution.

It is quite probable that the earlier group moved toward the lower Shabelle valley and the interior plains. Evidence from the oral tradition reveals two legacies that survived until today in the lower Shabelle region. One is the existence of the *Geledi* clan, who believe that they are the descendants of the *Julanda* 'Umani tribe. The Geledis established their center of activity in the Lower Shabelle Valley with headquarters in *Afgoye*. The second legacy is the phenomena of resistance on the part of some *Elai*[49] subclans towards paying the Islamic *Zakat* tax. This subclan is called *Seka Diid* ("Repudiators of the Tax").[50]

In general, societies with structured governments were most likely to adopt and absorb Islam into their systems. The oral tradition in the *Doi* belt of Somalia[51] suggests the existence of powerful pagan dynasties in the region, like *Ghedi Baabow, Dubka Baalow, Feyle Arow, Barambara* and others. The headquarters of these dynasties were mainly located on the tops of mountains, like *Bur Hakaba, Bur Haybe, Bur Gerwiine, Gelway,* and others. Such dynasties found in Islam a means of protecting their political power. Through proselytization, the place as well as given names of pagan historic sites were renamed in the Islamicization process. Even pagan sites became Islamic.

There are 114 historic mountains scattered in the *Doi* belt that have religious significance for the *Reewin* society. On the top of each mountain there are burial sites for holy men where annual pilgrimages, *syaro,* are still made by the local people. The names of these holy men are Islamic and Arabic, like *owul Qasim* at the peak of *Bur Haybe,*[52] next to *owul Qasim* tomb, there is the tomb of *Shaykh 'Abdulqadir al-Jilani* (the founder of Qadiriyyah order;) and not far from those two tombs, there is a cave site for *Abka Eden i Aboy Haawa* (Adam and Eve). About 60 miles northeast of *Bur Haybe* there is *Bur Gerwiine;* there are the tombs of the four holy *Ahmeds* and the holy woman *Edeegow,* known to the local people as *Affarta Emed Osobka yaala Abay Edeegow Shanaayti*[53] (the four Ahmeds and Edeego that are buried in the virgin land). It is striking also to find in the interriver region the popular cult of women saints which is alien to the male chauvinists of the world of Islam. In addition to *Abay Edeegow* of *Bur Gerwiine,* there are the shrines of *Oboy Imbiyow Hassan Diinow Ala* in *Abdurug*[54] and *Dada Ma Siti* in Barawa, just to mention a few.[55]

Evidently the number of the historic mountains is drawn from the 114 Qur'anic Surahs (or chapters). The local tradition holds that these mountains migrated from Arabia with their shrines. This is identical to the Shrine of Sayyidna 'Ali Ibn Abi Talib, the fourth Caliph of Islam, in *Aw-Barkhatle* near Hargeisa today. From these and other accounts it is clear that early Muslim migrants integrated the history of Islam with that of the strong local pagan cult. Accommodation of such practices was a common development throughout the world of Islam.[56]

North of the *Doi* region and up to southern Ethiopia are the *Bay* and *Harqan* territories, dominated by the *Asharaf cult*, which is a mixture of Islamic mysticism and local customary traditional *Heer.* The early Sharifs, accommodating local customs and coordinating with the local political authority, gradually succeeded in converting the people and helping them make a new socioeconomic order. The Ashrafs encouraged the warlike people of *Reewin* to come to peace, which is an Islamic ideal, and settle their disputes in an Islamic way. They counseled the clan authorities to forget their pre-Islamic lineages and join the wider Islamic identity. Boundaries were drawn between major clans, with grazing and water resources clearly defined. They also established public grazing and wells and *Wars* (artificial water reservoir) with rules and regulations inspired by the Islamic law that also accommodates aspects of the local customs of the *Heer.*[57]

To the Somali nomadic groups of the Peninsula, the situation was quite different. The nomadic organization was based on nested groups of egalitarian lineages assumed to descend from a common ancestor *Samale.* The relationship between each lineage rested on segmental opposition, that is, lineages were either supported by or opposed to one another based on their degree of relatedness. This ideal, though often more honored in the breach, produced the ethnographic cliche often cited by anthropologists: "I against my brothers; my brothers and I against our cousins; my brothers, cousins and I against the world." This egalitarian situation inhibited the development of a subverted hierarchal structure necesary to establish political authority and led to what Dr. Hersi described as "a state of chiefdom where central political authority meant nothing, as indeed it does not even to this day."[58]

Due to the harshness of the environment and the poverty of economic resources in the nomadic regions of Somalia, the Muslim migration was small and insignificant. Unlike the southern regions of the Peninsula, whose written and oral sources provide sufficient evidence on the arrival and activities of early Muslim migration, there is little reliable evidence relating to the nomadic societies, and what is offered is dubious and mythical stories of a few mysterious individuals.

There are two figures in the oral tradition of the northern nomadic groups of Somalia that are related to the early arrival of Muslim migrants. The first one is Sheikh Abdurahman Ibn Ismail al-Jabarti, and the second is Sheikh Ishaq Ibn Ahmed al-'Alawi. They both married local women and produced two of the larger clans in the north, the Darood and Issak clans. One would wonder, in the first instance, how the offspring of just two individual Arabs could become not only the dominant people of the northern part of the Peninsula, but also the majority of the whole Somali nation today. This point deserves examination but is beyond the scope of this paper. The focus will be the impact of Islam on the nomads of Somalia.

Although the universal message of Islam proscribes tribalism and racism — "the most honoured of you (mankind) in the sight of Allah is (he who is) the most righteous of you"[59] — the mere fact that the Prophet of Islam is an Arab by race and Qurayshi by tribe and that the language of the Holy Qur'an is Arabic ensures that the Muslim community as a whole pays special attention and respect to the Arabs in general and to the household of the Prophet (al-al-Beit) in particular. The history of the "glorious days" of Islam teaches its students that Arab tribes, previously divided, built states and empires and became dominant players in world history for centuries to come.

Like the nomadic groups of Somalia, Arabs before Islam were divided and lacked strong leadership and central authority; however, under the banner of Islam they become organized and found leadership in the Prophet Muhammad and his succeeding Caliphs. As Ibn Khaldun observed,

> Bedouins can acquire royal authority only by making use
> of religious coloring, such as prophethood or sainthood

or some great religious event in general. The reason is because of their savagery: the bedouins are the least willing of all nations to subordinate themselves to each other, as they are rude, proud, ambitious and eager to be leaders. Their individual aspirations rarely coincide. But when there is religion [among them]. . . then they have some restoring influence upon themselves. The qualities of haughtiness and jealousy leave them. It is, then, easy to unite them in [a social organization] . . . .

This is illustrated by the Arab Dynasty of Islam. Religion cemented their leadership with religious laws and ordinances which, explicitly and implicitly, are concerned with what is good for civilization.[60]

These glorious achievements attracted some non-Arab Muslims in different parts of the Islamic world either for prestige and protection or for more social and political gains. Many Somali nomads felt the need for the prestige that comes from an identification with Arab ancestry. They absorbed individual Arabs who provided them with new tribal lineages whose names were adopted as the tribal eponyms. Therefore, Ibn Khaldun's concept of *'Asabiyyah* (tribal bonding) prevailed more than Islamic solidarity among Somali nomads, which also caused Arab dynasties to fail. In the Islamic world, the Arabs, even today, remain divided by their obsession with *'Asabiyyah*, while the non-Arab Muslims established powerful Islamic empires and states, such as the Ottoman empire and the Pakistani state. Indeed, it was the non-Arab Muslim efforts that allowed Arab dynasties to survive even in the golden age. Without Persian, Indian, African, and European Muslims, the Umayyads and Abbasids could not have maintained power; and once they ignored that element, they soon lost power. Thomas J. Bafield warns scholars who overestimate religion's role in organizing tribal societies in the Middle East:

> ...the brilliance of the early Islamic conquests should not blind us to their exceptional nature. Both before and after this time neither the Arab tribes of the desert nor the

mountain tribes of north Africa and the Indian plateau
ever again established hegemony over the region. The
tribes that did were the Turco-Mongolian in origin and
their conversion to Islam . . . .[61]

The Arabic factors, therefore, were more influential among
the nomadic groups of northern Somalia. A glance at their
customary law, *Heer,* discloses more Arabic orientation than
in the south, which is more Islamic and African. The ethos
and patterns of life among the nomadic northern groups of
Somalia are very close to those of the Arabs. They are bel-
ligerent, less law abiding, arrogant, destructive, and look
down on any profession except herding. Ibn Khaldun,
describing the Arab Bedouins said,

> ...savagery has become [the Bedouin's] character and
> nature. They enjoy it, because it means freedom from
> authority and no subservience to leadership. Such a nat-
> ural disposition is the negation and antithesis of civiliza-
> tion . . . . The very nature of their existence is the negation
> of building, which is the basis of civilization. Furthermore,
> since they do not see any value in labor and craftsmen and
> do not appreciate it, the hope for profit vanishes, and no
> productive work is done. The sedentary population dis-
> perses, and civilization decays . . . The Bedouins are not
> concerned with laws, or with deterring people from mis-
> deeds . . . . They care only for the property that they might
> take away from people through looting . . . . Under the rule
> of Bedouins, their subjects live as in a state of anarchy.
> Anarchy destroys mankind and ruins civilization. . . . .[62]

The genealogy and lineage systems (*Abtirsiinyo*) are part and
parcel of the nomadic social life. They are in fact part of the
educational system in which children memorize their
Abtirsiinyo at the earliest stage. On the contrary, sedentary
societies of Somalia are not concerned with *Abtirsiinyo*. It is
noteworthy that *Abtirsiinyo* disappears the further south one
goes in Somalia and weakens as a linkage factor among the
Dighil and Mirifle people. In this part of Somalia, the bond

is more to the land that they cultivate or use as pasture, or to other forms of common interests.

In relation to the obsession with the Arabic elements in Islamic history on the part of some Somali nomadic clans, who constructed tribal lineage from mythical figures, the question of leadership in Islam and its interpretation could be another issue that might shed some light on the nomadic attraction to aspects of Islamic history, that they might use to enhance their social and political status. The Prophet of Islam, Muhammad, established in Medina the first central- ized Islamic state in which believers formed a single com- munity, an *Umma*. The commitment to the Islamic *Umma* ranked above tribal affiliations, in a new state structure based on an organized religion, Islam. However, immediately after the death of the Prophet, the Medina community disagreed over how to fill the leadership void.[63] The Arab tribes of non- Qurayshite clans articulated their right to the leadership posi- tion at the conference of *al-Saqifa*.[64] After a fiery debate, Abu Bakar — another Qurayshi — was chosen as the successor of the Prophet. This marked the beginning of the end of the Muslim solidarity. As Ibn Hisham eloquently stated: "The posi- tion of Caliph is the issue that causes Muslims to shed the blood of their coreligious people."[65] Because of the above dis- pute, three of the four orthodox Caliphs were murdered, namely Omar, Osman, and Ali. This power struggle contin- ues bloodily among Muslims today.

The impact of this struggle left a tremendous legacy on Islamic political thought throughout the Islamic world. A sig- nificant number of Muslim jurists required the Qurashite descent as one of the prerequisites governing the institution of Caliph. This view, though, was stubbornly advocated by the scholars of Qurayshite origin, such as al-Shafici'i and Ibn Khaldun.[66] Thus, the world of Islam was not free from these crucial distractions. In fact, concerning the non-Arab Muslims, it brought a new dimension to the power struggle. The closer one is to the household of the Prophet of Islam, the greater chance one has to be a leader of a non-Arab Muslim community.

The case of the Somali Arabized clans is, therefore, identical to the *Sadah* of Southeast Asian Muslims, the *Mawlanas* of Islamic India, the *Bani Ma'qils* of Egypt, or the Yemeni tribes in Northern Sudan, who each invented their own myth of descent from Prophet Muhammad's tribe, in order to dominate the position of leadership in their respective areas.

Conclusion

The purpose of this study has been to give some insight into the sociology of religion in Somalia. In my research on the reconstruction of Somali history and culture, I have been attracted to the enigmatic shrouding of that history and culture. Although Somalis claim they are homogeneous, the exact origin of their race remains mysterious. Some claim that their ancestors migrated from Arabia, but do not know the date or place of arrival. Others will tell stories about their past, about antiquity and about phir'onic civilization itself having been originated by Somalis in Puntland. The very word *Somali,* the name of the nation, remains ambiguous. Issues related to the "Somali" language remain most controversial and confusing. Most nomads today speak the official *Maxa* while the agro-pastorals speak several other languages, *Mai, Jiddu, Dabarre,* to mention just a few. These are some issues that have preoccupied this writer in trying to reconstruct that past.

In the present study, I have tried to show how religion in the experience of Somalia was both a divisive and a cohesive factor. My major concern was not how Islam arrived, but rather what factors led to the advent of Islam in Somalia. I examined the widely accepted notion that Islam arrived first in the northern regions of the peninsula and found the evidence far from conclusive. Previous hypotheses were based on the geographical proximity of the peninsula to Arabia and assumptions drawn from the early migrations of Islam into Abyssinia. However, authoritative historic accounts disprove that. The names and itineraries of the first and second migration to Abyssinia are well documented in the writings of Muslim historians of the time. And, after all, most of those migrants returned to Arabia to take part in the making of

Islamic states, after the migration to Medina, save those who died in Abyssinia. I showed four reasons why Muslim migrants could not settle in the northern region of Somalia:

1. The region's closeness to the enemy territory (Arabia), which forced dissidents to migrate further south
2. The region's lack of urban centers to accommodate the newcomers
3. The region's lack of natural harbors, and the hazards related to sailing on its coast
4. The region's lack of a viable economic resource

With regard to the issues related to the Islamic legacies and their influence and to how Islam is practiced in Somalia, I determined that Islam found a solid ground for survival and expansion along the Benadir coast and its hinterland. What is intriguing, though, is that Arabic elements associated with Islam prevail more in the northern region of the peninsula. Unlike Arabic factors in the Asiatic and North African groups, where physical and linguistic characteristics support Arab claims, in Somalia there is no such thing; those who claim descent from Arab sheiks speak Arabic less than the rest of Somalia and their features are no different in complexion or structure than other Somalis or the neighboring African races, such as the Afars, Amharas, or the Oromo. Therefore, I conclude that this is a cultural invention developed recently to gain political ascendancy.

Somalia's history, culturally or otherwise, has been seen mainly through the eyes of post-independence historiography, which interprets Somalia and its people with distorted generalization. For the past five decades or so, since the nomadic clans of Somalia started to dominate the nation's political realm, nomadization began to prevail in all aspects of Somalia's life. Efforts were made to carefully glorify nomadic language, culture, and history and destroy or denigrate the history and culture of the Somali sedentary societies. Institutions were created to propagate the nomadic tradition, ascribing to it a greater antiquity.

A good example of one of these institutions is the

Department of Culture in the Ministry of Education, created in the early 1960s for the enhancement of Somali history and culture. This department later developed into a Ministry of its own in the early 1970s, namely, the "Ministry of Culture and Higher Education," from which the Somali Academy of Culture eventually emerged as the custodian of the invented Somali tradition, which glorified the nomadic tradition but also ignored and degraded other Somali traditions.

Scholars of that period, Somali as well as foreign, contributed a great deal of research to this phenomenon of invented tradition and yet Somalia remained the least understood in the African context. Dr. Cassanelli, in his outstanding study, *The Shaping of The Somali Society,* described the situation as follows: "Preoccupation with them [the "invented tradition" phenomena] has diverted scholars from examining other important historical themes and from adopting alternative analytical perspectives in their study of the Somali past."[67] Efforts have been made to discourage scholars from studying other Somali themes. Valuable sources for the study of Somalia's past were ignored, among them, Arabic, Italian, French, and German sources, as I have pointed out in this study. The oral tradition of non-nomadic Somalia was *systematically ignored,* and their languages were not studied. Historical sites were set up where there were no signs of history. Religious heroes were made up where the practice of Islam has been insignificant. Truth is what is good for something and, in this instance, good for nomadism. The aim was, under cover of nationalism, to safeguard the interests of certain clans and suppress the aspirations of others.

The use of cultural alienation as a weapon of domination is as old as culture itself. The time has come to assess Somalia's history and culture in a more serious way. It is time to incorporate all Somalia's cultural heritage in all its diversity in a comprehensive and more meaningful future Somalia.

Notes

1. Ali Abdirahman Hersi,"The Arab Factor in Somali History: The Origins and the Development of Arab Enterprise and Cultural

Influence in the Somali Peninsula," Ph.D. diss., University of California, Los Angeles, 1977, pp. 56-60.

2. Despite the fact that there has been no accurate census, the figure above became widely accepted. See: Mohamed Haji Mukhtar, "The Emergence and Role of Political Parties in the Inter-River Region of Somalia from 1947-1960 (Independence)," *Ufahamu*, 17, no. 2 (Spring 1989):75; Hersi, "The Arab Factor," p. 109. Because of the relatively small number of families converted to Christianity and, perhaps, the assumed existence of a pagan community, some scholars started to diminish the figure to even 95%. See: Lee V. Cassanelli, *The Shaping of the Somali Society: Reconstructing the History of Pastoral People, 1600–1900* (Philadelphia: University of Pennsylvania Press, 1982), p. 119.

3. The Somali Language was a spoken language with no final written form until 1972. The development into a written form started early in this century. Due to the fact that Somali people speak different languages, there has never been a consensus on which language should be used as an official language. In the 1950s, when the Trust Territory of Somalia was consulted about the future of their language, they overwhelmingly chose Arabic. For more details about this, see: Mohamed Haji Mukhtar, "Arabic Sources on Somalia," *History in Africa*, 14 (1987): 151–152. Until 1960, Radio Mogadishu broadcast in two Somali languages: *Mai*, an agro-pastoral language, and *Maxa*, a nomadic language. However, *Mai* was eliminated for the sake of language uniformity. In 1972, the *Maxa* was adopted as the national language.

4. On how the Arabic sources that were written by Arabs, Muslim historians and geographers as well as Somali writers were ignored, see, Mukhtar, "Arabic Sources," pp. 141-172.

5. For more information about early Arabian presence in the peninsula, see: Enrico Cerulli, *Somalia, Scritti vari editi ed inediti*, vol. I. (Rome: Istituto Poligrafico dello Stato, 1957), pp. 147-8; and J.S. Trimingham, *Islam in Ethiopia* (London: Frank Cass and Co. Ltd., 1965), p. 214.

6. *Kitab al-Zunuj* is an anonymously authored Arabic manuscript found early this century on the southern coast of Somalia by Enrico Cerulli and later incorporated in his *Somalia*, Vol.I (Roma: Istituto Poligrafico Dello Stato, 1957), pp. 233-251; See p. 238.

7. *Ibid.*, p. 238.

8. *Ibid.*, p. 239.

9. Mohamed Haji Mukhtar, "The First Hijra (Islamic Migration) to Abyssinia 615 A.D. and Its Impact on Islam in Africa." *Proceedings of the 31st Annual Meeting of the African Studies Association*, Chicago, October 28–31, 1988.

10. Hassan Ibrahim Hassan, *Intishar al-Islam wa-al-Urubah Fima yali al-Sahra al-Kubra Sharq al-Qarra al-Ifriqiyyah wa-Gharbiha* (Cairo: Matba'at Lujnat al-Bayan al-Arabi, Cairo: 1957), p. 127.
11. 'Abdurahman Zaki, *al-Islam wa-al-Muslimuna fi Sharq Ifriqiya* (Cairo: Matba'at Yusuf,1960), p. 71.
12. Sharif 'Aydarus Sharif 'Ali al-'Aydarus al-Nudari, *Bughyat al-Amal fi Tarikh al-Sumal, li Ba'd Mulukiha wa-Sukkaniha wa-'Umraniha wa-al-Din al-Lladi Ya'budunahu Qabla al-Islam bi-Thamaniyah Qurun Ila al-An* (Mogadiscio: Stamperia AFIS, 1955), p. 42.
13. Cerulli, *Somalia*, vol.1, p. 9.
14. *Ibid.*, p. 9.
15. Abu al-Hasan Nur al-Din 'Ali Ibn Musa al-'Ansi Ibn Sa'id, known as Ibn Sa'id al-Maghribi (610-685 A.H.), *Nashwat al Tarab fi Tariikhi Jahiliyyat al-'Arab*, 2 vols., ed. Nasrat 'Abd al-Rahman, ('Amman: Maktabat al-Aqsa, 1982), p. 123.
16. Abu 'Abdalla Muhammad Ibn Muhammad al-Idrisi, *Kitabu Nuzhat al-Mushtaq fi Ikhtiraq al-Afaq*, MS. British Museum supplement 685, or 4636. The supplement is entitled: *Mukhtasar Nuzhat al-Mushtaq fi Ikhtiraq al-Afaq.*
17. al-Shaykh al-Imam Shihab al-Din Abi 'Abdalla Yaqut al-Hamawi, *Kitabu Mu'jam al-Buldan*, 5 volumes. (Beirut: Dar Sadir li al-Tiba'a wa-al-Nashr,1957), vol. 5, p. 173.. For more details, see also: Mohamed Haji Mukhtar, "Takwin 'Ula Marakiz al-Da'wah al-Islamiyyah fi al-Sumal," in: *The 20th Anniversary of National University of Malaysia*, (Kuala Lumpur: UKM Press, 1993), p. 282; and Hersi, "The Arab Factor," pp. 102-103.
18. al-Hamawi, *Mu'jam al-Buldan*, vol. 1, p. 543.
19. Freeman G.S.P. Greenville, ed., *The East African Coast: Select Documents from the First to the Earlier Nineteenth Century* (London: Oxford University Press, 1966), pp. 30-31.
20. In this study the term "north" or "northern" does not indicate a precise geographic delineation; it refers to the nomadic pastoral clans of the Somali people who predominantly inhabit territories stretching from the central regions of the peninsula to the Red Sea in the north and Indian Ocean in the northeast. The nomadic pastorals of the south, particularly those who inhabit the region south of the Jubba Valley known as *Oltre Juba*, are the offshoots of the previous ones. They migrated recently to the area, but historically belong to the northern regions, and, after all, their socioeconomic conditions remain as those of the north to this day.
21. Abu al-Hasan 'Ali Bin al-Husayn al-Mas'udi, *Muruj al-Dhahab wa-Ma'adin al-Jawhar* (Cairo: Matba'at Bulaq, 1866), p. 245; al-Hamawi, *Mu'jam al-Buldan*, vol. 3, pp. 164-165.
22. al-Hamawi, *Mu'jam al-Buldan*, p. 967.

23. Ibn Ishaq Ibrahim Bin Muhammad al-Farisi al-Istakhri, *al-Masalik wa-al-Mamalik,* (Leiden: E.J. Brill, 1927), p. 32.
24. al-Mas'udi, *Muruj al-Dhahab,* p. 245; al-Idrisi, *Nuzhat al-Mushtaq,* p. 52.
25. al-Hamawi, *Mu'jan al-Buldan,* p. 967.
26. George Fafdlo Hurani, *Arab Seafaring: In the Indian Ocean in Ancient and Early Medieval Times* (Beirut: Khayats, 1963), p. 7.
27. al-Mas'udi, *Muruj al-Dhahab,* vol.1, p. 65.
28. Lee V. Cassanelli, *The Shaping of the Somali Society, Reconstructing the History of a Pastoral People, 1600–1900* (Philadelphia: University of Pennsylvania Press, 1982), p. 42.
29. Hersi, "The Arab Factor," p. 123.
30. The northeastern part of Somaliland offers some aromatic products such as frankincense, *myrrh* and fishing, possibly for trade; see: Richard Punkhurst, "The Trade of the Gulf of Aden Ports of Africa in the Nineteenth and Early Twentieth Centuries," *Journal of Ethiopian Studies* 3, no. 1 (1965): pp. 56-57.
31. I.M. Lewis, "The Somali Conquest of the Horn of Africa," *Journal of African History* 1 (London: 1960): p. 74.
32. al-Hamawi, *Mu'jam al-Buldan,* vol. 2, p. 967.
33. al-Istakhri, *al-Masalik wa-al-Mamalik,* p. 32.
34. Yusuf Kamal Hassan, *Watha'iq Tarikhiyyah wa Jughrafiyyah wa Tijariyyah 'An Afriqiya al-Sharqiyyah* (a translation of Charles Gullain's *Documents: Sur l'histoire la geographie et le commerce de l'Afrique orientale)* 1st ed. (Cairo: the author, 1927), p. 712.
35. al-Hamawi, *Mu'jam al-Buldan,* p. 543.
36. The *Reewin* (pronounced and ascribed mistakenly as *Rahanweyn* or *Rahanwein)* are one of the largest groups in the Somali Peninsula. They occupy an area that extends from the Shabelle River in the east to Kenya in the west; and from the Indian Ocean in the south to southern Ethiopia in the north. They are agro-pastoral and speak a language of their own known as Mai *(Maay* or *Maaymaay).* Modern linguistic studies suggest that Mai is one of the oldest languages in the Horn of Africa. See H. Lewis, "The Origins of The Galla and Somali," *Journal of African History* 7 (1966): 27-46. Unlike the nomadic clans of Somalia in which the political identity is based on genealogical lines, the *Reewin* developed a political structure that transends lineage systems in favor of a system of territorial identity. Terms like *Reer Bay* (people of Bay), *Reer Dhooboy* (people of Dhooboy), *Reer Ghedo* (people of the other side of the Jubba river), *Reer Maanyo* (people of the sea), just to mention a few, explain how territorial identification is important in the *Reewin* political structure. For further details, see: Cassanelli, *The Shaping of the Somali Society,* pp. 15–25. The best general overview of *Reer Goleed* (people of Gosha), is Kenneth J.

Menkhaus, "Rural Transformation and the Roots of Underdevelopment in Somalia's Lower Jubba Valley," Ph.D. diss., University of South Carolina, Columbia, 1989, pp. 16–40. With regard to their political thought, see: M. Mukhtar, "The Emergence and the Role of Political Parties in the InterRiver Region of Somalia," pp. 75-95.

37. K. John Menkhaus, "Rural Transformation," p. 33.

38. Abu 'Abdalla Muhammad Ibn 'Abdalla al-Tanji Ibn Battuta, *Tuhfat al-Nazar fi Ghara'ib al-Amsar wa-'Aja'ib al-Asfar*, known as Rihlat Ibn Battuta (Beirut, 1960), pp. 574–84.

39. Hersi, "The Arab Factor," p. 166.

40. Ibn Battuta, *Rihlat*, p. 253.

41. Wilfred H. Schoff, *The Periplus of the Erythraean Sea* (London: 1912), pp. 60-61.

42. *Ibid.*, p. 3.

43. Hersi, *"The Arab Factor,"* 179; for more information, see also: Muhammad Abd al-Fattah Hindi, *Tarikh al-Sumal* (Cairo: Dar al-Ma'arif, 1961), pp. 7-12.

44. Hamdi al-Sayyid Salim, *al-Sumal Qadiman wa Hadithan*, vol. 1 (Cairo: al-Dar al-Qawmiyyah li al-Tiba'ah wa al-Nashr,1965), p. 321. See also: Muhammad Abd al Fattah Hindi, *Tarikh al-Sumal fi al-'Usur al-Qadimah*, in: *Somalia, Antologia Storico-Culturale*, No. 4. (Hamar: Dipartimento Culturale, 1967), p. 6.

45. Neville Chitick, "An Archaeological Reconnaissance of the Southern Somali Coast," *Azania: Journal of British Institute of History and Archaeology in East Africa*, 4 (Nairobi, 1969):10–14.

46. al-Shaykh Ahmad 'Abdalla Rirash, *Kashf al-Sudul 'An Tarikh al-Sumal wa-Mamalikihim al-Sab'ah* (Muqdishu: Madbacadda Qaranka, 1974), p. 12.; Mukhtar, *"Takwin 'ula Marakiz al-Da'wah al-Islamiyyah,"* p. 274.

47. There are hundreds of Italian colonial records, published and unpublished, describing the social, economic, and political conditions of the area. For a sampling, see: Ugo Ferrandi, *Lugh: Emporio commerciale sul Giuba* (Rome: Societa Geografica Italiana,1903,) which provides remarkable information about the political administration of Luq and its economic activities and lists the successive ruling families in the area, especially the Gasara Gude monarchy. Massimo Colucci, *Principi di diritto consuetudinario della Somalia italiana meridionale* (Florence: Societa Editrice, 1924) offers solid material on the socioeconomic realities of southern Somalia and various forms of governing systems in the interriver region. Charles Guillain, *Documents sur l'histoire, la geographie et le commerce de l'Afrique orientale*, 3 vols. (Paris: Arthus Bertrand, 1856) has impressive accounts on the coastal zone of Somalia, especially Benadir and the lower Shabelle Valley.

Otto Kersten, ed., *Baron Carl Claus Von der Decken's Reisen in Ost Afrika in den Jahren 1862–1865* (Leipzig: C.F. Winter, 1871) provides tangible information on the economic activities along the Jubba valley.

48. 'Abdurahman Zaki, *Al-Islam wa-al-Muslimun fi Sharq Ifriqiya* (Cairo: Matba'at Yusuf, 1960), p. 71.

49. The nomadic pastorals of Somalia refer to the *Reewin* people as *Elai (Eelay)*; they also refer to the Mai language that is spoken by the *Reewin* as *Af Elai (Eelay* language). It is a common mistake, widespread in Somalia during the last century when constant contacts between pastorals and agro-pastorals became frequent. The *Reewin* people, on the other hand, refer to the pastorals with terms such as Fara Dheer (long fingers), *Lama Goodle* ("two-cloth," indicating the two pieces worn only by nomads), *Reer Badiye* ("bush people"), etc., and some times they refer to all of the Somali pastoral nomads as *Hawiye*. However, the *Elai* are among the largest *Reewin* clans. They are predominantly farmers with some interest in cattle herding. They are divided into three major sub-clans, known as *Seddi Gember* (three seats): the *Bohorad, Nasie,* and *Gedefade*. See: M. Collucci, *Principi di diritto consuetudinario della Somalia meridionale* (Florence, 1924), p. 181, and also I.M. Lewis, *Peoples of the Horn of Africa; Somali, Afar and Saho* (London: 1969), p. 36.

50. Mohamed Haji Mukhtar, Field notes and Interviews with Elders and Religious Figures in *Afgoye, Wanle Weyn* and *Bur Hakaba,* Summer 1977.

51. *Doi* is a zone located between *Adabla* in the north and *Dhooboy* in the south, very good in its pasture. It extends from *Buur Haybe* in the east, to *Dinsor* in the west.

52. The name derives from the Arabic *Abul Qasim* ["the father of Qasim"], which is the nickname of the Prophet of Islam, Muhammad.

53. Note that *Emed* and *Ahmed* are the same. Unlike *Maxa (Maha)*, it is necessary to bear in mind that Mai has no pharyngial or glottal sounds, such as *ha (xa)* and *'a (ca)*.

54. Abdurug is a village located twenty miles southwest of Baidoa.

55. The terms *Oboy* and *Dada* mean "grandmother," whereas *Abay* means "elder sister." The term *Siti* comes from the arabic sayyidati, which means "my lady."

56. J.S. Trimingham, *The Sufi Orders in Islam* (Oxford, 1971), p. 28.

57. Cassanelli, *Shaping of Somali Society*, pp. 122-129.

58. Hersi, "The Arab Factor," p. 177.

59. *Qur'an*, Suurah al-Hujurat (49), Ayah 13.

60. 'Abd al-Rahman Ibn Muhammad Ibn Khaldun, *al-Muqaddimah,* trans. Franz Rosenthal (Princeton, 1967), p. 120.

61. Philip S. Khouri and Joseph Kostiner, eds., *Tribes and State Formation in the Middle East* (Berkeley: University of California Press, 1990), p. 164.
62. Ibn Khaldun, *al-Muqaddimah*, pp. 119–120.
63. Abu Muhammad 'Abdalla Ibn Hisham Ibn Ayyub al-Himyari Ibn Hisham, *al-Sirah al-Nabawiyyah*, 4 vols. (Cairo: Mustafa al-Bab al-Halabi) vol.1, pp. 322–323.
64. About the Saqifa Conference, see: Montgomery Watt, *Islamic Political Thought* (Edinburgh, 1968), p. 32; for more detailed accounts, see also: al-Shahristani, *al-Milal wa al-Nihal* (Cairo), vol. 1, p. 18; and also, *Encyclopedia of Islam*, vol. 1, (Leiden: E.J. Brill, 1986), pp. 381–386; vol. 4, pp. 937–953.
65. Ibn Hisham, *al-Sirah al-Nabawiyyah*, p. 323.
66. Ibn Khaldun, *al-Muqaddimah*, p. 158.
67. Cassanelli, *Shaping of Somali Society* ,p. 28.

ASPECTS OF THE BENADIR CULTURAL HISTORY:

THE CASE OF THE BRAVAN ULAMA

∽

Mohamed M. Kassim

Historical Background

Historically, the Banadir coast is the coastal strip extending from Warsheikh to Ras Kiamboni in present day Somalia. The name "Benadir" is derived from the Persian word *Bendar*, which means "ports" but signifies the coastal areas where goods are exchanged. The history of the Banadir coast is part of the history of the East African Swahili coast. It is closely intertwined in all its economic, cultural, and historical evolution to the Swahili coast. Contemporary historians have concentrated their research on the Kenyan, Tanzanian, and Mozambican parts of the Swahili coast and neglected or did not give due merit to the Banadir coast. The Banadir coast has been treated as merely the coastal area where the first Arab-Persian settlements were built and whence some of these settlers later migrated to the southern Swahili coast.

This paper[1] surveys the rich cultural history of this coast and calls for the archaeological study and the anthropological and ethnographic investigation of this much neglected part of the northern Swahili coast.

Most coastal historians agree that the Banadir coast is the first Swahili settlement on the East African coast settled around the 9th and 10th centuries.[2] Tradition, coastal chroniclers, and Arab geographers suggest that the first settlers came from the Persian Gulf. Archaeological and linguistic evidence suggests that there was also a Bantu population in the nearby fertile river valleys of the Jubba and Shabelli.[3] The Swahili culture that evolved in this coast was the result of the contact between this Arab-Islamic civilization on the coast with the Bantu culture of the hinterland.

According to coastal traditions, the Arab-Persian immigration reached the Benadir coast in successive waves. This coastal area was also the first foothold of Islam in the East African coast.[4] Oral traditions relating to the foundation of the Benadir coastal cities by Arab and Persian immigrants are supported by the historical sites in these areas.[5] Even the selection of the sites of these cities indicates that they were built by a maritime and mercantile community.[6] We will not indulge in the discussion of who the founders of these cities were and whether their foundation was in the 10th or the 12th century. What is important to note is that all the early historic sites found today are all credited to Arab-Persian settlers.

There is strong evidence that Swahili was originally spoken throughout the Banadir coast.[7] Several communities on this coast and some villages along the Jubba River have retained their Swahili language and culture. In addition to the coastal city of Brava and the Bajunis in the Kismayo zone (which are areas of Swahili literature and culture), the native inhabitants of Mogadishu and Merka have retained the Swahili culture, traditions, and personal names.[8] Also, the origin of the place names of Mukadisho (*mui wa mwisho* = the end city), Shangani (on the sand), Marika and Kismayu (*kisima iu* = upper well) indicates that these were all Swahili cities.[9] The linguistic Somalization of the Banadir coast started around the 13th century, when the first Somali-speaking nomads appeared there.[10] This has gradually eroded the Swahili language in the cities of Warsheikh, Mogadishu, and Merka. The impact of the Somali language diminishes as you move south along the Benadir coast.[11] For example, the northern Swahili dialect of Chimini (or Chimbalazi, which is spoken in Brava) has acquired some Somali vocabulary. The Bajuni dialect (also northern Swahili) has less Somali vocabulary than the Chimini, while all the rest of the southern Swahili dialects have no Somali vocabulary.[12]

Town Islam and Civilization

To describe how the Benadiri coastal towns were run during the 9th to 12th centuries is a matter for future research. What is known from travellers' accounts and early chronicles is that both Mogadishu and Brava were ruled by councils of elders representing all the clans of these city-states.[13] This joint leadership has probably ensured prosperity for the inhabitants and a comparatively more peaceful coexistence amongst themselves. The rule by town councils can also be attributed to the fact that some of these immigrants came to these shores to escape persecution and hence longed for a more peaceful climate. Others came to trade or settle in a more prosperous environment. Whatever their reasons for immigration, one thing is clear: they did not come to conquer or pillage this area, nor did they aspire to build an empire.[14] The first settlers of this coastal region came from diverse parts of the Arabian peninsula and the Persian Gulf with an urban and literate cultural background and were, as Cerulli described, "bound together by ties of citizenship and not by tribal relations."[15]

The Ulama and traders from this area spread the Islamic urban civilization southwards to the rest of the East African coast.[16] During this period the Benadir coastal towns developed into important trading centers. Similar to the other Swahili towns, the pursuit of wealth through trade and other vocational activities was the main objective of these townspeople. Even today, the two lifelong goals to be attained by a "civilized" *(uungwana)* townsman are the fulfillment of his religious obligations and the pursuit of wealth, mainly through overseas trade. But the pursuit of wealth and the access to religious education were available to all and, up to the present

20th century, these towns witnessed the upward mobility of many families and the emergence of brilliant religious scholars from the poorest members of their communities.

Another factor that may have contributed to the harmony and peaceful coexistence of these towns is that wealth was dependent upon family or individual profits and not upon taxation, leaving their rulers little authority.[17] Obviously, East African coastal civilization, with its Islamic mercantile culture and diverse ethnic composition, has managed to glean a common interest in trade and wealth building.

Between the 10th and 13th centuries, the Banadir coast enjoyed a period of prosperity and cultural efflorescence.[18] Mogadishu was a splendid and prosperous city during Ibn Battuta's visit around 1330.[19] Recent coin finds also indicate that Mogadishu minted its own local currency from 1300 to 1700.[20] But this economic affluence was very much dependent on international trade, and the economic decline of these coastal city-states started when the Portuguese began intercepting the trade from these cities during the 16th century. This economic calamity was followed by the overthrow of both the Ajuran dynasty of the Banadir hinterland and Muzaffar dynasty of Mogadishu by Hawiye clans.[21]

Although the Banadir coastal cities gradually lost their economic clout and Mogadishu, by the 19th century, had become "a shadow of its former splendid self,"[22] the influence and work of the Ulama from this coastal area proceeded unabated.

The Ulama of the Benadir Coastal Towns

Throughout the history of the East African coast, the Ulama and Mashaikh have been the pillars of town society.[23] The towns of the Banadir coast were no exception. The Ulama, by operating both the legal and educational systems and by their involvement in trade, exercised political power in these city-states. In Mogadishu, for example, the Chief Qadi was chosen from among the "Reer Faqi" of Hamar Weyn.[24] Similarly, in Brava and Merka, the Chief Qadi was also chosen from among the religious scholars.[25] Although the trade needs of these towns have determined ecological choices,[26] the Islamic civilization, propagated by the Ulama, gave these towns an identity and a unique character.

To illustrate the influence of the Ulama in the Banadir coast, the profiles of five Ulama and poets from Brava will be discussed. All five lived between 1847 and 1958 and had a strong influence on this town.[27] The first of these Ulama, and an *alim* (religious scholar) whose influence spread throughout the whole of East Africa, is Shaikh Uways Bin Muhammad Al-Barawi.[28] Shaikh Uways was born in Brava in 1847 and studied under Shaikh Muhammad Zayini Al-Shanshi. He later continued his studies in Baghdad under the Qadiri master Sayyid Mustafa ibn al-Sayyid Salman al-Kaylani, son of Shaikh Salman al-Kaylani.[29]

Upon Shaikh Uways's return to Somalia, he established a mosque-school that became the most important Qadiriya education center in East Africa. From 1881 to his death in April 1909 Sheikh Uways was involved in the spread of Islam in southern Somalia and throughout East Africa (as far as eastern Congo). The Uwaysiya, a branch of the Qadiriya brotherhood (*tariqa*) founded by Shaikh Uways, were involved in the Muslim resistance to European colonization in Buganda in the 1880s, and in German-controlled Tanganyika in the 1890s.[30] Besides his missionary activities, Shaikh Uways composed several poems in the Somali and Arabic languages.

The second *alim* and a distinguished jurist was Shaikh Nurein Ahmed Sabir al-Hatimy (1247H–1327H).[31] Shaikh Nurein was born in Brava and received all his education there. Shaikh Nurein was from the Hatimy clan of Brava and a follower of the "Ahmadiya" *tariqa*.[32] Although he was trained in all the religious sciences, Shaikh Nurein was considered an expert in *Fiqh* (jurisprudence). This had earned him an appointment as the Chief Qadi of Brava during the reign of Sultan Barghash. Shaikh Nurein was well known as an honest, pious, and just jurist who trained many Bravan scholars.[33] Today, Shaikh Nurein is a revered saint whose mosque-tomb is the site of an annual commemoration known as "Ziyara za Sh. Nureini."

The third *alim* and poet was Shaikh Qassim bin Muhyiddin

al-Barawi (1295H –14 Ramadan, 1340H). Shaikh Qassim, one of the most prolific religious poets, was the author of many *qasaid* (religious poems). Shaikh Qassim, who was from the Wa'ili clan, composed poems in Arabic and Chimbalazi. One of Shaikh Qassim's popular *qasida* is called "Chidirke," a poem imploring the Prophet Muhammad's "intercession." Shaikh Qassim also composed a Chimbalizi version of Al-Busiri's "Hamziya" and, as a follower of Shaikh Uways, authored "Ta'nis Al-jalis fi manaqib al-Shaikh Uways" and "Mujmu'a Al Qasaid."

The fourth poet-*alim* is Dada Masiti (1219H–17 Shawal, 1339H),[34] a contemporary of both Shaikh Uways, Shaikh Nurein, and Shaikh Qassim. Dada Masiti, who was from the Al-Ahdal clan of the Asharaf (descendants of the Prophet Muhammad), was born in Brava and as a six-year-old child was kidnapped and taken to Zanzibar. After approximately ten years, she was found by relatives who brought her back to Brava. Upon her return, Dada Masiti became immersed in religious studies and Sufi mysticism. She composed many religious poems, including "Shaikhi Chifa isiloowa," a powerful eulogy for Shaikh Nurein Ahmed Al-Sabir Al-Hatimy.[35] Dada Masiti is the only known female saint[36] and was a prolific poet in Somalia.

The fifth poet-*alim* is Shaikh Moallim Nur Haji Abdulkadir (1299H–27 Muharam, 1379H),[37] better known as Moallim Nuri. Moallim Nuri, a native of Brava and a member of the Tunni clan, studied under Shaikh Qassim Al-Barawi and Shaikh Nurein Sabir Al-Hatimy. Shaikh Moallim Nuri was a "Chimbalazi" literary genius who composed a "Chimbalazi" translation in versified form of "Matn az-zubad fi al-fiqh." The "Matn az-zubad" is a classical *"fiqh"* (jurisprudence) work written in Arabic by Shaikh Ahmed bin Raslan. Moallim Nuri's "Zubadi," which is more than a thousand verses, is a didactic *"tenzi"* that has the same metre as Shaikh Raslan's "Az-Zubad." The "Zubadi" prescribes the basic tenets of Islam and the correct procedure of performing the daily prayers, the Zakat, the Ramadan fasting, and the Haj pilgrimage. In Brava, for many years, Moallim Nuri's "Zubadi" was a required reading and was memorized by most Qoranic school students.

There are several interesting points to be noted from these brief biographies. The first is the fact that coastal *Ulama* used several media to teach. In conjunction with their teaching in the Qoranic schools (Chuo, Ziwo in Chimbalazi) and the mosque-schools, these *Ulama* used religious poetry to teach the basic tenets of Islam, the religio-legal laws *(Fiqh)* and all the Islamic rituals and beliefs. Another fact is that this education was so extensive and accessible, to both men and women, rich and poor, that certain towns like Brava had, up to the present, an illiteracy rate of zero. This exceptionally high rate of literacy in Brava may also be due to the fact that Qoranic schools in Brava are taught mainly by women teachers.[38]

Finally, there was a strong feeling of respect, friendship, and understanding between these *Ulama*. Their close friendships have in turn built cohesiveness in this multiethnic community. This can be gleaned also from their poetry. In one of Shaikh Qassim Al-Barawi's poems, "Chidirke," he states:

> *Shaikhi Uwayso Shaikhuna*
> *Shaikhi ya Masharifuna*
> (Shaikh Uways is our Shaikh.
> He is the Shaikh of our Sharifs.)[39]

In another poem, Shaikh Qassim praises Dada Masiti as follows:

> *Khusifawe skhadiri sifazo*
> *Ni Kathiri ntazimo Buldani*
> *Ni Sharifa afifa saliha mana*
> *wa sadati masultani*
>
> (I cannot give your rightful description,
> The description of your qualities is not mentioned even
> in the Buldan.[40]
> She is noble, she is chaste, she is pious,
> And the daughter of noble descendants.)

Besides their influence within these towns, the *Ulama* from the coastal towns of the Banadir have been travelling to the coastal cities of East Africa to spread Islam since the Middle Ages.[41] This has continued up to the early part of the 20th century. Two of the most prominent Ulama from Brava who trained other East African Ulama were Shaikh Muhyiddin Al-Qahtani Al-Wa'ili and Shaikh Abdulaziz bin Abdulghany Al-Amawy.

Shaikh Muhyiddin Al-Qahtani Al-Wa'ili (1794–1869) was born and educated in Brava. Shaikh Muhyiddin, who was from the Wa'ili clan in Brava, wrote several books in Arabic and several poems in Swahili. He later moved to Mombasa and served as a Qadi in the courts of Sayid Said.[42]

Shaikh Abdulaziz bin Abdulghany Al-Amawy (1834–1896)[43] was also born and educated in Brava. Shaikh Abdulaziz, who was from the Al-Amawy[44] clan of Brava, was one of Shaikh Uways's *"khalifas"* (deputies or adherents).[45] Shaikh Abdulaziz was a distinguished scholar who became the Qadi of Kilwa in 1848 at the age of eighteen. He was later appointed the Qadi of Zanzibar during the reign of Sultan Barghash. Shaikh Abdulaziz was an active and vocal opponent of European expansion in East Africa.

The Charisma of Shaikh Uways

The history of the Banadir coast provides many instances of how important the influence of the Sufi saints was in its cultural history. Shaikh Uways is considered as one of the great Sufi saints and a trailblazer in the introduction of the Qadiriya *tariqa* in Somalia. His efforts and enthusiasm were unsurpassed in his relentless drive to spread Islam. But what distinguishes Shaikh Uways from all the great Ulama of Somalia is Shaikh Uways's charisma. This can be illustrated by the following incident[46] that took place in Mogadishu right after Shaikh Uways's return to southern Somalia.

One of the most prominent *Ulama* of the Banadir coast was Shaikh Abdurahman Bin Shaikh Abdalla (1245H–1323H) better known as Shaikh Hagi Sufi.[47] Shaikh Sufi, a native of Mogadishu, was a distinguished scholar and was considered an authority on the Islamic religious sciences (*Funun*) in the whole Banadir coast. Initially Shaikh Sufi was reluctant to join the Qadiriya movement, but Shaikh Uways was able to convince Shaikh Sufi, after a long and arduous discussion, to join the Qadiriya *tariqa*.[48]

During the mid 19th-century a new form of dance became popular in Mogadishu. The dance was known as *"Manyas."* This dance featured men and scantly dressed women dancers dancing at very close proximity. The dance was considered by the town's *Ulama* as very profane and indecent. But the *Ulama,* including Shaikh Sufi, could not stop these dances. What disturbed Shaikh Sufi more was that the two main quarters of Mogadishu, Shangani and Hamar Weyn, were in competition with each other. The merchants and the wealthy families of each quarter were the patrons of the dance competitors and paid them to compete. Apparently, the merchants were also profiting from the business generated by the large crowds who came to watch these dances. Shaikh Sufi preached regularly at the Jami' Mosque of Hamar Weyn, the quarter where he was residing. In his daily sermons Shaikh Sufi implored the merchants and the dancers to stop, but the dances were so lucrative that both the merchants and dancers did not heed the revered Shaikh's request.

Shaikh Sufi was so distressed by this that in one of his popular religious poems he asked God to rid his people of this indecent dance. In this poem, written in Arabic, he states:

> With your power rid us of the *"Manyas"* ritual and the
> *"Kufr"* (Unbelief) and Satan's way
> And guide our leaders to the right path.
> And teach us the sciences and do not make us like one
> of the ignorant
> And give us the patience to stay with the virtuous.

Some time after Shaikh Sufi composed the above poem he received a *"Ru'ya"* (revelation) on this matter. In this revelation Shaikh Sufi saw a great and charismatic Shaikh coming from the west and ridding the town of this "evil" dance. Shaikh Sufi informed his disciples about the revelation. After several months, Shaikh Uways came to Mogadishu from Baghdad through Berbera and Ogadenia (the west) to the Shangani quarter of Mogadishu. In Mogadishu, Shaikh Uways was received by the Sultan of the Ya'qub of Mogadishu (one of the Abgal clans) and stayed at the Sultan's residence.

Shaikh Uways then met Shaikh Sufi who asked for Shaikh Uways's intervention. Shaikh Uways and his entourage went to the site of these dances in Shangani where his followers made a circle and started one of his popular Uwaysiya *"Dhikr."*[49] Shaikh Uways's *Dhikr* and preaching were so impressive that the whole audience left the dancers and joined Shaikh Uways's congregation. The crowd, the dancers, and merchants were so moved by Shaikh Uways's preaching that they immediately vowed to stop the dances. Later several merchants and dance *"Kabirs"* (leaders) joined the Uwaysiya movement and became *"Khalifas."*

Shaikh Uways exemplifies how a man of humble origins could exact the respect and veneration of disparate communities that were spread out in many parts of Somalia. There are also two remarkable factors about Shaikh Uways's missionary work that are worth mentioning here. The first is the strict use of nonviolent methods in spreading his message, unlike other *tariqas* in Somalia. The other is the phenomenal success of his *tariqa,* which spread over a vast area (from the northern regions of Somalia to the eastern Congo).

Conclusion

The Benadir coastal towns were, until the 16th century, very typical of other traditional Swahili towns, such as Lamu, Mombasa, and Malindi. Although there has been a gradual erosion of the Swahili culture since that period, several communities along this coast still retain this culture and language. It is also significant that the Benadir coast is the birthplace of the Swahili civilization and has also been the cultural, trade, and religious center that spread this civilization to the rest of the East African coast. Here we suggest that the *Ulama* of the Benadir coast were the real force that drove this civilization and propagated it southwards to the rest of the East African coast. We have cited, as a case example, the rich contribution made by the *Ulama* of the town of Brava during the 19th and 20th centuries. With the destruction of some of the historic sites in this area and the mass exodus of the native inhabitants of these coastal towns, there is an urgent need to investigate the history and culture of this part of the Swahili coast.

Notes

1. I extend my thanks to Prof. Lee V. Cassanelli, Prof. M. Mukhtar, and others for reviewing this paper and for their suggestions.
2. G.S.P.Freeman-Grenville, ed., *The East African Coast: Selected Documents from the First to the Nineteenth Century* (London: Oxford Univ. Press, 1966), pp.83-84. Also N.Chittick, "The Peopling of the East African Coast," *East Africa and the Orient* (1975), p.41. Refer also to E. Cerulli,"Inscrizioni e documenti Arabi per la storia della Somalia," *Somalia: scritti vari editi ed inediti*, vol. 1 (Rome, 1957), pp. 1–24.
3. J.Trimingham, *Islam in East Africa* (Oxford: Clarendon Press, 1964),pp. 6–7. Also D.Nurse,"A Linguistic Reconsideration of Swahili Origins," *Azania* 18 (1983): pp. 136–137.
4. R. Pouwels,"Islam and Islamic Leadership in the Coastal Communities of Eastern Africa, 1700 to 1914," PhD thesis, University of California at Los Angeles, 1979, p.13.
5. E. Cerulli, *Somalia: scritti vari editi e inediti* vol.1 (Rome, 1957), p. 304. This includes inscriptions on mosques and tombs recorded by Cerulli.
6. William Puzo, "Mogadishu, Somalia: Geographic Aspects of Its Evolution, Population, Functions and Morphology," PhD thesis, University of California at Los Angeles, 1972, p.20. Note that Mogadishu was built on a slightly raised coral promontory with defensive walls on the landward side.
7. J.Knappert, "Four centuries of Swahili verse" (London: Heinemann, 1979), p. xvi. Also Middleton, *The World of the Swahili* (Yale Univ. Press, 1992), p.22.
8. The names of Bana (Bwana), Mana (Mwana), Munye (Mwenye), which are only used by the native people from the Banadir coast, are all Swahili names.
9. There is also an Arabic version of some of these names. But several scholars have doubted their validity (see: N. Chittick, "Mediaeval Mogadisho," *Paideuma* 28 (1982):1.
10. Vinigi L. Grottanelli,"The Peopling of the Horn of Africa," *East Africa and the Orient* (1975), p.74.

11. With the exception of Kismayo, where there has been an infusion of new immigrants.
12. M. Abasheikh, "The Grammar of Chimwi:ni Causatives", Ph.D. thesis, Univ. of Illinois at Urbana-Champaign, 1978, p.4.
13. Yaqut,"Mu'jam Al-Buldan," (c.1228). Also E.Cerulli, *Somalia: scritti vari*, vol. 1, pp. 135–136. According to traditions, Mogadishu was ruled by a federation of 39 clans: 12 from the Mukri ("Reer Faqi"), 12 from the Djid'ati ("Shanshia"), 6 from the Aqabi ("Reer Shaikh"), 6 from the Ismaili, and 3 from the Afifi ("Gudmana"). Brava was also ruled by 12 elders (Freeman-Granville,"Medieval History of the Coast of Tanganyika," pp. 31–32, in reference to Joao de Barros, "Decadas da Asia," I, Book 8).
14. Middleton, *World of the Swahili*, p.20.
15. E. Cerulli,"Somaliland," *Somalia: scritti vari editi ed inediti*, vol. I, p. 148. There were of course economic distinctions between the poor and rich and prestige and rights given to the founders of each town.
16. R. Pouwels,"Islam and Islamic Leadership," p. 461. Also Trimingham, *Islam in East Africa*, p. 6. According to Freeman-Grenville, merchants from Brava were seen trading in places like Malindi.
17. Middleton, *World of the Swahili*, p.44.
18. Puzo, "Mogadishu, Somalia," p. 25.
19. H.A.R. Gibb, *The Travels of Ibn Battuta*, vol. 12 (Cambridge, 1962), p.373.
20. G. Freeman-Grenville, "East African Coin Finds and Their Historical Significance," *Journal of African History 1*, 1 (1960): 31-42.
21. L.Cassanelli, *The Shaping of Somali Society* (Philadelphia: Univ. of Pennsylvania Press, 1982), pp.92–93.
22. E.Alpers, "Muqdisho in the Nineteenth Century: A Regional Perspective," *Journal of African History*, 24(1983): 442.
23. R. Pouwels, *Horn and Crescent: Cultural Change and Ttraditional Islam on the East African Coast, 800–1900* (Cambridge Univ. Press, 1987), p.93.
24. Cerrina-Ferroni, *Benadir*, 28. The "Reer Faqi" were one of the founding clans of the city of Mogadishu. They were originally known as the Muqri clan (E. Cerulli,"Makdishu," *Somalia: scritti vari*, p. 136).
25. Shaikh Nureini Ahmed Sabir Al-Hatimy (1247H– 1327H), one of the most revered saints in Brava, was also the Chief Qadi of the town during Sayyid Barqash's reign.
26. Middleton, *World of the Swahili*, p.16.
27. The Banadir coast has produced many distinguished scholars, which should be the topic of another paper.

28. C. Ahmed, "God, Anti-Colonialism and Drums," *Ufahamu* 17, 2 (1989).
29. B.G. Martin, "Muslim Politics and Resistance to Colonial Rule: Shaikh Uways B. Muhammad Al-Barawi and the Qadiriya Brotherhood in East Africa," *Journal of African History* 10, 3(1969): 471–486.
30. *Ibid.* Also see: C. Ahmed, "God, Anti-Colonialism."
31. Interview with Shaikh Saidi Sh. Faqihi Shaikh Nurein, Mombasa; September 1993. Shaikh Saidi is a distinguished Bravan scholar and the grandson of Shaikh Nurein Ahmed Sabir Al-Hatimy.
32. Most of the inhabitants of Brava follow the Qadiriya *tariqa*. The Hatimy clan follow the "Salahiya" while a few Bravans follow the "Ahmadiya."
33. Among them were Sh. Abba Shaikh Haj Talha, Shaikh Moallim Nur Haj Abdulqadir, Sharif Sufi Habib, and Shaikh Qassim Al-Barawi.
34. Discussions with Dada Hajiya Shegow (101 years old) in Brava, February 1984; also interviews with Dr. Khalif Mowlana Sufi, Mombasa, September 1993.
35. This poem was composed to prevent the followers of Shaikh Nurein from crying and to ease their sorrow. But the poem has such a powerful emotional effect that even today most people shed tears when it is recited.
36. Dada Masiti's tomb is a site for *"ziyaara"* or annual commemoration.
37. Interviews with Shaikh Saidi Sh. Faqihi Shaikh Nurein, Mombasa, September 1993.
38. Arab League Educational, Cultural, and Scientific Organization (ALESCO), "A Survey of Qoranic Schools in the Somali Democratic Republic," January 1983.
39. The Sharifs or Masharifu clan-family are the descendants of the Prophet Muhammad. They are considered the religious elite and for Shaikh Qassim to describe Shaikh Uways as the Shaikh of all "their Masharifu" is the utmost complement that can be attributed to any scholar.
40. Here Buldan means "in all our books" (i.e., nobody has covered).
41. R. Pouwels, "Islam and Islamic Leadership," p.460.
42. *Ibid.*, p. 462. Also B.G. Martin,"Notes on Some Members of the Learned Classes of Zanzibar and East Africa in the 19th Century," *African Historical Studies* 4, 3(1971).
43. *Ibid.*, pp. 463-467.
44. The Al-Amawy clan-family of Brava are also known as the *"Ra Moallim."* Traditionally, they had the privilege of performing most of the religious functions, such as the Friday *"Khutba"* (ser-

mon), officiated marriage ceremonies, hereditary entitlements, etc.

45. B. G. Martin,"Muslim Politics and Resistance," p.474.
46. This incident, which is well known in the Banadir coast, was related to the author's father by Shaikh Mohamed Sufi Bin Al-Shaikh Qassim Al-Barawi (1908–1968). Shaikh Mohamed Sufi is the son of Shaikh Qassim Al-Barawi (discussed above) and the person who compiled Shaikh Sufi's collective works.
47. A brief biography and a collection of some of his works was compiled by Shaikh Mohamed Sufi bin Al-Shaikh Qassim Al-Barawi in "Dalil Al-Ibad Ila Sabil Al-Irshad" (Cairo: Al-Kilani Al-Sagir Press, n.d.).
48. Oral sources indicate that Shaikh Uways had a deep respect for Shaikh Sufi and referred to Shaikh Sufi as *"Abbe"* (father) when addressing him.
49. *Dhikr* is a Sufi litany that invokes the Remembrance of God or the Prophet Muhammad. For more discussion on Sufi *Dhikr*, see: Martin Lings, *What is Sufism* (London & Boston: Unwin Paperbacks,1981).

The Invention of Gosha:

Slavery, Colonialism,

and Stigma in Somali History[1]

∽

Catherine Besteman

The image of Somalia as an homogenous nation of one people who speak one language, practice one religion, and share one culture has been pervasive in the media as well as in scholarly writings. Only recently have divisions based on language, religious brotherhoods, and occupation been recognized[2] as significant distinctions[3] in Somali society. Somalia can no longer be represented as a "nation of nomads" or "a pastoral democracy" since the majority of contemporary Somalis have settled into the relatively sedentary lifestyles of farming or urban dwelling. Additionally, the perception of an homogenous population of cattle-and-camel herders is historically incorrect because it excludes the significant number of farmers who have lived along the banks of Somalia's two major rivers, the Jubba and the Shabelle, for generations. The riverine farmers speak Somali, practice Islam, share Somali cultural values, are legally Somali citizens, and most consider themselves members of Somali clans. Despite outward trappings of being Somali, however, many look different, and so are considered different by Somalis.

The majority of the riverine farmers of the Jubba Valley

are descendents of slaves acquired by Somalis in the 19th century.[4] The stigma of an enslaved past continues to mark Jubba Valley farmers, because the non-Somali physical characteristics shared by many valley farmers have been maintained by endogamous marriage patterns. Known as the Gosha after the geographical area in which they live, Jubba Valley farmers hold a distinct place in Somali social and cultural life. (*Gosha* is glossed as "dense jungle" and denotes the forested banks of the Jubba River stretching from above Kismayo to below Saakow. The geographical term *Gosha* has been extended to refer to the people who live in the Gosha.) Assigning group or tribal names and delineating supposed social groups on the basis of geography has been fairly common practice among both colonialists and ethnographers.[5] The present paper demonstrates how this process began for the farmers of the Jubba Valley by investigating the creation of "The Gosha" as a social category by colonial governments through official discourse and political practices, and by Somalis through ideologically constructed perceptions of difference and hierarchy. As the Gosha have a shared history of slavery (and thus non-Somali origins) but are "Somali" in other respects (language, culture, religion, custom), the ambiguity of their status as Somali and non-Somali at the same time has perhaps facilitated their representation as a distinct and unified social group within Somali society.[6] My analysis will test the validity of this representation by investigating its roots and by exploring Gosha people's perceptions of their own identities.

Most intriguing, perhaps, are the issues that lie beyond the analysis offered here, namely, the potential for the development of a Gosha group political consciousness in the wake of civil unrest. The Gosha, and other groups like them in southern Somalia, have been especially brutalized in the rural violence of the past three years and were certainly the victims of "silent violence" under Barre's regime. The extent to which such victimization has had the effect of unifying those victimized is an open question, which I cannot answer. But I can raise the question, and provide a historically-based analysis of the invention of the Gosha which, hopefully, will prove useful for evaluating contemporary and future political configurations of this population.

Slavery and Settlement — A Brief History

With the rise of Zanzibar as a trade center in the 19th century, Somali entrepreneurs began purchasing East African slaves through the Indian Ocean slave trade in order to develop plantation agriculture in the Shabelle River region. Reluctant to farm themselves, Somali plantation owners relied on slave labor to produce a surplus of grain and cotton to sell in the burgeoning Indian Ocean trade.[7] Slaves were bought or captured from a wide variety of East African groups, including Yao, Zegua, Nyasa, and Makua, and brought by dhow to Somali ports by Arab traders. Slaves purchased by Somali plantation owners lived and labored on family-owned farms in the Shabelle Valley.[8] Cassanelli estimates that the riverine areas absorbed somewhere around 50,000 slaves between 1800 and 1890.[9]

During this period of expanded agricultural production in the Shabelle Valley, the more remote Jubba Valley remained largely uninhabited. Partially utilized by small groups of hunter-gatherers, the forested portion of the valley was largely avoided by Somali pastoralists because of tse-tse fly infestation, which is lethal to cattle. Its jungle cover, abundant wild foods, and arable land provided a refuge for slaves escaping from Shabelle plantations. Local lore reports that the first fugitive slaves reached the lower valley and established villages around 1840.[10] They were followed by a constant and increasing stream of runaway and manumitted slaves. Reports by European travelers suggest the lower valley population of ex-slaves had grown from several thousand by 1865 to between 30,000 and 40,000 by the turn of the century.[11] Abolition decrees introduced after 1900 prompted a massive flight of slaves from Shabelle plantations, and perhaps 20,000 to 30,000 ex-slaves made their way into the Jubba Valley after the turn of the century.[12]

Ex-slaves arriving in the Jubba Valley initially settled in villages along lines of East African ethnic affiliations: Yao in one village, Nyasa in another, etc.[13] By the late 19th century, maroon villages stretched up into the middle valley, and the settlement pattern had begun to change. Somali clan affiliation emerged as an important force in shaping village identity, as ex-slaves entering the valley after about 1890 began settling in communities of people who had been enslaved to the same Somali clan. Many people entering the valley around the turn of the century had been enslaved as children or had been born into slavery and thus held only tenuous connections to their original ethnic groups. For them, Somali clan affiliation provided a degree of social organization and identity.

The role of Somali clan affiliation in shaping settlement patterns was strengthened by the influx of pastoral slaves in the early 20th century. Pastoral slavery has been overlooked in the literature on southern Somalia, but was an integral part of Somali life during the 19th and early 20th centuries.[14] Oromo pastoralists, especially women and children, were captured by Somalis during wars and raids. Captured Oromo women became wives, concubines, and domestic slaves, and captured children were brought up as part of the household, but with a slave or servant status. In some cases, entire Oromo groups were absorbed as serfs or clients of Somali clans. Manumitted Oromo who settled into Jubba Valley farming villages often maintained ties with their former masters, strengthening the bonds of clan affiliation between Gosha villages and Somali clans. Oromo settled in large numbers in the mid-valley area around Bu'alle, and their immigration has been continual since the earliest decades of the 20th century. While Oromo are not considered to share physical characteristics with descendents of plantation slaves, much intermarriage in the Jubba Valley between the two has occurred.

Beginning in the late 1920s and continuing into the 60s, an additional immigrant group began filtering into the Jubba Valley. These immigrants, known as "*reer* Shabelle," were fleeing bloody tribal wars in their homeland around Kalafo on the Shabelle River across the border in Ethiopia. While their history is obscure, *reer* Shabelle speak Somali, practice Islam, and are closely affiliated with the Somali Ajuraan clan in the Kalafo area, yet in physical appearance resemble the cultivators of the Shabelle Valley and the descendents of plantation slaves in the Jubba Valley. Many *reer* Shabelle settled in Ajuraan-affiliated villages in the mid-valley area.

This brief historical sketch demonstrates the varied backgrounds of the people who settled the Jubba Valley, displacing or incorporating remnant preexisting hunter-gatherer groups. While derogatory terms such as *adoon* ("slave") are still used to describe the valley population, the neutral term *Gosha* has become more prevalent as an inclusive identifier. In what follows, I will first discuss the contemporary symbolic associations which unite Gosha in a particular social category, and then investigate how this term, originally geographic in reference, was extended to represent a distinct, unified, cohesive social group with perceived physical and/or cultural similarities.[15]

"Hard Hair" and Racial/Religious Ideology

References to the people of the Gosha in contemporary conversations (during my 1987–88 visit) seemed to favor two characteristics: their reputed fearsome magical abilities, and their physical appearance. In describing the Jubba Valley farmers, terms referring to physical characteristics were prevalent, especially the term *jareer,* glossed as "hard hair."

While *jareer* literally denotes hair texture, it encompasses other traits, such as particular kinds of bone structure and facial features, which are negatively valued. For example, the shape of the nose carries special significance, with broader noses being seen as significant markers. Gosha are said to be bulkier; more specifically, "pure" Somalis are said to have longer, more slender fingers.[16] The descriptive term used for "pure" Somalis in opposition to *jareer* is either *jileec* which means "soft" or, more commonly, *bilis* (which is the opposite of *adoon*).

Most significantly, people who are *jareer* are considered

more "African," as distinct from Somalis, who are considered more"Arabic." Taking the *jareer* distinction at its most overt level, then the ex-slave descendents[17] are singled out as a group, united under one label, based on their physical appearance. It is important to note that Oromo descendents are not considered *jareer.* However, in equating the Gosha with a *jareer* population, a separate Gosha Oromo identity has often been overlooked, especially by colonialists (a point to which we will return). Oromo descendents who have settled in the Gosha region have intermarried with slave descendents categorized as *jareer,* thus blurring the distinction. Even though many Oromo would not be individually identified as *jareer,* this label when generically applied to Gosha residents includes Oromo by association.

Analyzing how physical distinctions embodied in the *jareer* label became correlated with an inferior and stigmatized status is somewhat speculative, but the literature on the ideological construction of slavery and race in Islamic societies provides some interesting and thought-provoking points of comparison.[18] Throughout Northern Africa, the distinction of slaves being called "black" — regardless of the complexion of their masters — is prevalent.[19] As slaves — and populations from which they were taken — converted to Islam, a transition from equating "slave" with "infidel" to equating "slave" with "black" occurred, with "black" being negatively valued for its association with slavery and its real or purported connection with paganism. The use of the term *jareer* to indicate "African" in Somalia may thus be linked to the historic transition in Islamic slave-holding societies from emphasizing paganism to emphasizing racial difference in slaves. When used in Somalia, it is a resuscitation of the history of slavery of the referent, clearly rooting him in the legacy of subordination and inferior social status.

Writing about plantation slavery on the Kenyan coast, Cooper[20] argues that Islam was used by plantation owners to legitimize the social hierarchy in which the master has the right to dominate the slave. Being a Muslim, the master could conceive of his relationship to his slaves as benevolent (rather than overtly dominant) by seeing as his role the conversion of pagan slaves to Islam. Religion, Cooper says, was thus used to rationalize domination; ideology, in the form of religious beliefs, was "an active agent, as much a part of domination as whips or social dependence."[21] Willis[22] and Lovejoy[23] similarly discuss how the *jihad* (religious holy wars) could also become a raid for slaves, due to the ideology that enslavement, through conversion and eventual manumission, frees a person from the despicable status of unbelief. As Willis says, "parallels between slave and infidel began to fuse in the heat of *jihad*."[24]

In Somalia, "black infidels" were purchased as slaves. The transition from labelling slaves as "infidels" to labelling them as "Africans" (*jareer*) after their enslavement and conversion is clear. While I cannot claim that Somali slave owners were self-consciously using Islam to justify economic and social power structures, it is clear that Somalis saw the basis of their superiority as religious. Speke recorded in 1855 that Somalis believed the slave trade was their Quranic right,[25] an opinion found repeatedly in colonial documents from the era of abolition.[26] Oral histories indicate that the image of benevolence towards social dependents (slaves) certainly existed, especially among Somalis who captured Oromo for pastoral slavery (often in the context of *jihad*).[27] The duty of the master was to convert slaves to Islam. As Cooper says,[28] plantation slavery, and, to an even greater degree I would argue, pastoral slavery, was ideologically constructed as a form of (enforced) dependence (through slavery) and benevolence (through Islam). By converting the slave, the master ensured that the slave internalized the religious basis of his subordinate status[29]; the converted slave could never be "as good."[30]

The *jareer* label then, while referring to a complex of features believed to physically characterize the Gosha population, has as its greatest significance the cultural values embedded in being *jareer*. It is a term that refers to history — that of non-Somali pagan slave origins; a history devalued in Somali culture and ideology.[31] The effect in social terms of carrying a *jareer* identity is a denigrated status within Somali social structure. The people of the Gosha, collectively lumped together as *jareer,* thus collectively share a lower status within Somali society.

Colonial Contributions to the Creation of "The Gosha"

In the context of colonial intrusion and the imposition of classificatory labels based on imposed eurocentric racial categories, Somalis' abhorrence of being classified as "black African" was given a new, colonially created reality. During the 1920s, for example, there was a great effort on the part of Somalis and British administrators to have the classification of natives into racial categories revised so that Somalis could be categorized as Europeans or Asians rather than "black natives," as Somalis considered themselves derived from Arabia, not Africa. One letter written (in English) to the Chief Native Commissioner from Somali Darood elders in 1922 says:

> The government officials who have visited our country know we are descendents from Arabia, and this we have already proved and we can prove we assure you we cannot accept to be equalled and compared with those pagan tribes either with our consent or by force even if the government orders this we cannot comply with, but we prefer death than to be treated equally with these tribes for as the government knows well these tribes are inferior to us and according to our religion they were slaves who we used to trade during past years.[32]

The tribes to which the writers refer are all those living in what was then British East Africa which the British colonial authorities lumped together with Somalis as "Natives" under the authority of the Chief Native Commissioner.

British administrators in Somalia accepted the Somali vision of the social order and echoed their call for a separate category. The District Commissioner for Kismayu District wrote in 1922 that determining the "racial status" of Somalis was "the most important Somali question of today" and that Somalis should be taken out of jurisdiction of the Native Authority Ordinance and placed under an ordinance of their own.[33] The Senior Commissioner in Kismayu wrote the same year to the Chief Native Commissioner of British East Africa to emphasize that with Somalis, "You are dealing with the most advanced brain on the East Coast."[34] In 1924 Somalis rebelled against the Registration Act, believing that the Act would cause them to be treated like *Kikuyu* (a generic term used by Somalis to mean black Africans). Intelligence reports complained that Somalis refused to acquiesce to British desires that Somalis take up farming, saying: "A running story is being spread that if the Somali uses a hoe he immediately becomes a *Kikuyu,* the result being that agricultural operations have received a very severe setback."[35] The connection here between agricultural work, black Africans, and slavery should be obvious.

While upholding the perception of Somalis as distinct from and superior to "black Africans," colonial administrators clearly included the geographically defined people of the Gosha in the latter category. British colonialists applied the Swahili plural prefix and called them "The WaGosha," indicating their perceived status as a unified social group. Italian colonialists referred to all Gosha as *liberti,* or liberated slaves, thus emphasizing their non-Somali origins. Colonial authorities administratively separated the Gosha as a social category, delineating a separate Gosha political district called "Goshaland," proposing a native reserve for the Gosha, and during the Fascist years of colonial rule, singling out the Gosha for forced labor campaigns to which other Somalis in the region were not made subject.

Elderly Gosha remember how the colonial governments distinguished Gosha from Somali nomads ("pure" Somalis). In the words of one man: "After the British government came in... the government differentiated in this way: *reer goleed* (people of the jungle) and *reer badiya* (people of the bush; nomads), or *jareer* and *bilis.*" During another discussion he used different terms: " This is soft hair (*tin jileec*); this is slave (*adoon*) — during the time of the British they were separated in this way." Italian colonialists, desperate for labor on their plantations in the lower Jubba, began a campaign of forced labor in 1935, their target being the ex-slave communities of the Gosha. Gosha stressed how the Italians definitionally separated the ex-slave population from the "pure" Somali population for purposes of conscripting laborers. One Gosha informant imitated Italians scolding Gosha farmers trying to avoid conscription:

> I don't accept saying "I am Mushunguli," "I am Bartire," "I am Shabelle," "I am Cawlyahan," "I am Marexan." These don't exist for you. You are all lying. You all are Mushunguli Mayasid (Bantu). You have to participate (in the forced labor system).

While colonial authorities certainly did not create a separate ethnicity for the Gosha, their policies and actions encouraged the perception of Gosha and Somalis as highly distinct social groups. For Somalis, the symbolic basis of the subordination of the Gosha is rooted in the history of slavery and supported by a religious ideology of racial difference. For European colonialists, similar racially based conceptions of superiority and slave status were also undoubtedly influential in their categories of the Gosha.

The perception of the Gosha as a unified social group has dominated the infrequent mention of the Gosha population in the ethnographic literature as well: Cerulli, the most prominent Italian ethnographer of Somalia, refers to the "Wagoscia" as a "tribe" formed by ex-slaves[36]; Lewis, following colonial procedure and perhaps Cerulli, also refers to them as "the WaGosha"[37]; Nelson generically refers to them as *habash* and "non-Somali"[38]; and Luling also uses the term "Wagosha," but at least acknowledges that this is "apparently a name given collectively to a number of different groups."[39]

The creation of the Gosha as a category, a social group, a collectivity has thus had several incarnations. Colonial administrators saw the people of the Gosha as a tribe of ex-slaves.

Somalis, less prone to use the reified label "Gosha," see them as a group of inferiors with distinct history made clear by physical differences. Ethnographers have exhibited some uncertainty as to how to label the people of the Gosha — as a tribe (*WaGosha*), as a social category (*habash*) — but the impression of the Gosha as a collectivity has remained.[40] Because of their unique history, distinct physical characteristics, geographical contiguity, and farming lifestyle, the inclination to consider the people of the Gosha as a separate, unified, and even internally homogenous social group has been constant. A consideration of the Gosha view of who they are reveals the complexity of Gosha identity kept hidden by these externally created and imposed perceptions.

Gosha Self-Identity

How the Gosha see themselves is quite different from this external perception of the Gosha as somehow a clan of their own. They see themselves as a group of people of very different origins living and working together in one geographical area. While Gosha themselves will say things like "we came to live here with the Gosha," or "We Gosha believe...," this use of the group term is based primarily on geography and recognition of outside perceptions of Gosha unity.

While most people of the Gosha are products of subjugated ancestors (and some of the oldest Gosha were themselves slaves), these ancestors came from different regional areas, experienced different forms of slavery and clientship, and came to settle in the Gosha in different ways. While acculturation to the host society continued with every generation (far outpacing assimilation), slave children and free descendents of slaves retained a knowledge of the distinction between being of East African (Yao, Nyasa, etc.) and being of Oromo heritage. Somali clans could have slaves of both Oromo heritage and East African heritage, used for different purposes. Once these slaves attained their freedom, they and their children could then be affiliated to the same Somali clan, despite their separate areas of origin. In this way, villages formed along Somali clan lines in the Jubba Valley could contain people of both Oromo and East African heritage, who claimed affiliation to the same Somali clan. Within a village, while working together and cooperating on village matters, people of different ancestries tend to live separately, and marry endogamously, although this is changing.

In addition to these settlers with a recent history of slavery were *reer* Shabelle immigrants. Unlike other Gosha, *reer* Shabelle have a very long history of acculturation to and affiliation within Somali society, as well as a well-known area of origin (in Ethiopia) to which strong attachments are still held. *Reer* Shabelle define themselves as a group, and see themselves as distinct from other Gosha of East African or Oromo heritage. As one example, many of the adult men living in one middle Jubba village in 1987–88 who had grown up together in a *reer* Shabelle village continued to converse in their own "secret language," which is not understood by other, non-*reer* Shabelle villagers.

For Gosha individuals, their sense of who they are is quite complex, with many social and cultural components. At base is their knowledge of their ancestry — Oromo, reer Shabelle, or other East African groups. By the 1930s Somali clan identity had emerged as the most important intra-Gosha organizing force in the villages north of Jilib. Clan affiliation was based either on deep ties resulting from clientship to Somali families, or on more pragmatic choices made in order to join a village or receive protection from a neighboring clan. For the younger generations, their Somali clan identity is a very important part of their self-identity.

One's village affiliation is also an important component of Gosha personal identity. Territorial ties are emphasized much more among Jubba Valley villagers than among their nomadic Somali neighbors. Villages, rather than lineages or clans, hold and allocate land, and the village functions as a single entity in the payment of blood money, which among Somalis is a lineage affair. With outsiders, often the village will stand as a single unit. Within mixed villages above Jilib, however, Somali clan identity becomes important. In mixed villages, neighborhoods tend to be organized such that members of one clan live near each other. If conflicts occur between members of the same clan, original tribal identities define potential supporters: such as Ajuraan of Oromo ancestry versus *reer* Shabelle Ajuraan.

While different ethnic backgrounds are thus recognized and relevant in all Gosha villages, in many villages — especially those above Jilib — ethnic commonalities are increasingly deemphasized so as to stress Somali clan affiliation, which provides a far more important basis of social interaction, and which for most individuals has been their life-long orientation. The younger Gosha in particular are struggling with where they belong in Somali society. A group identity has not been actively forged by the Gosha because of the variety of backgrounds and slavery experiences. The primary factor that could serve to unite them — historical experience of subjugation — is viewed as something to be buried, forgotten, rejected as a source of personal identity, and not to be resurrected merely to fashion some kind of group unity.

It is difficult to predict what form personal and group identity for Gosha villagers may take in the future. Conceptions of identity — from both an internal and an external perspective — continue to change, as Somali society has changed with the development and disintegration of the State. It has only been a generation or two since the last slaves obtained their freedom, so clearly the process of identity formation is dynamic and continuing.

Concluding Comments

In this chapter I have attempted to probe the "Gosha" representation — to see what it means in Somali society, where it came from, whom it refers to. In doing so, I have attempted to demonstrate that the group to which the term "Gosha" refers is not internally unified at all, except geographically. Exclusion from consideration as ethnically Somali, however, does not provide the Gosha with an ethnic identity of their own. A stigmatized identity does not create ethnicity.

Nevertheless, the term *Gosha* does refer to a group of people with certain distinctions within Somali society. As such, I find myself arguing against the reification of a label that suggests group unity, while at the same time recognizing that distinctions which are real and important in contemporary Somali society and politics do exist. We would do everyone a disservice — especially perhaps the Gosha — by denying the unique histories and contemporary social position of the Gosha. Indeed, such a term as *Gosha* is a far preferable identifier of these people than some alternatives, such as the ponderous and needlessly divisive "descendents of ex-slaves who inhabit the Jubba Valley." As the people of the Gosha are, without question, Somali, perhaps taking a nationalistic perspective and referring to riverine farmers as minorities is the best approach.

All of this becomes politically relevant rather than merely academically interesting in terms of the potential for the development of a political consciousness. The Gosha community historically has not been a politically unified force in Somalia. Any political action taken by Gosha individuals above the village level (such as *diya* payments) was mediated through their Somali clan affiliations, not their identity as Gosha or as minorities. There is much evidence to suggest that a separate political consciousness may be developing among not just the Gosha, but among all so-called minority groups in southern Somalia as a result of the brutality and abuses these groups have suffered during the civil war. There is certainly precedent for such an emergent political consciousness, as subjugated peoples around the world have found their history of subjugation to be a galvanizing force in the development of group unity. The ties of affiliation Gosha individuals felt to their Somali clans may very well be overridden by the lack of protection these clans provided Gosha villagers during the years of pillage and violence. In the wake of rural chaos, the Gosha may in fact emerge, together with other groups like them in southern Somalia, as the newest "ethnopolitical" group on the Somali political scene. If this happens, they will certainly be a force to be reckoned with on the basis of population number alone.

Notes

1. This paper is based on ethongraphic fieldwork conducted during a one-year period of residence in a farming village in the Middle Jubba Region during 1987–88. Fieldwork was funded by the Land Tenure Center and was carried out with the assistance of Jorge Acero and Ali Ibrahim. I would like to thank them, the villagers and herders of the Jubba Valley, and Ali Jimale Ahmed for his insightful comments. Any errors remaining are my responsibility.

2. Cf., I. M. Lewis, "From Nomadism to Cultivation: The Expansion of Politcial Solidarity in Southern Somalia," in Mary Douglas and P. M. Kaberry, eds., *Man in Africa* (London: Anchor Books, 1971); Kenneth Menkhaus, "Rural Transformation and the Roots of Underdevelopment in Somalia'a Lower Jubba Valley," Ph.D. diss., Univ. of S. Carolina, 1989; and Lee Cassanelli, *The Shaping of Somali Society* (Philadelphia: Univ. of Penna. Press, 1982).

3. Specifically, I am referring to the distinction between the *max-aadtiri* and *maay-maay* dialects, the distinction between the different Sufi brotherhoods, and the cultural differences among people practicing different occupations in contemporary Somalia (the most basic of which are farming, agropastoralism, pastoralism, and urban jobs).

4. As this paper is limited to a discussion of the population of the Jubba Valley, I will not address the farmers of the Shabelle Valley, who have a distinct history and a somewhat different position in Somali society. For discussion of Shabelle Valley inhabitants, see: Enrico Cerulli, *Somalia: Scritti vari editi ed inediti*, 3 vols., (Rome: Istituto Poligrafico dello Stato, 1957, 1959); Cassanelli, "Ending of Slavery"; and Virginia Luling, "The Other Somali — Minority Groups in Traditional Somali Society," in Thomas Laban, ed., *Proceedings of the Second International Congress of Somali Studies* (Hamburg/Buske: Univ. of Hamburg, 1983), pp. 39–55.

5. Examples are the Igbo of Nigeria — see: Richard Henderson, *The King in Every Man* (New Haven: Yale Univ. Press 1969) — and the Kofyar of Nigeria see: R. M. Netting, *Hill Farmers of Nigeria: Cultural Ecology of the Kofyar of the Jos Plateau* (Seattle: Univ. of Washington Press, 1968).

6. Only one group living in the Gosha has retained a shared non-Somali identity and language: descendents of Zegua slaves. They represent a special case and have been desribed by Menkhaus, "Rural Transformation"; F. Declich, "I Goscia della regione del medio Giuba nella Somali meridionale. Un gruppo etnico di origine bantu," *Africa* 42, no. 4 (1987): 570-599; Adrianna Piga de Carolis, "Il quadro etnico traditzionale nelle prospettive di svilup-

po della valle del Giuba," *Africa* anno 35 (1989):17–42; and Enrico Cerulli, "Gruppi etnici negri nella Somalia," *Archivo per l'antropologia e la etnologia* 64 (1934):177–184.

7. Cassanelli, *Shaping of Somali Society.*

8. Ibid., p.173, no.71.

9. Lee Cassanelli, "The Ending of Slavery in Italian Somalia: Liberty and the Control of Labor, 1890–1935," in Suzanne Miers and Richard Roberts, eds., *The End of Slavery in Africa* (Madison: Univ. of Wisconsin Press, 1988), p. 319.

10. Menkhaus, "Rural Transformation."

11. Otto Kersten, ed., *Baron Carl Claus von der Decken's Reisen in Ost Afrika in den Jahren 1862 bis 1865,* vol.2 (Leipzig & Heidelberg: C.F. Winter, 1871); Clifford H. Crauford, "Mr. Crauford to the Marques of Salisbury" (letter, Mombasa, 13 July 1896), in *Archivo Storico del Ministero degli Affari Esteri*(Rome, 1896), Position 68/1 f.6; Menkhaus, "Rural Transformation"; and Declich, "I Goscia del medio Giuba."

12. Catherine Besteman, "Land Tenure, Social Power, and the Legacy of Slavery in Southern Somalia," Ph.D. diss. (Ann Arbor, Mich: University Microfilms, 1991). Population estimates by travelers and colonial administrators are highly suspect. European travelers did no systematic surveys, and population data recorded by administrators were, by their own admission, based on guesswork. These figures should be taken as general estimates only.

13. Some villages in the Lower Jubba continue to retain a sense of ethnic distinctiveness, especially those settled by Mushunguli (see: Menkhaus, "Rural Transformation," and Declich, "I Goscia"). For the settlement process of the Lower Jubba, see: Cerulli, *Somalia: Scritti vari;* de Carolis, "Il quadro etnico"; Declich,"I Goscia"; Menkhaus, "Rural Transformation"; and Cassanelli, "The Ending of Slavery."

14. For more detailed discussions of pastoral slavery in Somalia, see: Besteman, "Land Tenure, Social Power," and Hillary Kelly, "Orma and Somali Culture Sharing in the Juba-Tana Region," in Thomas Labahn, ed., *Proceedings of the Second International Congress of Somali Studies* (Hamburg/Buske: Univ. of Hamburg, 1983), pp.13–38.

15. By my use of the term "Gosha" I do not intend to encourage or support a perception of group unity of the ex-slave population of the Jubba Valley. On the contrary, an investigation of this perception is the main point of this paper.

16. For lack of a better term, I will use "pure" Somali to refer to people of Somali heritage, as opposed to immigrants who have been absorbed into Somali society. As noted, the latter, such as descen-

dents of slaves, are legally and culturally Somali. My use of the term "pure" is not in any way a value judgement.

17. The *"jareer"* description is also used for the farmers of the Shabelle Valley whose history is unclear but who, like the farmers of the Jubba Valley, have "Bantu" physical characteristics.

18. Cf., John Ralph Willis, ed., *Slaves and Slavery in Muslim Africa*, 2 vols. (London: Frank Cass & Co., 1985); Frederick Cooper, "Islam and Cultural Hegemony: The Ideology of Slaveowners on the East African Coast," in Paul Lovejoy, ed., *The Ideology of Slavery in Africa* (Beverly Hills, Calif.: Sage, 1981), pp.271–307; and Alan Fisher and Humphrey Fisher, *Slavery and Muslim Society in Africa: The Institution in Saharan and Sudanic Africa and the Trans-Saharan Trade* (London: C. Hurst & Co.,1970).

19. John Ralph Willis, "The Ideology of Enslavement," in Willis, ed., *Slaves and Slavery in Muslim Africa*, pp.1–15.

20. Cooper, "Islam and Cultural Hegemony."

21. *Ibid.*, p. 278.

22. John Ralph Willis, "Jihad and the Ideology of Enslavement," in Willis, ed., *Slaves and Slavery in Muslim Africa*, pp. 16-26.

23. Paul Lovejoy, *Transformation in Slavery: A History of Slavery in Africa* (Cambridge: Cambridge Univ. Press, 1983).

24. Willis, "Jihad and Enslavement," p.17.

25. Fisher and Fisher, *Slavery and Muslim Society in Africa*, p.22.

26. While I believe the data support the argument for a religious justification of slavery, the writings of 19th century Europeans should not be treated uncritically, as Europeans were partly using the Indian Ocean slave trade as a basis for invading East Africa.

27. Somalis in the Jubba River Valley frequently referred to the raiding of Oromo camps for slaves as *jihad.*

28. Cooper, "Islam and Cultural Hegemony," p. 284.

29. *Ibid.*, p. 290.

30. *Ibid.*, p. 291.

31. My argument demonstrating the connection between slavery and physical representations is also obviously relevant for people who do not live in the Gosha but who would also be identified as *jareer.*

32. Darood Somalis, Letter to the Chief Native Commission, 1 August 1922, in *Kenya National Archives* (KNA), Arens Reading Room, Bird Library, Syracuse University: Miscellaneous Correspondence, Reel 2804, Roll 8.

33. D.C. Jennings, Letter to the Senior Commissioner, Kismayo, re "Racial Status of Somalis," 8 August 1922, in KNA (1922), Reel 2804, Roll 8.

34. Hastings Horne, Letter to the Chief Native Commissioner, Nairobi, 30 October 1922, in KNA (1922), Reel 2804, Roll 8.

35. Kenya Colonial Intelligence Reports, 1924, in KNA (1924), Reel 2805, Roll 4.
36. Cerulli, *Somalia: Scritti vari,* p. 144.
37. I.M. Lewis, *Peoples of the Horn of Africa* (London: International Affairs Institute, 1955).
38. Harold Nelson, *Somalia: A Country Study,* Area Handbook Series (Washington, D.C.: Foreign Area Studies, The American University, 1982).
39. Luling, "The Other Somali," p. 42.
40. This portrait of the Gosha has been bolstered by the stories of Nassib Bundo, a man of almost mythic proportions who was treated as a Gosha chief by colonial authorities in the late 19th century. His precise role is debated in the ethnographic literature. Declich ("I Goscia") argues that Bundo's leadership culturally and politically solidified a Gosha community (by which she means only the lower Jubba). Menkhaus ("Rural Transformation") disputes this picture, suggesting that during this time Gosha villages retained a high degree of linguistic, cultural, and political independence and autonomy, with sometimes bitter rivalries existing between village or ethnic leaders. In Menkhaus's view, Bundo's leadership skills helped Gosha communities work together to overcome the threat posed by local pastoralist Ogadeen Somalis, but he was not a 'chief' of a united Gosha confederacy.

Bibliography

ASMAI (Archivo Storico del Ministero degli Affari Esteri, Rome, Italy). 1896. Crauford, Clifford H. "Mr. Crauford to the Marques of Salisbury." Mombasa, 13 July 1896. (Position 68/1 f.6.)

Besteman, Catherine. "Land Tenure, Social Power, and the Legacy of Slavery in Southern Somalia." Ph.D. dissertation. Ann Arbor: University Microfilms. 1991.

Cassanelli, Lee. "The Ending of Slavery in Italian Somalia: Liberty and the Control of Labor, 1890-1935." In *The End of Slavery in Africa.* Suzanne Miers and Richard Roberts, eds. Pp. 308-331. Madison: University of Wisconsin Press. 1988.

——.*The Shaping of Somali Society.* Philadelphia: University of Pennsylvania Press. 1982.

Cerulli, Enrico. "Gruppi etnici negri nella Somalia." *Archivio per l'antropologia e la etnologia* 64 (1934): 177–184.

——. *Somalia: Scritti vari editi ed inediti,* 3 Volumes. Rome: Istituto Poligrafico dello Stato. 1957, 1959.

Cooper, Frederick. "Islam and Cultural Hegemony: The Ideology of Slaveowners on the East African Coast." In Paul Lovejoy, ed. *The Ideology of Slavery in Africa.* pp. 271–307. Beverly Hills: Sage. 1981.

de Carolis, Adriana Piga. "Il Quadro Etnico Tradizionale nelle Prospettive di Sviluppo della Valle del Giuba." *Africa,* anno 35 (1989): 17-42.

Declich, Francesca. "I Goscia della Regione del Medio Giuba nella Somali Meridionale. Un Gruppo Etnico di Origine Bantu." Africa 42, 4 (1987): 570-599.

Fisher, Allan and Humphrey Fisher. *Slavery and Muslim Society in Africa: The Institution in Saharan and Sudanic Africa and the Trans-Saharan Trade.* London: C. Hurst and Co. 1970.

Henderson, Richard. *The King in Every Man.* New Haven: Yale University Press. 1969.

KNA (Kenya National Archives, Arens Reading Room, Bird Library, Syracuse University) Letter to the Chief Native Commission, 1 August 1922, from Darood Somalis. Miscellaneous Correspondence. (Reel 2804, Roll 8).

——. Letter from Mr. Jennings, D.C., Kismayo, to the Ag Senior Commissioner, Kismayo, re "Racial Status of Somalis." 8 August 1922. (Reel 2804, Roll 8).

——. Letter From Mr. Hastings Horne, SC, Kismayo, to Chief Native Commissioner, Nairobi, 30 October 1922. (Reel 2804, Roll 8).

——. Kenya Colonial Intelligence Reports. 1924 (Reel 2805, Roll 4).

Kelly, Hilarie. "Orma and Somali Culture Sharing in the Juba-Tana Region." In Thomas Labahn, ed. *Proceedings of the Second International Congress of Somali Studies.* pp. 13–38. Unversity of Hamburg. Hamburg: Buske, 1983.

Kersten, Otto. ed. *Baron Carl Claus von der Decken's Reisen in Ost Afrika in den Jahren 1862 bis 1865.* Volume II. Leipzig and Heidelberg: C. F. Winter, 1871.

Lewis, I. M. *Peoples of the Horn of Africa.* London: International Affairs Institute, 1955.

——. "From Nomadism to Cultivation: The Expansion of Political Solidarity in Southern Somalia." In Mary Douglas and P. M. Kaberry, eds. *Man in Africa.* London: Anchor Books, 1971.

Lovejoy, Paul. *Transformations in Slavery: A History of Slavery in Africa.* Cambridge: Cambridge University Press, 1983.

Luling, Virginia. "The Other Somali—Minority Groups in Traditional Somali Society." In Thomas Labahn, ed. *Proceedings of the Second International Congress of Somali Studies.* pp. 39-55. Unversity of Hamburg. Hamburg: Buske, 1983.

Menkhaus, Kenneth. "Rural Transformation and the Roots of Underdevelopment in Somalia's Lower Jubba Valley." Ph.D. dissertation, University of South Carolina, 1989.

Nelson, Harold. *Somalia: A Country Study.* Area Handbook Series. Washington, D. C.: Foreign Area Studies, The American University, 1982.

Netting, R. M. *Hill Farmers of Nigeria: Cultural Ecology of the Kofyar of the Jos Plateau.* Seattle: University of Washington Press, 1968.

Willis, John Ralph, ed. *Slaves and Slavery in Muslim Africa.* Two Volumes. London: Frank Cass and Co., 1985.

Willis, John Ralph. "The Ideology of Enslavement in Islam." In Willis, ed., pp. 1-15, 1985.

———. "Jihad and the Ideology of Enslavement." In Willis, ed., pp. 16-26, 1985.

CAMELS, INTELLECTUALS, ORIGINS, AND DANCE IN THE INVENTION OF SOMALIA: A COMMENTARY

∞

Irving Leonard Markovitz

Unfortunely, I must disavow the too kind words of Mohamed Haji Mukhtar, the moderator of our panel, and reject any claims of special knowledge. Indeed, I must give my special thanks to the organizer of these seminars on "The Invention of Somalia," Ali Jimale Ahmed, for being willing to take a chance on a non-specialist to be the commentator, and for having provided the opportunity to say a few words.

At the Horn of Africa Conference in New York in 1992, at the Seattle meeting of the African Studies Association, and now in the written report that appears in these proceedings, I have had the privilege of observing Abdi M. Kusow deepening his — and our — understanding of "The Somali Origin: Myth or Reality." On each occasion, he has further elaborated his argument and added to his evidence. His work on this most important topic clearly continues to develop. His current remarks promise to be a major theoretical and empirical contribution to the understanding of political, national, and personal identities. Kusow follows the path laid down by

T.O.Ranger in *The Invention of Tradition* and V. Mudimbe in *The Invention of Africa.*

Kusow has not only demonstrated the historical context within which identities are formed; he has also revealed how *theorizing* about identity formation is also historically conditioned. His analysis does not stop with such broad concepts as "historical context," because such terms are only words and categories transferred from one social or cultural arena to another; he *specifies* which forces and interests were involved.

Kusow challenges the dominant paradigm and view that the Somali people originated from overseas, from outside of Africa, from the "other." From the pyramids of Egypt to the ruins at Great Zimbabwe, "authorities" have frequently attributed great accomplishments on African soil to foreigners, on the assumption that mere Africans could not have done those great things.

Others, such as Herbert Lewis, Fleming, and Turton have brought out facts from linguistic and historical materials that have cast doubt on the theory of the Arabic origins of the Somali.

Kusow has added to the empirical record by focusing on the hitherto neglected role of the southern Somali clan families in the "ethnic" development of "the Somali speaking people." But he has done more. He has enabled us to understand that choosing a people's history, that determining one's past, is a matter not merely of *fact,* but of *power.* When outsiders called the tune, when Somali intellectuals looked overseas for their role models, theories of overseas origins rose to the fore and appeared to be "objectively" correct. Kusow convinces us that this was not the case.

It is remarkable that Kusow's work should appear at this historical juncture. It is a time that must be disheartening to most Somalis. It is a time of great suffering, of foreign occupation, of great internal turmoil. And yet Kusow's study, and this volume itself, are evidence that beneath the surface of this apparent chaos, a powerful effort of self-discovery and self-assertion by a new generation of self-confident Somali intellectuals is well underway.

Kusow's work is "political" in the highest, most old-fashioned sense of patriotic identity — and I must confess to a distrust of patriotisms that can become self-righteous, avenging nationalisms, committed to persecuting minorities. But at this moment of Somalia's suffering peoples, if I were a Somali, I would find Kusow's work a tonic, a basis for a renewed dignity.

Kusow's serious studies, among those of many other Somali scholars, raise basic difficulties with Ahmed Qassim Ali's essay "The Predicament of Somali Studies." Ahmed Ali is, I think — and again this comes from an outsider — too hard on his fellow Somali intellectuals.

Durkheim, who was exceedingly critical of the ideas of Karl Marx, nevertheless said: "Marxism is a cry of pain." He meant that one could examine each of Marx's ideas, one could consider the idea of "exploitation," or of "alienation," or of the "labor theory of value," and one could tear those ideas to pieces. However, one would not have understood "Marxism" unless one understood the industrial revolution in England in the middle of the nineteenth century, the wretched misery of child labor, the exploitation of women, the living and working conditions of the industrial workers and of the poor.

When Ahmed Ali declares, "During this period of dramatic need, the Somali people have not heard from the national intelligentsia which instead has fallen into absolute silence and estrangement from the reality of its people," I want to protest. A number of difficulties exist with this statement: *Which* Somali people? Were they *able* to hear? Were all of the intellectuals silent? Under what conditions *could* they be heard?

If we wish to understand the tragedy of Somalia, must we not first situate that tragedy in the pre-existent conditions of great poverty, of the newness and the smallness of the indigenous bourgeoisie, of the limited and underdeveloped nature of the productive forces, of the international pressures from imperialism and of the conflicting pressures (in the past) of East and West, of the tons and tons of arms left behind in Somalia when those external forces departed.

Yes, leadership is important. And, yes, individual leaders must be held responsible. However, to condemn *all* leaders, to condemn the entire "national intelligentsia," is to risk too sweeping a judgement, and to suffer a possible descent into a debilitating negativism.

It is not my business to defend Somali intellectuals who are perfectly capable of defending themselves. As a non-Somali, however, my impression has been that many Somali intellectuals have struggled continually to make an impact on achieving a peaceful and rapid resolution of the conflict at home, and that they have done this at great personal cost and sacrifice.

Somali intellectuals have also contributed critical, substantial analyses that go beyond anything written by Westerners. To mention only a few works in this limited space would be presumptuous; but if one considers, for example, how lengthy is the gestation period of a book or a monograph or even a serious article born of a doctoral dissertation, then from any comparative perspective Somali intellectuals have indeed accomplished a great deal.

As I said at the beginning of these remarks, all of this was my original reaction to Ahmed Ali's essay. However, if what we are hearing is really "a cry of pain," of unbearable affliction from the present circumstances of Somalia, then of course, I, especially as an outsider, can only be silent and appreciative.

Abdalla Omar Mansur, in "The Nature of Somali Clan System," has produced genealogies of extraordinary detail. (See pp. 117-134 of these proceedings.) These genealogies will provide a new basis for recasting the study of Somali political and historical development. This work is, therefore, invaluable. His second contribution, "The Cancer of the Somali State" is another matter. (See pp. 107-116 of these proceedings.)

Abdalla Omar Mansur in "The Cancer of the Somali State" has considerably nuanced the presentation of the first draft of this essay which was originally called "The Camel Herder and the Modern State." The basic thesis, however, remains the same: "But the nomadic population, moving into the cities and constituting the new ruling class, kept their nomadic mentality which became, in my opinion, the major obstacle to the growth of a modern state." These former camel herders, he tells us, regard manual labor jobs as humiliating: "Culturally they are not trained to work hard." At the same time, "their desire is to get rich in the shortest possible time, even if this means by illegal methods." "Remember," he cautions, "these are the people who see nothing wrong in stealing camels."

Once they — these nomads — transfer to the city, they apply the same cultural practices to this modern system, and they do so with disastrous results. His conclusion is that "the most serious problem in Somali society today is that cultural traditions are not compatible with a modern state. We, Somalis, are prisoners of a culture that we created, in the past and in the present time."

This is an intriguing thesis. However, if Professor Mansur really thinks that these are the main problems that have led to what he previously called "the rampant corruption, nepotism and inefficiency which helped propel the country into the chaotic mire," I must hesitate to accede.

There are countries that do not have camels that have similar problems.

Not all camel herders, I suspect, are thieves.

Professor Mansur's contentions about the background of Somalia's leaders and those who engage in various crimes and misdemeanors are assertions of fact. They are not presented as matters of opinion. Where is the evidence? Where are his facts?

In traditional Somali society, countervailing forces and institutions restrained cattle-rustling. These included customary laws enforced by the councils of elders. Even traditional feuds had their limits. Although it might be hard now for outsiders to remember, there were indeed in premodern society powerful traditions of cooperation. Who is to say that strong modern Somali leaders cannot call upon, and adopt for contemporary purposes, those socially beneficial elements?

The modern state, in any event, has different functional requisites. It requires the type of institutionalization that restructures and constrains behavior in ways that go beyond anything in "traditional" societies. The scale of activities, the numbers of people, the range of responsibilities creates new possibilities for a better life, as well as opportunities for new antisocial activities that go qualitatively far beyond previous horizons and boundaries.

Professor Mansur's thesis reminds me of two books with the same name: *Imperialism*. Joseph Schumpeter wrote one volume with that title; V.I.Lenin, the other.

Schumpeter argued that the basic cause of imperialism — which he defined as unlimited expansionism, no end, no limit — lay in what he called certain warrior traits. These traits of great ferocity and appetite might once have been functional for the protection of small groups of people, of bands attacked by marauders. But now these warrior traits, Schumpeter claimed, were atavistic. People with these traits, however, still pushed to the fore. They came to control modern states. They were still aggressive. And they were responsible for imperialism.

Lenin, on the other hand, found the source of imperialism rooted in the internal contradictions of capitalist development, especially the crisis of overproduction because of the inability of capitalism to equitably distribute the products of social production.

How is one to choose between Schumpeter's and Lenin's interpretation of imperialism? Cultural variables are clearly very important. However, with imperialism, as with the causes of the present crisis in Somalia, I would want to situate cultural factors within a broader framework.

Finally, only a brief word about Francesca Declich's "Identity, Dance and Islam Among People with Bantu Origins in Riverine Areas of Somalia." That study provides wonderful insights into social structures, politics, and power. She reveals to us the building up of sets of supports, of structures, in places where we don't ordinarily think to look. Power, she indirectly tells us, is always locally constructed. Status is installed by degrees, not by one momentous blow. She shows, for instance, how the playing of drums and the participation in dance are not individual acts but social activities, that is, they are structured in enduring patterns. They are part of reinforcing structures, of microstructures that bulk up the dominant bases of society. They help create values that become internalized in the construction of new identities.

When Dr. Declich tells us that she "shall attempt to reveal the conflicting and interacting identities underlying dance performances in rural areas," she is actually too modest about her objectives. More than a conflict between Islam and Bantu traditional beliefs, dance and drums express class conflicts as well. Dr. Declich recounts a historical episode of how "Dances with drums are also remembered as playing a very powerful role during the escape from slavery." She analyses how "Both traditional and Islamic ancestors are considered sources of power and having one's own ancestors invoked by many people also conveys power," but, "the important point is which dead or whose ancestors are revered."

While it is true, as Declich tells us, that "a whole social organization carrying its own hierarchal structure underpins dancing," she also points out that "dances are closely related to both individual and group identities." Declich then offers another case study of how power intrudes upon personality, and of how the politics of identity is never a purely individual matter.

In the struggle between Islam and tradition, and different forms of Islam and different types of traditional societies, and in the conflict between different social classes, Professor Declich in her study of dance and drums goes to the roots of a Gramscian struggle for cultural hegemony.

These studies together, therefore, have provided powerful contributions to understanding the continuous process of the invention of Somalia.

THE PREDICAMENT OF
THE SOMALI STUDIES

∞

Ahmed Qassim Ali

I

The tragedy of the Somali nation, which has caused the loss of thousands of lives, widespread starvation, and an unprecedented diaspora, is approaching its fifth year, and today, like yesterday, its ending is uncertain. Almost four years have elapsed since the downfall of the dictator M. Siad Barre, yet the country is unable to find its way toward even a provisional solution for peace, let alone the establishment of the foundations of the long dreamed of third republic. The country has been precipitated into a downward spiral of chaos. A middle-class political leadership incapable of leading the people in a victorious war of liberation and a swarm of greedy power-seekers are paralyzing the nation and holding the people hostage in an unyielding grip of terror. Undoubtedly, the tragedy of Somalia is one characterized by a struggle for power and a lack of valid leadership.

While the peoples of the international community have shown support and reacted promptly to alleviate the plight of the Somali people, the United Nations and governments close to Somalia have failed to provide effective relief or to help achieve a political solution of the crisis. Although the Somali crisis is undoubtedly a difficult one, it is not impossible to resolve.

In a time in which world attention has focused on Somalia,

the library shelves, the prolix columns of the international newspapers, and the reverberant sounds of television sets have been unable to offer any reasonable answer to the genuine desire of the millions of readers and viewers around the world to understand the causes of such a tragedy. During this period of dramatic need, the Somali people have not heard from the national intelligentsia, which instead has fallen into absolute silence and estrangement from the reality of its people. The Somali intellectuals have fallen short of their role and responsibility, dashing the hopes of the people who look to them as the vanguard of their liberation.

The purpose of this article is the thankless one of examining the prevailing attitude of the Somali intelligentsia toward the struggle of the people and of attempting to define their present role and tasks.

II

From its beginnings, the military regime of M. Siad Barre established a powerful and merciless apparatus of repression which prevented the Somali people from exercising their rights to freedom of speech and movement at home and abroad. The intelligentsia was targeted by the regime's security service, the NSS, as a dangerous category whose persecution was justifiable if its support could not be obtained. In its desire to have docile intellectuals, the regime generated a handful of opportunists who, in return for privileges, covered up for the socio-economic failure of the regime, minimized its repressive policies, and predicted better days to come. The example of these intellectuals was supposed to have an effect on the younger generation: principles are not worth suffering for; instead *dadkaaga dhinac ka raac* (flow with the tide). On the other hand, the majority of the Somali intellectuals who chose not to sell their souls were subjected to persecution.They were refused access to the university institutes, the research centers, and other public offices; or, if already there, they were expelled with the label of *kacaandiid* (antirevolutionary). In addition to the NSS offices, this policy had its "centers" in the Ministry of Information and National

Guidance, the national university, and the Ministry of Higher Education. To genuine scholars the road was barred not only for research and teaching activities but also for publication, no matter how valuable their works were to the country.[1] The repression was not limited to exclusion from career advancement, but included well-known instances of threats, arrests, and detention. One cannot forget the suffering inflicted on the great poet, playwright, and patriot Mohamed Ibrahim Warsame "Hadrawi." The great poet and scholar Mohamed H. "Gaariye" also was prevented from teaching Somali literature.

These unbearable conditions compelled hundreds of intellectuals to flee the country, leaving behind them families, friends, and their most precious property, books and documents which they had gathered jealously over a lifetime. The asylum did not offer an easy life; they had to endure difficulties of all sorts in order to earn a living. Yet, their situation was in general better than that of those who remained within Somalia; at least they were safer and freer.

After the failed coup of April 1978 following the 1977 *Galbeed* fiasco, a widespread repression was undertaken by security forces against those with affiliations with the organizers of the attempt. In the early 1980s the country suffered a severe "brain drain." Once abroad, the intellectuals confirmed that Somalis have a preference for oral literature and do not indulge in writing down what can be conveyed orally. Except for a few who joined other intellectuals in organizing alternative journals, the bulk of the Somali intellectuals abroad never exceeded a sporadic article showing great erudition on matters of no significance to the Somali people. In the U.S., Dr. Said S. Samatar, perhaps the most prolific of all Somali intellectuals, endeavored to set an example by publishing his articles in the journal *Horn of Africa*.[2] In France, *Revue d'Etude Somalienne,* through the efforts of Dr. Omar Osman Rabeh, attracted some Somali pens. More recently, *Ufahamu,* a journal of the African Studies Center of UCLA, has published a few Somali articles.

Most of the time, however, the Somali scholars have not

produced materials relevant to the national situation. Often their erudite works were conceived to impress foreign scholars and had little impact on the Somali reader, who could neither have access to them nor understand them. These intellectuals have never endeavored to contribute to the clarification of the socioeconomic and political situation of Somalia.

The attitude of the Somali intelligentsia (inside and outside) toward the political opposition movements born after 1978 was a blend of scorn and suspicion which resulted in a " wait and see" policy. Often the intelligentsia engaged in subtle criticism, mainly to justify their lack of commitment. This attitude was extremely detrimental to the movements, which desperately needed the support and the intellectual contributions of Somali thinkers. Therefore, the whole matter of the resistance of the Somali people to the dictatorship was left to the political and military figures of the opposition movements without any input or analysis from the intelligentsia. In fact, there is a conspicuous absence of any noteworthy document on any specific situation or sector of the nation prepared by any of the opposition movements. This lack of analysis has contributed substantially to the current crisis in leadership.

This passive "wait and see" attitude on the part of the intellectuals and artists inside the country changed in the years 1988–89. The courageous activity carried out by the poets, actors, singers, and other artists in appealing to the people and inciting them to oppose the dictatorship, resist, and support the armed struggle is remarkable. They were undoubtedly inspired by the bravery of the masses in the northern regions, in Lower Jubba, Bakol, Mudugh, etc., as well as by the appeals of patriots and poets in exile. Certainly, together with the "Bayaan," they played a great role in unifying the various resistances.

In the meantime, the intelligentsia abroad were becoming estranged from the reality of Somalia and its resistance, perhaps due in part to the rapid evolution of events. This alienation is best described in the following lament by one of these intellectuals: "No less shunned by the populace are members of another group of intellectuals. These preach aloofness from the humdrum of daily life. Instead, they advocate a life of research, not knowing that any research which does not jolt one from apathy is not worth the name. They, in their own ways, succumb to historical catalepsy. Erudition as an end in itself only furthers estrangement from reality." [3]

III

Abroad, this abdication of the Somali intellectuals from their proper role left a vacuum in analyzing and writing about Somalia. In reality there was no vacuum, for the Somali intelligentsia had never occupied this role. Thus, a continuity exists from the 19th century to today with colonial and neo-colonial pens: Burton, Jardine, Hanley, Collins, Lewis, Bottego, Cerulli, Petrucci, etc.

The so-called International Congresses on Somali Studies, started under the auspicies of Siad Barre in 1980 and limited to social science, natural science, and the humanities, are foreign dominated, although some members like to mention the increase in Somali scholars. For instance, at the last conference, held in Rome in 1986, about 30% of the papers were presented by Somalis. Only a handful of these papers were worthy of the name. A cursory examination of the proceedings of the Third Congress, issued in September 1988, suffices to demonstrate its nonrelevance to the Somali people and their problems. These "scholarly research" papers are striking examples of the poverty of the so-called Somali studies.[4] Thanks to an effort made by Dr. Said S. Samatar, who denounced the holding of the Fourth Congress in Mogadishu in 1989, and other Somalists who boycotted the congress in solidarity with Samatar, the Fourth Congress was not held.[5] (Siad did stage mock Fourth Congress a few months before his downfall.)

Apart from the proceedings of Somali studies, the works which have become "classics" and available for consultation by those interested in Somalia consist of a few books, profoundly influenced by the colonial literature, whose main concern is to rationalize the aggression and domination of one nation by another. More than a hundred years ago, when Britain took control of part of Somalia, the Somalis were described as savages, bloodthirsty and constantly at war for unceasing "blood feuds whose origins cannot be remembered, only honoured in the stabbing by the Somali."[6] "The Somalis," Hanley comments, "have had to try and survive hunger and thirst while prepared to fight and die against their enemies, their fellow Somalis for pleasure in the blood feud, or the Ethiopians who would like to rule them or the white men who got in the way for a while."[7] That "while" for the Somali people is three quarters of a century.

Prof. I. M. Lewis, in his "classic" on Somalia, *A Modern History of Somalia,* minimizes the British occupation in the following fashion : "The British government was only interested in Somaliland's meat supply [sic!] as a necessary ancillary to the garrisoning of Aden. Only if this were severely threatened would any occupation of the Somali coast be justified."[8] Britain by 1886 took control of the north of Somalia and after a few years undertook a war with the Dervishes which lasted about 20 years, resorting for the first time in Africa to air bombardment. When Corfield was killed during an operation of excess zeal to defeat the resistance of the Dervishes, M. Abdille Hassan composed his famous poem *"Koofilow!"* Fifteen years ago, I.M. Lewis called the poem "savagely brilliant." Lewis' racist position became very clear in 1992 when, in the columns of the *The Times* of London, referring to the resignation of the Algerian diplomat Mohamed Sahnoun from his UN post in Somalia, he wrote: "Nearly 80 years ago a brave servant of the empire called Richard Corfield also tried to bring order to the Somalis, when they were rebellious under a religious leader dubbed the Mad Mullah by the British. All Corfield got for his pains was a bullet in the head in battle and a place in the epic poetry of Somalia — a bloodthirsty hymn to victory that has lived on in a society steeped in antagonism to outsiders." He continues his indoctrination on Somalia by saying, "first to understand about the Somalis is that they are not as other men....they take orders from nobody; and their sense of independence is matched by a supremely uncentralized and fragmented degree of political organization, a kind of ordered anarchy."[9] This rhetoric reveals unequivocally Lewis' deep racism and his defense of colonialism and domination. It is hard to believe that he is talking about human beings and not about wild horses. It should be noted that he specifies that Corfield was not killed in his bed, but in battle, because for the author he is a hero. I.M. Lewis "the Somalist" does not care in the same way about those killed by the British who resorted to air bombardment against the Somalis; he merely says, *en passant:* "But the rebellion of the Mad Mullah (Mohamed Abdille Hassan) lasted 20 years and eventually had to be put down by air power." The colonial literature is full of such obscenities, in which there is no condemnation of the atrocities committed by the European powers but rather an emphasis on the ignorance, the violence, and the barbarism of the natives. Some may use a milder rhetoric which blends paternalism with contempt, but in essence they are the same.

IV

The issue is not whether these writers have the right to write about Somalia; it is rather our inalienable right to criticize and reveal their real essence to the reader even though sometimes these authors may be giants by others' standards. Chinua Achebe has criticized and labelled as a racist one of the giants of the English novel, Joseph Conrad, in his essay *"An Image of Africa: Racism in Conrad's Heart of Darkness."*[10] Similarly, perhaps more violently, Ngugi wa Thiong'o criticized the colonialist literature in Kenya, including that of the venerated Karen Blixen, the author of *Out of Africa,* who also gave Somalis a terrible image. Ngugi criticizes this author for having written "not a single word of condemnation for this practice of colonial justice. No evidence of any discomfiture. And for this, generations of western critics from Hemingway to John Updike showered her with praises. Some neocolonial Africans too."[11]

Morever, if criticizing is our inalienable right, our moral obligation is to write about our reality. It is in the interest of our people and country to do so, for this subtle literature will be there to confuse the many readers who have the genuine desire to know about the country. In fact, it is not realistic to expect the disappearance of such writings for they respond to a real demand.[12] Whitehall, Palazzo Chigi, and others have their own requirements and sources. M. Siad Barre had a similar purpose when he tried to use docile intellectuals who would shape history and society to his will.

Indeed, there are friends of Somalia who have written and will write good works about Somalia just as there will be national intellectuals whose works will be less valuable. Hoddar-Williams explains that the fact of being African does not imply a clear understanding of the politics there and adds that an African "should rightly feel aggrieved at the oversimplified and exaggerated portrayal of [his/her] continent in the North," but he/she should not assume that "indignation leads to true knowledge," which requires questioning, analysis, and endeavor.[13]

Ultimately, the difference between bad and good work depends on the point of view of the writer. For instance, for Lewis, Corfield is a hero, while in the eyes of Somalis he is not. Indeed, the issue is not to replace John, Paul, and Giovanni with Guuleed, Libaan, and Mohamed; it is where we stand on the struggle of the people for their liberation from the enslavement to nature, from foreign domination, from dictatorship or power-greedy local cliques. The choice of many intellectuals to suffer the privations of asylum rather than enjoy an easy life and privileges was the first step of a just response. But consistency demands reasonable commitment to work. The accumulation of erudition for its own sake cannot bring about self-actualization of the person; on the contrary, in the long run it will backfire in neurosis or the like.

The tens of thousands of Somali refugees in the U.S., Canada, Sweden, Germany, Italy, etc. are divided and frustrated, unable to unite to help each other and to overcome their problems (health, education, language, etc.). Feigning ignorance of this compelling situation is escaping from reality. Can the Somali intellectual live in peace with the Western media which every day presents a distorted image and an exotic interpretation of the reality of his/her country? He/she knows that the universal explanation of "ancient feuds" fails to explain the simple fact that *Habar Gidir* and *Abgaal* never had such fighting in the past and does not explain the existing alliances. He/she knows that borrowing exotic terms like "warlords" from the history of other peoples does not explain much more than the "ancient feuds." He/she also knows that what is at stake today — or what the various factions and cliques are pursuing — is not something buried in the past; it is rather something that is tangible and concerns the present and the future, and it is called power. Clan militias, *baraha, mooryaanta,* etc., are all instrumental to the power struggle.

It is time for Somali intellectuals in exile to heal the wounds they opened in the past, fill the gap they left in the study of their own country, resume their role in national reconciliation, and aid their fellows in exile who are in need of unity and help.

Notes

1. A prime example is Mohamed Hashi "Gaariye," author of valuable discoveries in Somali poetry. His work was not published and he later was expelled from the University.
2. Said S. Samatar, professor of African history at Rutgers University, is author of many publications on Somalia. He is co-author with David Laitin of a book on Somalia, *Somalia: A Nation in Search of a State* (Boulder: Westview,1987). Some of his articles are found in the journal *Horn of Africa.* Although one may disagree with his point of view on some issues, Samatar is an authoritative scholar in Somali studies and possesses an immense knowledge of Somali culture and tradition.
3. Ali Jimale Ahmed, Editorial, *Ufahamu* 17, no.2 (1989):1.
4. Annarita Puglielli, *Proceedings of The Third International Congress of Somali Studies* (Rome: Il Pensiero Scientifico, 1988).
5. Said S. Samatar, An Open Letter to Somalist Scholars, *Horn of Africa,* 13, no.s 1& 2 (1990): 88-95.
6. Gerald Hanley, *Warriors and Strangers* (London: Hamish Hamilton,1987), p. 19.
7. *Ibid.,* p.20.

8. I. M. Lewis, *A Modern History of Somalia* (Boulder: Westview Press,1987), p. 40.
9. I. M. Lewis, "In the Land of Mad Mullah," *The Times*, (London) Aug.31,1992.
10. Chinua Achebe, *Hopes and Impediments* (New York: Anchor,1989).
11. Ngugi wa Thiong'o, *Detained: A Writer's Prison Diary* (London: Heinemann, 1981), p. 36.
12. These foreign Somalists are often hired for sociological studies for development-related projects in Somalia funded by International Agencies such as FAO, World Bank, etc. The UN operation UNOSOM has hired as experts on Somalia: I.M. Lewis, J. Drysdale, B. Helander, P.Dieci, etc.
13. R. Hoddar-Williams, *An Introduction to the Politics of Tropical Africa* (London: G.Allen & Unwin, 1984), p.xv.

THE SOMALI ORIGIN:
MYTH OR REALITY

∞

Abdi M. Kusow

This paper is a fairly radical reinterpretation of the early
Somali origin and history. Such appraisal is largely based on
the long neglected and misinterpreted ethnography and oral
traditions of the Reewin clan families of southern Somalia,
and the implications of a number of published works on the
origin of the Somali-speaking people. This appraisal does not
in any way claim to be definitive, yet tentatively suggests that
Proto-Reewin[1] Somali occupied almost all of southern
Somalia prior to any Cushitic or Bantu-speaking groups until
recently, when the population of the region increased dramatically, creating a great shortage of land and resources.
This population pressure forced more and more people to
migrate to the more arid regions with more extensive use of
camel as the sole mode of subsistence. It was probably at this
time that the Hawiye Somali diverged from the Proto-Reewin,
later splitting itself up into Dir, Daarood, and Isaaq. These
three groups later expanded northward until the 16th century, when they started a reverse migration to the south mainly for economic reasons. Both the Reewin language and the
socioeconomic structure of the Proto-Reewin confirm their
being the historical, linguistic, and the sociocultural link
between the early Cushitic speakers and the modern-day
northern Somali language. Thus, the main thrust of this
paper is to examine the role of the Reewin-speaking clans of

southern Somalia in the historical, linguistic, and ethnic development of the Somali-speaking people.

Introduction

Traditionally, it has been accepted that the Somali people originated from the shores of the Red Sea, expanding southward since the start of the 10th century, driving out the Oromos, who were thought to have been the first Cushitic-speaking occupants of the Horn of Africa. The Oromos in their turn were thought to have pushed the Bantu-speaking peoples further south from the Jubba River area. This implied that almost all of northern Somalia was occupied by Oromo. Similarly, southern Somalia was said to have been occupied by Bantu-speaking groups with a well established kingdom known as "Shungwaya" located in Bur Gabo along the Jubba River. The early history of the Horn of Africa has thus been commonly seen as a result of contacts between Africa and southern Arabia. Support for such history was mainly found in the writings of early Arab geographers and in the northern Somali oral tradition which emphasized the supposed arrival of some Arab individuals who married local Somali women. This union supposedly produced the first ancestors of the current Somali ethnic population. Also, the descendants of these unions were said to have later overwhelmed most of the Horn of Africa region through conquest, migration, and southward expansion.[2]

But the written records suggest the existence of Hawiye clans before the name Somali itself appeared in the written documents. The first appearance of the name Somali in a written historical record was in the victory-claim song of Negash Yeshak (1414–1429) of Ethiopia over the neighboring Islamic Sultanate of Adal. In this, the Somali groups were mentioned as one of the enemy groups of the King.[3] Another document containing Somali elements is found in the Arab chronicle dealing with the Jihad wars of Ahmed Gurey. The Somali groups which are found in this chronicle are the ones that are found in today's northwest Somalia.[4] However, Ibn Said, the 14th century Arab geographer, wrote about Merka as being the capital of Hawiye country, which consisted of more than 50 tribal villages.[5] Even though these early records are fragmentary in nature, they at least contradict the suggestion that non-Somali groups occupied the area prior to the alleged Somali conquest from the north. This is supported by the fact that most of the current Somali clans have occupied and maintained separate geographic locations until recently. The Somali clans of Hawiye, Dir, Isaq, and Reewin, for example, inhabited relatively restricted areas.[6] Somali clan politics in the past also indicates a clear segmentation of political authority in the region. There have been regional sultanates, Imams, or Malaqs between the 16th and the 18th centuries, but the Somali people never came under the control of a single political authority until 1960.

Also, the nature of the Arab influence in Somalia has been exaggerated. This is not to say that there was no Arab influence or migration to the Horn of Africa shortly after the first century of Islam, but their capacity for dramatically changing the ethnic configuration of the Somali people has been exaggerated, especially in the north.[7] The early Arab immigrants who arrived before the 16th century were mainly disjointed individual families who came as a result of economic and political pressures within their homelands. In fact, if there was any recognizable Arab migration and settlement, it was in the south rather than the north. The northern part of the country has never attracted any sizable Arab immigrants because of its harsh environment, among other things. Indeed, Mukhtar gives us four convincing reasons as to why the Arab immigrants were not interested in settling anywhere around the Red Sea in large numbers. First, because the runaway Muslim migrants were concerned for their safety and thus would not take the risk of settling in a neighboring area such as that of northern Somalia. Secondly, unlike southern Somalia, there were no significant urban centers to attract these immigrants. Thirdly, the lack of natural harbors and the frequent violent cyclones discouraged Arab immigrants from traveling to that part of Africa. And fourth, the lack of viable economic resources made it unattractive for the Arabs to settle there permanently. Thus, the Somali claim that they are the descendants of immigrant Arabs remains, as Mukhtar accurately characterizes, "enigmatic, perhaps more accurately 'puzzling.' "[8]

Since 1966, however, several scholars have attacked this view, suggesting that the original dispersal point of the Somali-speaking people must be located somewhere between southern Ethiopia and northern Kenya.[9] This view has radically reversed the earlier belief that the Somali-speaking people migrated from north of their present settlements. Nevertheless, these scholars, despite their great contributions to the development of Somali history, neglected the role of the southern Somali clan families in the historical and ethnic development of the Somali-speaking people.

Literature Review

In the mid to late 1950s, Western anthropologists, particularly Cerulli and I. M. Lewis, postulated well-organized and rather elaborate north-south migration routes and trends based on an otherwise highly mythical but ideologically enduring northern Somali oral tradition. This tradition claims that a long time ago, one Sheikh Jabarti and later another Sheikh Isaq, came to northern Somalia and each married one of two Dir women. These two unions, the story goes, started what later became the basis of the identity and ethnic composition of the current Somali population — one nation half Arab, half Dir.[10] By about the 10th or the 11th century, it is suggested, the descendants of Sheikh Jabarti and 200 years later those of Isaq started their migration and expansion from the shores of the Gulf of Aden to the plains of northern Kenya. This alleged migration and expansion is said to have been halted only by colonial officers early this century, by their establishment of fixed grazing lands.[11] It was also suggested that prior to the Somali conquest most of northern Somalia was occupied by "Galla" and the south by Bantu-speaking groups.[12] The most disturbing part of the whole concept is the source of its evidence, which is based purely on Somali oral tradition, on the presence today of supposedly residual pockets of Galla among the northern Somali, and on the existence of place names such as Gaalkayo, Gaala-Eri, and Gaala-ood to supposedly indicate that some Galla groups lived in this area and gave these place names prior to the Somali occupation."[13]

Recently, however, Herbert Lewis and others have challenged the north-south migration concepts by suggesting that both the written records and the application of the language dispersal and migration theories contradict the traditional north-south migration concepts. For example, Ibn Said's association of the Hawiye with Merka, where the Hawiye live today, suggests to Lewis that they have been in that area for the last 700 years, if not more. This is further substantiated by the existence of other, later written documents such as *Futuh-al-Habasha,* referring to some particular Somali groups without using the name Somali. This, according to Herbert Lewis, is a good indication that the settlement and the distribution of the Somali population in this area has remained substantially unchanged since the 16th century. The most interesting aspect about the obscurity of the Somali name, though, is its different oral interpretations. In the north it is said to reflect *soo-maal,* which means "go milk," with an undertone of camel being the beast involved. In the south, particularly among Reewin clan families, it is said to reflect *sa-maal, sa* meaning "cow," and *maal* "milk," indicating a cattle nomadism. Lewis also examines the oral traditions of both Galla and Somalis. According to him, the Galla do not claim to have lived in northern Somalia before the Somalis, or at any other time; and they do not claim a homeland other than South Central Ethiopia. As for the Somalis, their claims about their descent from Arabic sheikhs and their migration from the north to the south are tales invented to suit prevailing sociopolitical conditions. "There can be no doubt that the Somali oral tradition contains little reliable historical material; but even if we accept the contention that they mirror actual settlements of Arabs among Somalis, this would leave unanswered the question of where the indigenous Somali had come from."[14] The traditions of the Darood and Isaq, which are treated in more detail in the literature, are silent on this point lest they associate themselves with a dark indigenous group and lose their racial ranking. Even after the supposed migration of the sheikhs, the Darood and Isaq movements have been — with few exceptions — minimal.[15] There is therefore no indication that they did not come from the south.[16] Lewis further indicates that the Somali oral traditions about their origin are suspect, first because of the great time depth involved — 1000 years — and the importance they place on a descent from Arabia.

In addition to oral references and early written documents, Herbert Lewis utilizes language distribution and migration theories, according to which it is possible to derive from linguistic data the genetic relationships among languages, dispersal centers, origins of population settlement, and directions of population movements and migrations. Esidore Dyen outlines this theory as follows: "Any related languages imply the former existence of a single language, which by an accumulation of change in different areas have diverged into distinct languages".[17] Moreover, "since related languages are divergent forms of one language, it follows that all of the forms can be traced to a movement from a single continuous area."[18] In short, Dyen indicates, the postulates of migration theory are: 1) "the area of origin of related languages is continuous, and 2) the probabilities of different reconstructed migrations are in an inverse relationship to the number of reconstructed language movements that each requires."[19] Following these principles, Lewis concludes that "since today 21 of the 24 languages of the eastern Cushitic groups are spoken in southern Ethiopia and northern Kenya, if the Galla and Somali and their relatives had originated in northern Somalia, we would account for 21 population movements. If, on the other hand, we assume that the original homeland was in the area of southern Ethiopia-northern Kenya, we need only to postulate three movements to the northeast : those of the Afar, the Saho, and the Somali."[20]

Building on H. S. Lewis's analyses, Turton (1975) examines the evidence relating to the migration of the three main ethnic groups involved in this area, namely, 1) the Meji Kenda and other Bantu-speaking groups, 2) the Orma or Warra Deya, and 3) the Garre, a section of the Pre-Hawiye Somali. First Turton examines the migration and origin of the Meji Kenda in view of their well-publicized assertion that they came into the general area of their present homeland in eastern Kenya and northern Tanganyika after a dispersal from Shungwaya (somewhere in southern Somalia). This thesis has been based largely on an Arab manuscript, the *Kitab-Al-Zang*, which mentions the existence of a group of Blacks (*Zang*) set-tled around the Jubba River.[21] Exactly when this document appeared is not known, especially the portion that deals with the origin and culture of the so called Shungwaya people, as older Arabic manuscripts from the coast do not include sim-ilar accounts. Thus, it is suggested that these descriptions were mainly insertions intended to protect the actions of the coastal slave holders desiring to continue child slavery, post-poned bride wealth, female pawnship, and other activities under attack by the colonial administrators at the time.[22] Other evidence came from the existence of Negroid groups on the Shabelle river, such as the Shidle, Eile, and Dube. However, a question remains as to whether these groups were Bantu speakers. According to Turton, "there are no evidences that show these Pre-Cushitic inhabitants were Bantu speakers because both archaeologists and linguists have failed to pro-vide any reliable information to support such conclusions."[23] The survival of these groups so far can be explained by their fishing occupation, which filled an ecological gap without competing with the surrounding Somali communities.[24] Based on the information we have thus far, it would be high-ly speculative to indicate, let alone conclude, the existence of a well-established Bantu state in southern Somalia before the Somalis came to occupy the region. This thesis becomes even more unlikely in view of the overwhelming information regarding the existence of early Somali communities in this region prior to any other group.[25] The traditional Arab ances-try cannot stand careful scrutiny either. As H. Lewis suggests, this is probably a function of the desire of the Somalis to associate themselves with the people of the Prophet. "People who know enough and care enough to fabricate genealogies tracing their ancestry back to the prophet's uncle are not likely to claim to have come from southern Ethiopia."[26] As for the existence of a Galla group before the Somalis in the region, Turton argues that they came to the Somali coast only in the 16th century, and not from the north via the Jubba; but through the Lorain Swamps and the Tana River.

The traditional evidence for the presence of a Galla group prior to the Somalis, i.e., place names containing the word *galla*, is no longer viable either. As Mansur pointed out, the word *gaal* does not mean geographical Galla (modern day Oromos in Ethiopia) as Lewis suggested, nor "infidel," as Herbert Lewis suggested, but means "camel" in the Reewin language of southern Somalia. H. S. Lewis' and Turton's reconstruction of the migrations of the Galla and Somali, and Mansur's definition of the word *gaal* are good indications that the Oromo never lived anywhere in Somalia prior to the Somalis.[27]

Turton's main argument, though, is his assertion that the Garre Pre-Hawiye group must have been the first group to occupy the land between the Jubba and Tana rivers prior to the Oroma. Support for such a thesis was based mainly on the fact that the Garre group is the most widely dispersed among the Somali clans. These Garre clans are said to be found on the lower reaches of the Shabelle River; around Dolo on the upper Jubba; between Webi Gesho and Webi Mana; and in the upper reaches of the river Dawa on the borders of Ethiopia and Kenya.[28] This in turn is based on the Garre oral traditions (collected at the beginning of this century) that they migrated several centuries ago from the upper reaches of the Jubba River along the west side of the river to Afmadu. This scattering of the Garre is also supported by the small remnants they supposedly left along the routes they took in their migration. These include some so-called Boon Garre at Afmadu, other Boon Garre at Gelib near the mouth of the River Jubba, and still others on the River Tana who spoke not the dialect of their Darood neighbors, but rather the southern Somali dialect of the Garre. This last group is interesting in that the dialect they spoke could have been that of the Reewin Somali language. It is also noteworthy that the concept Boon is mainly used by the Reewin and southern Hawiye groups. (This in fact raises the question as to whether these Garre groups could have been a Reewin-speaking group, a point to which we will return later.)

More recently, Mohamed Nuuh Ali (1985) has tried to reconstruct the social and economic development of the Horn of Africa over the past three millennia. The primary sources of Ali's reconstruction are linguistic evidences drawn from some 40 Somali languages and dialects. Based on these languages and dialects, he undertakes a cognate counting of some 100 core vocabularies which are said to be resistant to change and borrowing. Using this list of words, he employs a lexicostatistical analysis for each member language and dialect in order to calculate how many words they share in common as a percentage measure of how closely related they are.[29] Thus, two or more languages that share a large number of words with the same meaning — cognates — are usually said to be closely related, while languages with lower percentages are more distantly related. Based on this linguistic and lexicostatistical analysis, Ali deduces and reconstructs the past history of the Horn into six stages of migration and group divergence as follows:

The Proto-Somali society splits into two communities, Proto-Bayso-Jiiddu and Proto-Somali II, during the first half of the first millennium B.C. Proto-Bayso-Jiiddu splits into Pre-Bayso and Pre-Jiiddu late in the first millennium B.C. At around the same time, Proto-Somali II splits into Pre-Rendille and Somali II. Early in the first millennium A.D., Proto-Somali III breaks down into Proto-Somali IV, Garre-Aweer, and the Jubba groups. At around 500 A.D., the Somali IV further splits into Pre- May and Proto-Somali Benadir. Ali continues to subdivide the Proto-Benadir into Shabelle Northern and several other dialects, but nevertheless gives no clear indication of the first identifiable Somali community from which modern Somali speakers are derived.

We agree with H. S. Lewis's suggestion that the Somali expanded to the east and north much earlier than the Galla, and the Galla lived only in southern Ethiopia and northern Kenya until their famed migration in about 1530. This study also complements Turton's suggestion that the Galla came to the Somali coast only in the 16th century; that they did not come from the north via the Jubba River, but through the West via the Lorain swamps and the Tana River. However, we disagree with Turton's suggestion that the Garre, Pre-Hawiye group were the original occupiers of the region; we also disagree with Ali's description of what he calls Somali IV as diverging into Pre-May and Proto-Benadir in around the first century B.C. Instead, we tentatively suggest that the Reewin and Proto-Reewin who currently occupy most of southern Somalia south of the Shabelle river entered southern Somalia at the end of the second millennium B.C. This group adopted dry-land farming to complement their cattle nomadism. It is also suggested that camel nomadism was first adopted in this area as a supplement to dry-land farming until the Proto-Benadir group, probably the Hawiye, diverged from their Reewin ancestors and took up more extensive camel nomadism and migrated further and further north starting at about the middle of the first millennium A.D. The main thrust of this paper is to examine the role of the Proto-Reewin Community of southern Somalia in the historical, ethnic, and linguistic development of the Somali-speaking people.

The Pre-Hawiye (Garre)

The Pre-Hawiye group first suggested by Collucci provides an interesting candidate for the link that the Proto-Reewin provides to the origin of the Somali-speaking nation. In the past, the Pre-Hawiye group was thought to have preceded the modern Hawiye clans. They were also seen as quasi-ancestors of the Hawiye clans. Turton, for example, justifies his conclusion that the Hawiye occupied the area between the Jubba and Tana rivers before the Galla arrived in this area, on the assumption that the Garre were a Pre-Hawiye group. We do not disagree with Turton's suggestion that a Somali group occupied this area before the Galla, but we disagree with the implication of the existence of a Pre-Hawiye Group that pre-ceded the modern Hawiye. Looking at the original list of the Pre-Hawiye group as suggested by Collucci, we find all of them — except the Hawadle — to be part of the current Reewin clan families. The Gilale are part of the current Reewin clan families. They speak Reewin language and live in the Doi region (the heart of the Digil and Mirifle country). They are also found among the Geledi and Eelay areas, both Reewin clans. The Hober is one of the main Reewin clan families. They settle with Hadamo Reewin in the Bakool region. The Hon are a subclan of Harien. The Harien are a major clan of the Reewin clan families. Even the Garre are linguistically and socioculturally part of the Reewin. specifically they are part of the Digil Reewin known as the *Toddobaadi Aw Digil* . Thus, based on the above analysis, we can infer that the Pre-Hawiye groups are in fact part of the Reewin, clan families. At least the oral and social structure of the Reewin Somali clan fam-ilies seem to support this inference, as does a comparison of the following chart (Figure 1) with that of the social structure of the Reewin clan families (Figure 2).

Figure 1.

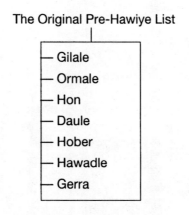

The Original Pre-Hawiye List

— Gilale
— Ormale
— Hon
— Daule
— Hober
— Hawadle
— Gerra

Kusow

Figure 2.

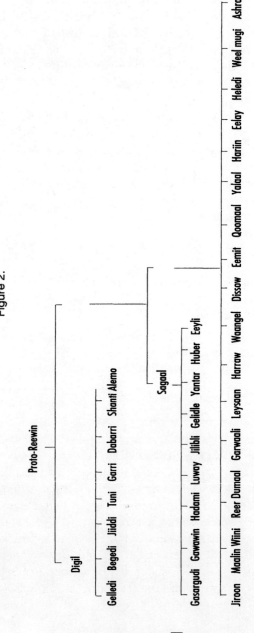

Kusow

The Proto-Reewin

Before we discuss the role of the Proto-Reewin in the historical development of the Somali-speaking people, a brief introduction to the current Reewin population in Somalia might prove helpful for the reader. The modern Reewin groups occupy the area south of the Shabelle River, crossing Jubba all the way to Kenya and Ethiopia. They have settled and established such important cities as Afgoye, Dafeed, Luug, Baidoa, Barawe, and Bardera. The Reewin are divided into two major clan segments known as Digil and Mirifle. The Mirifle is divided into two main groups, Sagaal and Siyeed. Each subgroup divides into several clans, which in turn each divide themselves into a dozen subclans. Similarly, the Digil are divided into seven clans which subdivide into a dozen subclans each. Together they constitute about 40% of the Somali population. They are culturally and linguistically distinct from the rest of the Somali population. They practice agropastoralism — a mixture of dryland farming, some irrigation, and pastoralism on the plains south of the Shabelle River. They speak the Reewin Somali language as opposed to northern Somali. These two languages are not intelligible to each other, differing to the same extent as Spanish and Portuguese.[30]

The Proto-Reewin, the ancestors of the modern Reewin clan families (Digil and Mirifle), occupy a unique position both linguistically and culturally in the historical development, migration, and settlement in the area south of the Shabelle River. This is despite a successful academic campaign over the past 100 years to dismiss their history and language. The Proto-Reewin groups were probably the first Cushitic group to enter what is the southern part of modern-day Somalia, around the end of the second century B.C.. For one thing, the socioeconomic culture of the Proto-Reewin and the modern Reewin clans is similar to that of earlier Cushitic groups. The Proto-Somali community, which represented the eastern Cushitic of the Omo-Tana, still practiced the eastern Cushitic mixed agricultural economies that included the raising of cattle, sheep, goats, and donkeys.[31] In terms of agriculture, a fairly large number of reconstructable cultivation terms attest to their practice of farming. Ecologically, the nature of the land between the two rivers, especially the western plains of Bay and Bakool, attest to the practicability of such socioeconomic culture. The richer soil and the greater rainfall in this area makes agropastoralism a desirable economic activity. Thus, the modern socioeconomic culture of present day Reewin clans is more similar to that of the earlier Cushitic groups than is the culture of any other Somali clan.

The name Reewin itself lends further credence to this proposition. Anthropologists and northern Somalis who helped define the name have coined the name *Rahanweyn*. This name was said to combine *rahan* ("grindstone") and *weyn* ("large") for a meaning of "the large grindstone," referring to or indicating the name's semantic relationship to the Reewin economy. Another, more romantic definition is said to combine *rahan* ("crowd") and *weyn* ("large") for a meaning of "the large crowd," mainly suggesting that the Reewin clans are aggregates of diverse clans most of which migrated from the north, but, in the course of their settlement in the south, absorbed both other incoming Somali migrants from the north and elements of Bantu groups whom they defeated as part of their great migration and settlement to the south.[32] All these definitions are based on the northern Somali dialect rather than the southern, on which the name is and must be based. The name is not pronounced "Rahanweyn" as traditionally suggested, but "Reewin." It is a compound name which can be divided into *ree=reer=*Family; *win=weyn=*old: "the old family." This definition of the name Reewin might indicate that the Reewin (Digil and Mirifle) might have once been the first Somali-speaking group that established itself in what is today modern Somalia, whence the rest of the Somali clans diverged slowly and through time developed their distinct northern dialect.

A possible indication of the Reewin as the ancestral clan family of the Somali-speaking people can be found in a lexical comparison of the southern Somali, northern Somali, and Proto-East Cushitic languages, of which the Somali language is one. But since the northern Somalis were separated from the Reewin-speaking people for at least 1500 years, their language might have undergone a mutation process. Nevertheless, thousands of southern Somali-based words have been preserved either in northern Somali poetry, in compound names, or in words that are used with shifts in meaning, as can be seen in Table 1.

Table 1.

English	E. Cushitic	S. Somali	N. Somali
soul	*rubaz*	*rubud*	*naf* (Ar. *nafs*) *rubadjar*, deprive of soul.
face	*fool/Fuul*	*fool*	*weji* (Ar. *wajh*) *fool xume*, ugly face
time	*amm(-an)*	*amman*	*waqti* (Ar. *waqt*) *ammin*, time

Southern Somai-based words preserved in northern Somali.
Mansur

Based on these reconstructions, professor Mansur concludes: "This overwhelming identity of lexical elements [demonstrated above] between southern Somali, northern Somali and East Cushitic languages leads us to conclude that southern Somali (Reewin) is in some aspects more archaic linguistically, and can be considered as a link between Omo-Tana or East Cushitic languages and the standard Somali. Thus confirming the idea that, from a linguistic point of view, the older speech community of early Somalis expanded from the south." Once more, we can infer that Reewin who currently speak the above-mentioned Somali language are to be regarded as the true ancestors of all the Somali-speaking groups today.

An examination of the relationship between certain Hawiye clans (Abgaal and Gaaljecel) and the word *gaal* will attest to this assertion. Traditionally, this word was used to mean Galla, to indicate the earlier presence of some (Galla) Oromo-speaking groups in northern Somalia prior to the conquest by the Somali-speaking group. In other cases it was used to mean "infidel," but, as we have seen, the word *gaal* means "camel." This being said, let us examine the relationship between this word and the above-mentioned two Hawiye groups. For example, if we take this word to mean "infidel" or Galla as in Oromos, do we also take the name of the Somali tribe Gaaljecel to mean "that which loves the infidel or the Galla?" For the word *jecel* means "love" in the Somali language. What about the Abgaal? Do we also here take the word *abgaal* to mean "the ancestor of the infidel or the Galla?" For the word *ab* means "ancestor" in the Somali language. The true linguistic relationship between the word *gaal* and the names of these two clans is that in the case of the Abgaal it could mean "the ancestor of the camel," for the word *gaal* means "camel" in the southern Somali language and *ab* means "ancestor." Similarly, the definition of the name *gaaljecel* would be "that which loves the camel." This could also mean that the Abgaal and the Gaaljecel were the first groups to diverge from the Proto-Reewin and start to extensively use the camel as the sole mode of survival. Furthermore, because both the Abgaal and the Gaaljecel have used the base-word *gaal* in their names, they must have been familiar with the Reewin dialect.[33] Even though we do not have any conclusive evidence about the relationship between the southern Hawiye clans and the Proto-Reewin, it is likely, as we said earlier, that they were the first group to diverge from the Proto-Reewin and set the bases for the divergence of the rest of the Somali groups. Nevertheless, pursuing such questions as "What was the past relationship between the Hawiye and the Proto-Reewin clans?" will help us reconstruct a truly reliable Somali history and origin.

An even more convincing factor for the possible indication that the Somali-speaking people originated and diverged from the Proto-Reewin clans is found in the concept of language distribution and migration theories. The basic principle behind this theory, as pointed out earlier, is that any group of related languages implies the existence of a former single language; that the probabilities of different reconstructed migrations are in an inverse relation to the number of reconstructed language movements each requires. This means that if two reconstructed migrations differ in the number of necessary language movements, the one with fewer movements has the higher probability; this principle Dyen calls *the Postulate of the Least Moves.* This concept was first applied to the Horn by H. S. Lewis, who concluded that since the Somali language is a member of the Eastern Cushitic languages and since the majority of the Eastern Cushitic languages are today spoken in southern Ethiopia and northern Kenya, the Somali people must have originated from this area. More recently, Ali, using the same theory with an extensive lexicosostatistical analysis, reached a slightly different but essentially similar conclusion. Furthermore, Ali uses this theory to examine the internal linguistic and dialectal differences within the Somali language itself and concludes that most of the earlier historical development of the Somali-speaking people took place in the area between the two rivers Jubba and Shabelle.

Following the concept that the motion of linguistic and population migrations is from diverse to uniform areas, one could conclude that southern Somalia is the home of the early Somali-speaking groups because of its linguistic diversity. Comparatively, the southern Somali language has more diverse dialects than the northern Somali. Almost all the speakers of northern Somali can understand and communicate with each other regardless of their location. Southern Somali, on the other hand, contains several dialects that are not mutually intelligible. These include the Dabarre in Diinsor, the Somali-speaking Tunni in Baraawe, and the Hadamo in Hudur, to mention a few. Thus, following the language distribution and migration theory, it is apparent that the Reewin dialect was the Somali language that separated from it's East Cushitic ancestral language possibly some 2,000 years ago and established itself in the area between the two rivers. Later, around 500 A.D., the Hawiye diverged from its Reewin parent language, as a result of their extensive practice of camel nomadism which allowed them to move further northwards. The Hawiye later diverged into more groups such as Dir, Darood, and Isaaq. The Reewin first adopted the camel as a complement to dry-land farming. During this time, population movements were very limited within the area between the rivers, until the Hawiye started to use the camel more extensively. The reason for this analysis must lie between the ecological and population increase. Maybe around 500 A.D., the population of the area started to increase. This phenomenon created a shortage of land, which led to more extensive use of camels, which in turn led to more and more people migrating north to secure a more suitable climate for camel breeding.

Towards An Ecosystem Approach

The term "Ecosystem" generally refers to the structural and functional relationships among living beings and the physical environment.[34] Our interest in this concept is not that of all living organisms, but that of the human populations only. We are interested in the causal connections between social structures and modes of subsistence, particularly in the ways by which human populations cope with disturbances in their subsistence strategy. By disturbance we mean the occurrence of environmental catastrophes such as floods or earthquakes. In the case of Somalia, we mean long-term droughts caused by a lack of rainfall over several consecutive seasons and/or the human overuse of an essential environmental resource, such as locally available water or topsoil, and the impact of this on the social structure of the population. The imbalance of resources resulting from such disturbances may cause the reduction of the local population, or the intensification of efforts to acquire the resources from alternative sources, such as, in the Somali case, the camel. In order to apply this concept to the Somali situation, we will examine the roles of such environmental essentials as water and rainfall and the adaptive strategies that people used to cope with such disturbances. Our suspicion is that the early Somali populations in southern Somalia found the camel to be an alternative source of resources.

In order to understand the ecological reasons behind the divergence of the northern Somali clans from their Proto-Reewin ancestors, one must look at the traditional norms regulating water and territorial rights among the Reewin clan families of southern Somalia. There are two important elements involved in these rights, namely, water and farming rights. Water is a very important commodity in Somalia as a whole. Apart from the banks of the Jubba and Shabelle rivers, the only source of water is rain and, as we know, rain itself is a scarce commodity. Given these conditions, the Somali people, particularly the southern groups, have devised an elaborate system of water sharing depending on the amount of water available at a particular season. There is of course less water available during the dry seasons than in the rainy season; hence most conflicts occured during the dry season. In general, there are variations on the norms regulating the use of wells (*waro*). However, the most generic form is that in which several clan sections share water rights, the firstborn[35] lineage group has the ultimate authority over that particular *war*.[36] As long as there is enough rain, and thus enough water, every clan can use the *war*. But in the case of water shortages, the firstborn lineage group, who are in almost all cases the most powerful, can revoke the rights of the non-firstborn lineage's use of the *war*. Thus, if the shortage persists, the non-firstborn lineage groups have no choice but to migrate further and occupy a land that was not occupied before. This group then becomes the firstborn lineage to their new area. If another group migrates and joins this group, a relationship of firstborn and non-firstborn is established again in which the newer group is forced to migrate further upon persistent shortage periods. The same thing is true with dry-land farming. As long as there is extra land for farming, the firstborn group accepts incoming immigrants. However, when the population density of a particular area increases, the newest group migrates further up to find an unoccupied land. Initially, this process was very slow; however, two factors have increased the speed of the process: (1) population increases, and (2) the introduction of the camel in southern Somalia around the middle of second half of the first century A.D.[37] At that time, perhaps, the population densities of southern Somalia started to increase, pressing the available resources. This population pressure has created a situation of constant conflict between firstborn and non-firstborn groups which typically results in waves and waves of small group migrations. At around the same time, the camel was slowly being introduced into the region, providing an alternative mode of survival to the weaker who could not acquire land. This allowed more people to migrate further to the more arid areas of the country without being restricted to settling a particular area.[38] This process of accelerated migration due to the introduction of the camel continued until some Somali groups reached the shores of the Indian Ocean and the Red Sea. By the 16th century, however, some Somali groups remigrated to the South once more due to ecological changes such as dessertification and less rainfall in the northern part of the country. This is based on the assumption that the northern part of Somalia had higher rainfall 1,000 years ago than it does today. To summarize, the whole process of the Somali migration from the south to the north and their remigration to the south was forged between the anvil of the prevailing ecological conditions of a particular era and the hammer of the survival strategies of the people.

Also the following lexicostatistics of the Somali dialects as presented by Ali fairly show the position that the Reewin dialect held as the link between the East Cushitic languages and the modern northern Somali dialect. Lexicostatistics determines the relationship between two or more languages on the bases of the number of words that they have in common. The higher the number of words two languages share, the higher the probability of relationship between them. Following this analysis, we can see that the Reewin dialect of Bardera, Dafeed, and Baraawe, or most of the Reewin dialects, are somewhat concentrated in the middle between, for example, the Jiiddu and Hargeysa dialects. Again the implication is very simple. It shows the Reewin language as a link between northern Somali dialects and the East Cushitic languages,

Table 2. SOOMAALI Lexicostatistical Analysis*

	Jiido	Rendille	Garre	Tunni	Baardheere	Daafeed	Luuq	Bay	Dhiinsoor	Baydhaba	Afgooye	Baraawa	Jamaama	Xamar	Cadale
Rendille	40														
Garre	48	52													
Tunni	55	49	65												
Baardheere	51	57	72	76											
Daafeed	50	52	64	68	79										
Luuq	52	54	65	70	79	84									
Bay	48	53	62	67	79	85	87								
Dhiinsoor	48	55	67	70	80	82	84	87							
Baydhaba	52	55	67	70	81	82	86	84	88						
Afgooye	49	54	61	65	76	81	85	82	81	87					
Baraawa	51	58	63	72	78	79	78	74	81	76	72				
Jamaama	46	54	65	68	69	70	72	66	71	73	72	77			
Xamar	47	51	64	62	64	63	69	62	64	68	64	73	81		
Cadale	43	50	58	63	63	65	64	62	68	66	65	69	79	75	
Hargeysa	39	51	58	57	61	60	65	60	65	68	63	69	72	65	78
Qardho	41	55	60	62	63	61	62	64	65	68	62	69	74	68	79

Qardho–Hargeysa: 88

* Source: Christopher Ehret and Mohamed Nuuh Ali, "SOOMAALI Classification," in Thomas Labahan, (editor), *Proceedings of the Second International Congress of Somali Studies*, (Hamburg: University of Hamburg, 1984).

confirming that the historical development of the Somali people took place in the area between the two rivers Jubba and Shabelle. Also, the two Somali languages may have separated as early as 2,000 years ago. This suggests again that southern Somalia represents the earlier location of the Somali-speaking people, where the greatest linguistic differences have occurred.[39]

Conclusion

Most of early Somali history writing has been based on some highly unreliable but ideologically enduring northern Somali oral traditions. This oral tradition was mainly based on the desire of the northern Somali group to link their ancestral origin to that of Southern Arabia in the hopes of raising their *Nasab*. This invented culture was later organized into a seemingly credible cultural aspect by the early social anthropologists of the Horn. Since then, all but a few students of Somali studies have accepted this tradition uncritically. Cerulli (1923, 1957) and I. M. Lewis (1955, 1960) became the holy scriptures of Somali history. Since 1966, however, several scholars have challenged Cerulli and Lewis by suggesting that the original homeland of the Somali-speaking people must be located in the area between southern Ethiopia and northern Kenya. Unfortunately, though, most of these scholars have ignored the role of the Reewin clan families of southern Somalia in the historical and ethnic development of the Somali-speaking people.

The purpose of this paper has been to provide some insights into the role of the Reewin clan families of southern Somalia in the linguistic, historical, and ethnic development of the Somali people. Both the linguistic and sociocultural structure of the Reewin Somali suggest that southern Somalia represents the earlier location of the Somali-speaking people.

This paper does not claim to be a definitive reassessment of Somali history, but tries to provide alternative approaches to the analysis of Somali history. It challenges linguists to look at the importance of the Reewin language in the development of Somali history by examining the relationship between the Reewin language and the East Cushitic languages, on the one hand, and that of the northern Somali. My suspicion is that the Reewin language is the main link between the Cushitic languages and the northern Somali. We also challenge archaeologists to come out of their trap of concentrating on the coastal areas or some imported wares as a means of investigating African history. Instead, we urge archaeologists to look at other indigenous cultural artifacts such as items relating to socioeconomic modes of production.

Notes

1. The Proto Reewin are here hypothetically considered the ancestral group of the first group that diverged from their Cushitic ancestors, thus setting the stage for the modern Somali identity.
2. For a good outline of this view , see E. Cerulli, *Somalia: Scritti vari editti ed inediti,* vol. I (1957) ; I. M. Lewis, "The Somali Conquest of the Horn of Africa," *Journal of African History* 1, 2 (1960): 213-229. See also I.M. Lewis, "The Galla in Northern Somaliland," *Rassegna di Studi Etiopici* 15 (1950-60): 21-38.
3. Cerulli, *Somalia,* vol. 1, p. 111.
4. Shihab Ad-Din, *Futuh al-Habasha,* ed. and trans. R. Basset (1897), quoted in Herbert Lewis, "The Origins of the Galla and Somali," *Journal of African History* 7 (1966): 27-46.
5. Cerulli, *Somalia,* vol. I, P. 94.
6. Herbert Lewis, " Origins of Galla and Somali."
7. For a good description of the Arab influences in Somalia, see: Ali Abdirahman Hersi, "The Arab Factor in Somali History: The Origin and the Development of the Arab Enterprise and Cultural Influences in the Somali Peninsula," Ph.D. diss., University of California, Los Angles, 1977.
8. Mohamed Haji Mukhtar, "Islam in Somali History: Fact or Fiction," p. 9 in these proceedings.
9. Among the scholars who attack this view are: Herbert Lewis, "Origins of Galla and Somali," *Journal of African History* 7 (1966):27-46; H. C. Fleming, "Baiso and Rendille: Somali Outliers," *Rassegna di Studi Etiopici* 20 (1964):35-96; E.R. Turton, "Bantu, Galla, and Somali Migrations in the Horn of Africa: A Reassessment of the Jubba/Tana Area," *Journal of African History*

16 (1975): 519-537; Hersi, "The Arab Factor in Somali History" (1977); Mohamed Nuuh Ali, "History in the Horn of Africa, 1000 BC to 1500 AD," Ph.D. diss., Univ. of California, Los Angeles,1985. Another convincing work, although slightly different from the rest, is Cassanelli, *The Shaping of Somali Society* (Philidelphia: University of Pennsylvania Press,1982). This work challenges most of the earlier analysis of the Somali history by suggesting that the history of Somalia must be examined from a regional perspective rather than one based on genealogical recounting.

10. The Dir are one of the major six Somali clan families. According to the Somali traditional myth, they are supposedly the indigenous clan whose daughters were married to the Arab shiekhs like Shiekh Jabarti and later Shiekh Isaq.

11. I. M. Lewis, "The Galla in Northern Somaliland," p. 22. See also, by the same author, "The Somali Conquest," p. 227.

12. I.M. Lewis, "The Somali Conquest," pp. 226-227.

13. I.M. Lewis, "The Galla in Northern Somaliland," pp. 21-38.

14. H. S. Lewis, "Origins of Galla and Somali," p. 36.

15. *Ibid.,* p. 36.

16. *Ibid.,* p. 36.

17. For detailed information about population distribution and migration theories, see: Esidore Dyen, "Language Distribution and Migration Theories," *Language* 32 (1956): 611–626; see p. 612.

18. *Ibid.,* p. 613.

19. *Ibid.,* p. 613.

20. H. S. Lewis, "Origins of Galla and Somali," pp. 39-41. Lewis's conclusion is similar to that of Fleming, "Baiso and Rendille Somali Outliers," p. 37, which states: "The Watershed of the Jubba River as far south as the present Somali border is the homeland of the Proto-macro Somali."

21. The *Kitab-Al- Zang* with an Italian translation appears in E. Cerulli, *Somalia, Scritti vari editti ed ineditti,* vol. I (1957), pp.231-255.

22. R.F. Morton, "The Shungwaya Myth of Miji Kenda Origins: A Problem of Late Nineteenth Century Kenya Coastal History," *The International Journal of African Historical Studies* 5 (1972): 397-424; see particularly p. 405.

23. Mohamed Nuuh Ali, "History in the Horn of Africa, 1000 B. C. - 1500 A. D. : Aspects of Social and Economic Change Between the Rift Valley and the Indian Ocean," Ph.D. diss., University of California, Los Angeles, 1985; see, p. 7; see also, Turton "Bantu, Galla, and Somali Migrations in the Horn of Africa," p. 524.

24. *Ibid.,* p. 8.

25. For the existence of early Somali communities in the region more than 1500 years ago, see, Mohamed Nuuh Ali, "History in the Horn of Africa, 1000 B.C.– 1500 A.D."

26. H. S. Lewis,"Origins of Galla and Somali," p. 36.

27. We can further assume that the word *Galla* itself is an invention, for the Oromos do not refer to themselves as Gallas.

28. I. M. Lewis, *Peoples of the Horn of Africa* (London: International African Institute,1955), p. 27.

29. Mohamed Nuuh Ali, "History in the Horn," pp. 14-15. Even though Ali uses the concepts *languages* and *dialects* as two distinct categories, he does not tell us which is a language and which is a dialect among those entities he investigates.

30. I.M. Lewis, *Peoples of the Horn*. See also, John Said, "Central Somali: A Grammatical Outline," *Afroasiatic Linguistics* 5, no. 8, issue 2 (1982): 1-43.

31. Ali, "History in the Horn," p. 57.

32. Lewis, *Peoples of the Horn*.

33. The most interesting point, again, is the existence of a group known as *Gaaljeel*, "camel-lovers," among the Reewin clans. This is a subclan of the Hadamo clan family which lives in the Bakool region.

34. Emilio. F. Moran, "Ecosystem Ecology in Biology and Anthropology: A Critical Assessment," in E. F. Moran, ed., *The Ecosystem Approach in Anthropology: From Concept to Practice* (Ann Arbor: The University of Michigan Press. 1990),p.3.

35. Firstborn and non-firstborn lineage systems are still common concepts among the Digil and Mirifle clans.

36. Garth Massey, *Subsistence and Change: Lessons From Agropastoralism* (Boulder: Westview Press, 1987), p. 34, defines *war* (pl., *waro.*) as "a hand dug pit into which shallow drainage channels (Ilo) empty, varying in size from 100 square meters in surface with a capacity of less than 200 cubic meters to a surface more that 2,000 cubic meters usually found in close proximity to villages. The amount of water stored in each pond is a major determinant of the number of people and animals in or near the village at any given time of the year."

37. There is some disagreement concerning the early socioeconomic structure of the Somali-speaking people. On the one hand, Murdock suggested that the socioeconomic structure of the Somali people was based on agriculture supplemented by livestock and by commerce along the coastal areas. Harold Fleming also suggested they adopted camel at the same time as the introduction of Islam. On the other hand, Hiene suggested that they have been using camel all along. More recently, however, on the bases of linguistic reconstruction, Ali demonstrated that the early Somali

groups were engaged in mixed economy, one that is based on farming *and* cattle raising. He also demonstrates that camel was only introduced during the second half of the first millennium A.D.

38. Camel was also probably adopted in the area between Afgoye and Baidoa. Initially the camel was used as a supplement to dry-land farming but because population was increasing and reaching new densities, pressing more and more on the available resources, more Somalis began to utilize camels more extensively. This rather increasing population also forced more and more people to move into the more arid regions north of the Shabelle River, which was probably occupied previously by hunter-gatherer groups. This process can be credited with the divergence and further migration to the north of a large number of Somali groups from the Proto-Reewin and the area between Afgoye and Baidoa.

39. Harold. C. Fleming, quoted in Lee Cassanelli, *The Shaping of Somali Society: Reconstructing the History of a Pastoral People* (Philadelphia: University of Pennsylvania Press, 1982), p. 123.

CONTRARY TO A NATION:

THE CANCER OF THE

SOMALI STATE[1]

∞

Abdalla Omar Mansur

Several factors have contributed to the destruction of the
Somali State. In my opinion, clanism, misconceptions about
the nature of the state, and international aid are the primary causes for the disintegration of the Somali nation-state.
The aim of this article is to elucidate in a brief and diachron-
ic manner these factors and their impact on a modern African
state.

Factors of Clanism

The Somali population, which has a common language, culture, and religion, is considered to be a real and unitary state
and is given the title of nation-state within the African context, but in reality it is contrary to a nation. The Somali people are internally broken up into clans and traditionally lack
the concept of state as a hierarchical power. To understand
this phenomenon it is necessary to examine Somali traditional culture.

   The Somali society can be grouped into four main communities: nomadic pastoralists; agropastoralists; agriculturalists; and coastal people, both urban dwellers and fishermen.

Nearly 60% of the entire population can be classified as nomadic. Most of the nomads are camel herders. These nomadic pastoralists are more deeply attached than the rest of the Somalis to the traditional system of clan divisions, due to the socioeconomic situation of the pastoral community life. Most of the nomadic pastoralist economy is based on camel husbandry, while the rest of the Somalis have more varied economies, such as agriculture, livestock breeding, small crafts, commerce, and fishing.

The Somali pastoralists give prime consideration to their camels, over all other domestic animals, because of the camel's usefulness and contribution to their basic survival. For instance, camels have abundant milk and flesh, which are the principal diet of Somali pastoralists. Male camels are the best transportation in the semi-desert of much of the Somali territory. Camels are also more able than other domesticated animals to endure extreme and harsh climatic conditions. They are the usual form of payment in cases of homicide: the clan of the killer pays to the relatives of the victim an agreed-upon amount of camels as compensation. Thanks to their high social and economic value, the payment of camels for murder often resolves bad blood existing between communities and individuals. Camels constitute the highest bride price paid by a bridegroom to the parents or relatives of the bride. The man who owns camels is accorded considerable honor and prestige in his society, and his opinion and advice are always sought. The famous Somali poet, Mohamed Abdulle Hassan, summed up the value of the camel in the following poem:

Hasha-geelu waa hooyadii
ninka lahoo hantiya
halka awrku yahay halbawlihii

A she-camel is a mother
to him who owns it
Whereas a he-camel is the artery
onto which hangs life itself....[2]

Therefore camels are considered the highest form of wealth acquired in the Somali pastoral society. For this reason these animals are coveted by all men of that society, making them the cause of perpetual conflict and serious clan warfare in the countryside.

To understand Somali culture, one must consider the extreme importance of oral poetry. A considerable part of oral poetry has been created by pastoralists about the role of the camel as the cause of bitter enmity among men of diverse clan groups, as expressed in the following lines by the poet Abdi-Gahayr:

> Bilash iyo cayaar looma helo bogiyo heemaale
> Nimaan sabarka baaruud ku xiran Baar ma foofsado'e
> Rag bireysan buun iyo rasaas boohin iyo qaylo
> Iyo laba bahood maalin ay boqol ku ruuxweydo,
> Belo iyo col baa lagu tabcaa Baarax weligeede.

> Men never easily acquired
> Boga and Heemaal [camels]
> Unless one's fully armed
> To defend Baar [his camels] unable he would be
> ....
> as two clans meet in deadly conflict
> where hundreds lay slain
> as possession of Baarax is always the cause
> of this enmity and destruction.(69)[3]

Looting other people's camels is not an illegal act for the Somali pastoralist. On the contrary, he regards the seizing of another's camel(s) as a source of honor and pride (although it is forbidden by Islam). A good example is the story of the poet, Ali Dhuux, who one day looted some camels belonging to religious men. He was severely criticized for this act by his clansmen. Defending his actions, the poet composed the following verses, pointing out that the greatest religious authority in his part of the country, Sayid Mohamed Abdulle Hassan, had permitted the looting of camels:

Sayidkii wadaad oo dhan xiray, Waris xalaaleeye
Xaaraan hadduu yahay xula ma qaadeene
Xoolaha kaleetiyo isaga waaba kala xeere
Nin kastoo xadreeyaba wuu u xusul duubaaye
Haddaan xaajiyadu weerareeyn xer uma duuleene.

...The Sayid, the wise one
who knows more
than all other men religious in the land
did sanction Waris [camel] by force to take
Xula [camel] he won't take
Should this act unlawful be
Laws superior camels govern
above other animals all
any preacher religious
camels to acquire desires
though pious pretends he to be
should Hajis ambitious
other men's camels raided not
I, too, would have done the same....(73)

According to Somali tradition, the conflict between pastoral communities caused by camels, both the looting of camels and skirmishes over the rights to water and pasture for camels, has a very long history. Men have fought over these animals ever since they were first used by the Somali people to populate the drier regions of the Somali territory. This is described in the following watering songs:

Sidii loo helay
loogu hadalyoo
laguma heshiin

...ever since camels were discovered
over them men quarrelled and disagreed.(70)

Qayib laba qolo
oo qabiilo ah

oon wax kala qabin
Qaata-qaatiyo
Qaylo geliyaay!

...it's you Qayib [camel]
that among the tribes [clans]
who hitherto in harmony together lived
bitter enmity inflamed
one another destroying in battles bloody....(66)

Cooperation between camel herders is needed in the pastoral society in order to defend one group's camels against the raids of another group of camel pastoralists. Therefore the camel creates, for mutual benefit, strong ties between relatives and clan members. The following lines by Cilmi Carab summarize this concept:

Xejin waayay geel nimaan tolkii lagu xurmaynayne
Kol hadday xigtadu kugu yartahay kuu xasili waaye

...He who into strong tribe [clan] isn't born
enemies to ward off
retains camels not for long....(34)

Misconceptions about the Nature of the State

All Somalis suffered harshly under colonial control, both prior to and during World War II. At that time, some Somali leaders came forward and mobilized the people to struggle for national liberty and the unity of all Somalis. But this was a new concept, not well understood by all the people. Since the camel dominated the mentality of the pastoralists, it was difficult to express the concept of nationalism without resorting to the figure of the camel. In fact, poets produced patriotic poetry in which they used the camel as a symbol of the country or independence. The following poems give us some insight into this new phenomenon:

Haruub nin sitoo
harraadan oo
hashiisa irmaan
laga horjoogaan ahay!

...am a starving man
milch camel his[4]
forbidden to milk
vessels empty carrying in hand....(80)

Tulad geeloo dhacan baa
Toban toban u dhintaane
Ma dhulkaa tegey baan
Dhagaxna loo tuureyneey?

... for the sake of a camel looted
tens of your compatriots you murder
yet, you throw no stone
for your motherland's liberation!(ibid.)

In 1960 Somalia became a republic, and this new nation was
symbolically compared to either a favorite she-camel called
Maandeeq which gave abundant milk to the people, or to a
herd of camels looted by thieves but later retrieved by the
owner.

Wataa curatoo mataanaysee
An maalno hasheenna
Maandeeq
Wataa magawdoo
Candhadi gollaa marisee
An maalno hasheenna
Maandeeq

...now that she has given birth
to twin calves cute
let's milk our camel Maandeeq
now that she is for milking ready

with the udder swollen huge
let's milk our camel Maandeeq....(81)

After a few years of independence, the Somali people became
dissatisfied with the way successive governments managed
their affairs. The following poem is a case in point.

Dambarkeeda Maandeeq kolkii weelka lagu duugey
Durdur iyo rakaad duul yar baa dhamaye
Dibjirkii u soo diriray iyo doorki la illowye.

...When Maandeeq the camel beloved
abundant milk produced for all
few people drank all of it
not once but many times more
dispossessing the hungry and the brave
who for the camel fought hard for long....(83)

The main problems of the newborn state were: first, the
Somali ruling class at the time was not well trained; they followed the same political line pursued earlier by the colonial
"protectors" who gave little value to the development of the
internal resources of the colony. So after independence there
was no serious attempt to develop or transform the basic
infrastructure of the country. Most of the budget was
absorbed by the expenses of the bureaucratic/administra-
tive/ military staff. Secondly, the Somali people believed that
after independence they would be living in paradise, as
reflected in the previous poems, without realizing that the
creation of paradise requires time and a great deal of sacrifice. Also, nomadic segments of the population, moving into
the cities and constituting the new ruling class, kept the worst
aspects of their nomadic mentality which became, in my opinion, the major obstacle to the growth and development of a
modern state. Traditionally the self-righteous and proud pastoralists believe they are more noble than other Somalis and
for this reason they regard as humiliating all manual jobs such
as blacksmithing, shoemaking, leather tanning, farming, and

fishing. Culturally they are not trained to work hard, for herding camels is not a sustained hands-on job. Yet, at the same time they are not easily satisfied and their desire is to get rich in the shortest time possible, even if this means by illegal methods. Often looking for easy work, the former nomads-turned-townspeople mostly work in the government sector as office workers. During the 1960s, the poet Ali Ilmi Afyare expressed this attitude in a poem: *"Dawlad wada karrani ahi dunidaba ma joogtee."* [There is not such a government solely composed of clerks]. Lastly, the transfer of the pastoral clan system had a corresponding adverse effect on Somali political life. Opportunistic individuals came to manipulate the segmentary Somali politics. It was no wonder therefore that in the last elections of the First Republic, more than 80 political parties registered to compete for parliamentary seats. It seemed that each Somali subclan had its own political party. This was democracy gone mad. That madness was that all Barre needed to stage his coup.

Foreign Aid

These are the main problems that have contributed to rampant corruption, nepotism, and bureaucratic inefficiency that helped propel the country into a chaotic mire. This led to the 1969 coup which for the first five years in power took a path of economic development. The new regime tried to "promulgate" deep social transformations. Barre's attempts to engineer a new Somali society, however, ran into trouble when he decided to go to war with Ethiopia against that strip of land called the "Ogaden." Somlia's defeat in the Ogaden war of 1977–78 accentuated economic and social problems in the country. This war also marks the beginning of a crisis of consent for the regime. Instead of devising plausible ways of defusing the situation, President Barre answered with repression and a concentration of power into the hands of his family. In 1980, 1 million refugees from the Ogaden looked for asylum in Somalia, and the country's resources (which were meager to begin with) were stretched even further. Starting in 1980, Somalia began to receive massive international aid. During the years 1980–89 international aid reached a level of $4.268 billion in cash, mainly from the Western world. The majority of this aid ended up in the pockets of the ruling clique or was used to build up the military, even in times of severe food shortages. One must remember that prior to the Ogaden war, the Soviet Union had armed the Somali military to the teeth. When the Soviet Union switched its alliance to Ethiopia, the United States started giving arms to Somalia. The result was that Somalia became the second, after Iraq, most armed- per-capita country in the Third World. Food and other emergency aid rarely reached the people who needed it. It is our belief that international aid worsened the political, economic, and social situation of the country for the following reasons. First, the aid given fostered the dictatorial regime, endowing it with a new life. Secondly, it created a dependency on imported foodstuff, discouraging local food production. Last, but not least, aid made thieves of nearly all the state employees, whose salaries were not enough to support their families even for a week.

The state property, which consisted in great part of foreign aid, became the best Maandeeq to raid. As in the past, one involves his own clan to get support. And this "aid raiding" has continued to the present time. The upshot of all this is that every clan leader, through his clan or subclan, is fighting to seize power in order to control the flow of future foreign aid. Their followers have mostly similar aspirations, and only a few give their support for purely clan reasons. To compound our problems, the present Somali clan system has lost its traditional *xeer* ("customary law"). In the absence of state laws, it was the customary law that helped minimize frictions among clans. Now we are, as they say, neither fish nor fowl, neither clans nor state.

Conclusion

The most serious problem in Somalia today is that our cultural traditions are not compatible with the constructs of a modern state. We Somalis are prisoners of a culture that we had created in the past and one which we refuse to reexamine. What is needed is to educate our people and exhort them to free themselves from the dependency of clanism, charity, and family parasitism. Only after we have created this new culture will it be possible for us to reinvent ourselves and in the process launch the construction of a new, viable state.

Notes

1. Presented at the 35th Annual Meeting of African Studies Association, Seattle, Washington, November 20th to 23rd, 1992. The author wishes to express his sincere thanks to the ASA for sponsoring him in 1992 in order to present his paper at its annual meeting in Seattle. I also wish to thank Ali Jimale Ahmed who nominated me for the program.
2. Ahmed Ali Abokor, *The Camel in Somali Oral Traditions* (Uppsala: Somali Academy of Arts & Sciences in cooperation with the Scandinavian Institute of African Studies, 1987), p.51. All the poems in this paper are from Abokor's book. Thus, all subsequent references are cited in parenthesis in the text.
3. Boga, Heemaal, Baar, and Baarax are the proper names of particular camels and they are used as symbols in general. We'll see more of this in the following poems.
4. Here the camel represents the country and the starving man the Somali people.

THE NATURE OF THE
SOMALI CLAN SYSTEM

∞

Abdalla Omar Mansur

The aim of this short piece is not to talk about the present Somali political system, but rather to elucidate some cultural aspects which are related to the nature and origin of Somali clan families. In doing this I realize that I am breaking the old rule of hypocritical silence which has lasted for the better part of a half-century.

According to tradition, the Somali nation symbolically consists of a vast genealogical tree (Figure 1). Nearly all Somalis descend from a common founding father, the mythical *Hiil* (father of *Sab* and *Samaale*), to whom the Somalis trace their genealogical origin. At the same time, a widespread Somali belief holds that most of them descend from the Qurayshitic lineage of prophet Muhammad. The clan and clan families which have high regard for this claim include: Daarood, Isaaq, Ajuraan, Shiikhaal, Geledi, and others (Figure 2).

To test the authenticity of such a claim, I will focus on two related aspects of the Somali lineage system. The first aspect examines the validity of the links genealogists attempt to establish between a forefather of a Somali clan and the Qurayshitic family of the Prophet. The second aspect of our examination tests the validity of the claim as it pertains to a forefather of a clan and his descendants. The first aspect of the test reveals a glaring contradiction that challenges the genealogist's ability to weave a coherent narrative. For instance, as for the forefather of Daarood, there are more than seven different versions of his genealogy up to Aqil bin Abitalib (the Prophet's cousin) (Figure 3). Another example is that of the Shiikhaal subclans—Qudhub, Looboge, and Gandershe who have a common Arab ancestor, Fiqi Cumar, but where each subclan has a different genealogy for the same ancestor (Figure 4).

The preponderance of the Qurayshitic lineage attests to the salient role of Islamic ideology in the formation and formulation of the early Somali identity. It is against this background that one could interpret the mushrooming of Arab progenitors related to the prophet and siring whole Somali clans. The progenitor of the Daarood Somali clan family is a case in point.

Legend has it that Daarood was expelled from Arabia. Seeking refuge, he arrived at the Somali coast. He dug a well near a large tree. Then, one day, he was discovered by Dir's daughter, Doombiro, who was tending her flock somewhere in the vicinity. He watered her animals at 'his' well. Noticing that the stock had been watered more than the usual times, Dir one day decided to follow his daughter and discover for himself where the water for the animals was coming from. Seeing that there was a third person in the vicinity, Daarood quickly closed the well with a large stone and climbed up the tree. Dir and his followers sought Daarood's aid after unsuccessful attempts to reopen the well. Daarood refused to come down until "the chieftain promis[ed] him his daughter in marriage" and allowed him to descend on his own shoulders.[1] From this marriage the Daarood clan family is said to have descended.

This story alludes to the scriptural tale of Moses found in the Quran. In escaping from Egypt, Moses found two sisters near a well. The girls wanted to water their flock, but the well was covered by a very heavy stone that could only be lifted by 4 to 6 people. Moses removed it by himself and helped the girls to water their flocks. The father of the sisters, Shuayb, gave Moses one of the girls in marriage.

There is, however, one conspicuous difference between the Quranic version of the story of Moses and the Somali legend, viz., the motif of the man in the tree. This motif is also found in the following Somali story, which explains the mythical feat of the ancestor of the Ajuuran clan, a subclan of the Hawiye.

One day a stranger was discovered by Faaduma, the daughter of Jembelle Hawiye, while she was grazing her flocks. He was sitting in the branches of a tree. He refused to come down until she summoned her people to the tree. Upon the arrival of the clan at the scene, the man on the tree asked for three things: a hundred camels, a slave, and Faaduma's hand in marriage. Moreover, he had to climb down onto the back of a man. All his conditions were accepted. From this marriage the Ajuuran clan descended.

This story is in a way similar to one that is prevalent among segments of the Afars of the Horn who claim to have descended from a common Arab ancestor who was discovered by local groups in the branches of a tree. The stranger agreed to come down from the tree only after the indigenous people accepted him as their chief and had made a fitting gesture of submission. The Asaimara Afars (nobles) supposedly descended from the union of the Arab and a local woman.

Also, among the Oromos (especially Borana and Guji), Sidamo Janjero, Bako, and others living in southern Ethiopia in the area of the lakes, which is said to be the ancestral home of the Eastern Cushitic-speaking peoples, the story of a clan ancestor, or king or priest endowed with supernatural powers, who descends from the sky and is discovered by the local people while sitting in a tree is a common occurrence in the lore of these people. In this case, the sky is considered as God. Accordingly, in the Oromo language, the sky and God are both called "Waaq."

Before the coming of the Islamic and Christian faiths to the Horn of Africa, the Eastern Cushitic-speaking peoples had an ancient common religion, which is still professed by the Borana. Aspects of the old religion are still extant in the new faiths adopted by the other groups. One of the most characteristic elements of that religion is connected with the notion of the sky-God called *Waaq*. This name is still used to mean God by the Oromo, Konso, Burji, Haddiya, Tasmai, Dasenech, Arbore, Elmolo, Bayso, Rendille, Dahalo, and Somali, all of whom speak Eastern Cushitic languages except the Dahalo. A number of these groups — Borana, Konso, Sidamo, Haddiya, Tasmai, and Afar — still consider some kind of trees as sacred. For instance, the sycamore is the Borana's temple. They believe that *Waaq* sometimes descends on that tree. Thus the ingenuity of some of the Somali mythic ancestors — or whoever the mythmaker was — to have molded the semblance of smooth transition, one that could bridge the old and the new religions. Needless to say, the old religion is adapted to reflect the hegemony of the new in that the ancestral home of the ancestor is in Arabia, the headquarters of Islam. Nonetheless, the ensuing myth is a living testimony to the syncretistic powers of African traditions (Figure 5).

Another Somali tradition that shows the merging of African and Islamic cultures is the rite that Somali women in the seventh or ninth month of their pregnancy perform, called *Kur* or *Madaxshub*. The invited women pour abundant oil on the pregnant woman's head, invoking Eve or Fatima, the daughter of the prophet, in order to safeguard the woman during delivery. This rite is not a part of Islam; it has its roots in the cult of the goddess of fertility and maternity practiced by the Borana women in the same way and for the same purposes. Here Fatima is a covering name for the ancient goddess Ateta, as the Arabian descendant was for the heavenly origin.

Now let us move to the second part of our examination, viz.,the authenticity of the claim of Arabian ancestry as it relates to a forefather and his offspring. Here the phenomenon of merging is more pronounced, although it seems to be less confused thàn in the first part, where we examined the authenticity of the Qurayshitic ancestry. Even in this part the ancestors of clan families represent a critical point. The forefathers that bear Islamic names, such as Fiqi Cumar of Shiikhaal, Ibrahim of Ajuuran, Cumar Diini of Geledi, and

Sheekh Cabduraxmaan Daarood, all married girls with Islamic names — Faaduma Mahdiyo, Faaduma Jambelle, Caasha and Doombiro, respectively. Even this last name seems Arabic since it resembles the name of the wife of Imam Ahmed Ibrahim Al-qasi, Dalombiro bintu Maxfud (in *Futuh-al-Habasha*). Now, one wonders how it was possible for these wives to have maintained Islamic names if they belonged to the local people who had been converted only by their husbands? If the assumption is that their names were changed by the Sheikhs after conversion — no doubt, a plausible one — then how do we account for the fact that their sons also did not bear Islamic names (Figure 6)? The names starting from the first-born sons of all ancestors up to nearly the tenth generation have obscure meanings because they belong to a remote linguistic stratum. But one thing is certain: these names are not Islamic. After the tenth generation, the fusion of Islamic and Somali names begins. This implies that the greatest number of Somalis seem to have converted to Islam by nearly the 15th century, perhaps brought about by the Audal kingdom, one of the greatest and most powerful Islamic states that existed in the Horn of Africa from the 15th to the 16th centuries.

Add to this the fact that in a variety of clan genealogies, the appearance of the name *Waaq* (sky-god) coincides with the initial adoption of Islamic names. Theophorous names are very common among all Semitic peoples from antiquity until today. So the Islamic tradition has introduced this form of name to the Horn (Figure 7). For instance, *BiddeWaaq* is a loan transition of the Islamic name Abdullaahi (the Servant of Allah). Here the name *Waaq* no more represents the traditional meaning of "sky-god," but stands for Allah. This fact underlines the validity of our assumptions about the Somali Islamicization period.

No less problematic is the actual lineage systems through which Somalis trace their genealogy. The actually memorized genealogy is not the crucial basis for determining one's clan identity, as is commonly believed among the Somalis. For example, Xawaadle, Gaaljecel, Degoodi, and Cawrmale are usually considered to belong to the Hawiye clan family, but genealogically they are not. The Xawaadle clan descended from Mayle Samaale and the other three clans from Gardheere Samaale. Other groups in a similar category are the Garre and Dabarre clans, which are considered to belong to the Digil clan family but genealogically descend respectively from Garre Samaale and Maqaarre Samaale (Figure 8). These examples do indeed strengthen the Somali saying *"Tol waa tolane"* ("Clan is something joined together"). We find several folk tales that talk about fission and fusion of subclans, as the following controversies reveal (Figure 9). The fission and fusion processes also explain the Somalization of non-Somali groups in the Horn of Africa. For instance, in 16th century *Chab-ddin* chronicle (*Futuh Al-Habasha*) distinguish explicitly the Somali clans (Geri, Mareexaan, Harti, Misirre, and others) from the Xarla clans (Barata, Barzara, Yaqula, Gaasar, and others). But today Xarla remnants in the Harar region of Ethiopia appear to have been already assimilated by the above mentioned Somali clans, who have inducted them onto their genealogy; thus the Xarla become Xarla Koomba, Kablalax Daarood.

In conclusion, what emerges from such analysis is that the Somali clan structure typically is not based on blood relationship, but rather it is a fruit of nomadic pastoral life. The necessity of defense, and the movement to new territory necessitated by a constant search for pasture and water have resulted over time in the formation of new alliances and, later, new clan identities. Thus, the need to fully examine the mythic nature of the Somali clan system is apparent. This short piece is only meant to provoke discussion and certainly is not an end to the discussion. It is perhaps important to critically sift through received traditions so that we might be able to reinvent new and more viable terms of reference for Somalia.

Notes

1. V. Luling, "The Man in the Tree. A Note on a Somali Myth," in Annarita Puglielli, ed., *Proceedings of the Third International Congress of Somali Studies.* (Rome: Il Pensario Scientifico, 1988), p. 331.

1: Somali nation symbolically consists of this vast geneological tree,
ept Jareer, Gibilcad and the other Sabs (Midgaan, Yibir, Tumaal, etc.)

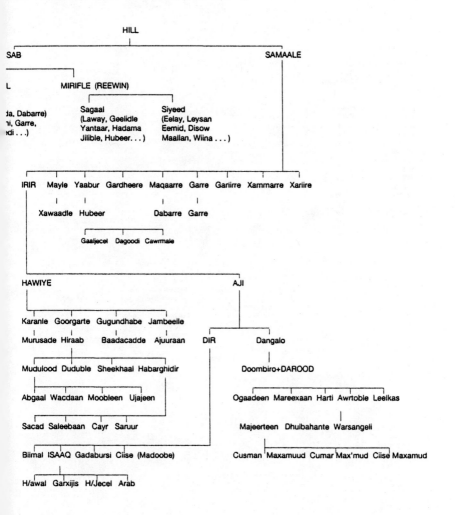

Fig. 2: The genealogies of some forefathers that claim to descend from Quraysh clan.

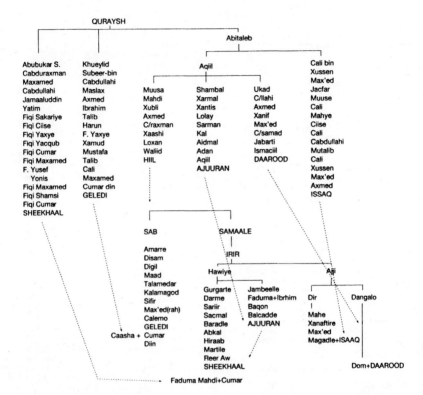

Figure 3: The seven different genealogies of Daarood

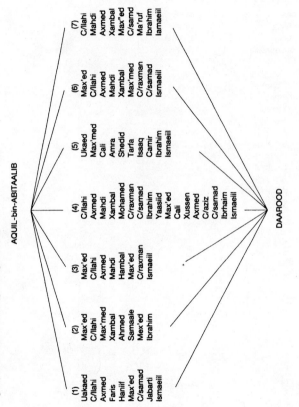

AQUIL–bin–ABITAALIB

(1)	(2)	(3)	(4)	(5)	(6)	(7)
Uakaed	Max'ed	Max'ed	C/llahi	Ukaed	Max'ed	C/llahi
C/llahi	C/llahi	C/llahi	Axmed	Max'med	C/llahi	Mahdi
Axmed	Max'med	Axmed	Mahdi	Cali	Axmed	Axmed
Faris	Xambal	Mahdi	Xambal	Amra	Mahdi	Xambal
Haniif	Ahmed	Hambal	Mohamed	Shedid	Xambal	Max''ed
Max'ed	Samaale	Max'ed	C/raxman	Tarfa	Max'med	C/samd
C/samad	Mex'ed	C/raxman	C/samad	Isaaq	C/raxman	Ma'ruf
Jabarti	Ibrahim	Ismaeiii	Ibrahim	Camir	C/samad	Ibrahim
Ismaeiii			Yaasiid	Ibrahim	Ismaeiii	lamaeiii
			Max'ed	Ismaeiii		
			Cali			
			Xussen			
			Axmed			
			C/aziz			
			C/samad			
			Ibrhaim			
			Ismaeiii			

DAAROOD

Informants:

1. Cali Max'ed Max'ud (Qandala)
2. Xagi Ibrahim Bul (Afgooy)
3. Xagi Cali Majeerteen (Marka)
4. Cabdi Xagi Yusef (Bari)
5. Sheekh Abubakar Sabola (Harar)
6. Sheekh Max'ed Wacays (Ogaden)
7. Sheekh Axmed bin Xussen (Cairo 1945)

Figure 4: The Three different stages of Sheekhaal ancestor (F. Cumar)

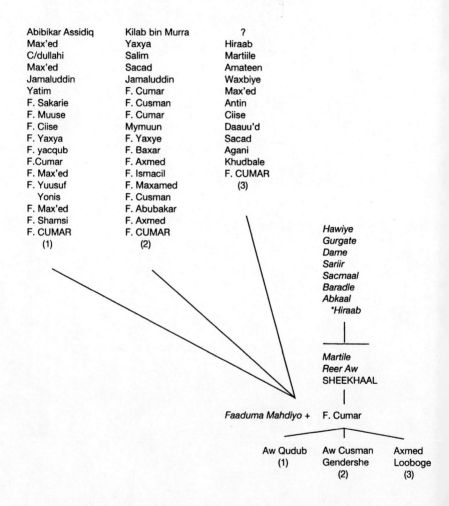

QUREYSH

Abibikar Assidiq	Kilab bin Murra	?
Max'ed	Yaxya	Hiraab
C/dullahi	Salim	Martiile
Max'ed	Sacad	Amateen
Jamaluddin	Jamaluddin	Waxbiye
Yatim	F. Cumar	Max'ed
F. Sakarie	F. Cusman	Antin
F. Muuse	F. Cumar	Ciise
F. Ciise	Mymuun	Daauu'd
F. Yaxya	F. Yaxye	Sacad
F. yacqub	F. Baxar	Agani
F.Cumar	F. Axmed	Khudbale
F. Max'ed	F. Ismacil	F. CUMAR
F. Yuusuf	F. Maxamed	(3)
Yonis	F. Cusman	
F. Max'ed	F. Abubakar	
F. Shamsi	F. Axmed	
F. CUMAR	F. CUMAR	
(1)	(2)	

Hawiye
Gurgate
Dame
Sariir
Sacmaal
Baradle
Abkaal
　Hiraab

Martile
Reer Aw
SHEEKHAAL

Faaduma Mahdiyo +　F. Cumar

Aw Qudub　　Aw Cusman　　Axmed
(1)　　　　　Gendershe　　Looboge
　　　　　　　(2)　　　　　(3)

Fig. 5: The fusion of the ancient and new faiths

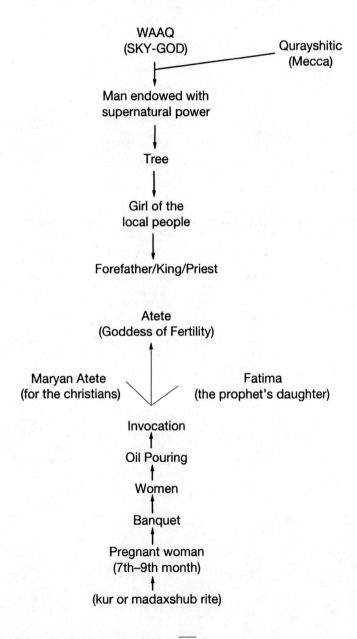

Fig. 6A: The fusion of the Islamic and non-Islamic names (Daarood clan family)

1. DAAROOD

2. Kabalax	2. kabalax	2. Kabalax	2. Sede
3. Koombe	3. Koombe	3. Kuumade	3. MAREEXAN
4. Amtalo	4. Amtolo	4. Absame	4. Awsame
5. Hantaale	5. Hantaale	5. OGAADEEN	5. Baalyere
6. HARTI	6. HARTI	6. Tagaal Waaq	6. Hadambari
7. Moorahante	7. DHULBAHANTE	7. Bar Waaq	7. Gaashireedle
8. MAJEERTEEN	8. Lamyaluum	8. Miyir Walaal	8. Isaaq
9. Awe	9. Sareer	9. Kaante	9. Amanreer
10. Cumar	10. Fiqi Door	10. Yuusuf	10. Raadimir
11. Noolaye	11. Falaqdoor	11. Muuse	11. WarWaaqJecel
12. Maxamed	12. Ibrahim	12. Siccid	12. Xussen
13. Xijiile	13. Facaye	13. Talamuge	13. Maxamed
14. Talareer	14. Gareen	14. Cabdi	14. Muuse
15. Xasan	15. UgaaYhan	15. Sunwaaq	15. Abaadi
16. Toljeclo	16. Siciid	16. Cabdi	16. Daauud
17. Umadnabi	17. Muuse	17. SiinWaaq	17. Maxamed
18. Jibree'iil	18. Cabdalle	18. CabudWaaq	18. Axmed
19. Ibrahim	19. Habarwaa	19. SiinWaaq	19. Ciise
20. Maxamed	20. Shirshoore	20. AwMahadle	20. Mataan
21. Saleebaan	21. Faarax	21. C/kariin	21. Yuusuf
22. Maxamuud	22. Cabdalle	22. Yaxye	22. Xussen
23. Cusman	23. Axmed	23. Nagaaye	23. Khalaf
24. Yuusuf	24. Aadan	24. Maxamed	24. Sharmarke
25. Maxamed	25. Hagar	25. Xussen	25. Guuleed
26. Cumar	26. Faarax	26. Rooble	26. Faarax
27. Cali	27. Cigaal	27. Geeddi	27. Diini
28. Maxamed	28. Maxamed	28. Nuur	28. Sharmarke
29. Yuusuf	29. Axmed	29. Kamaal	29. Warsame
30. Maxamuud	30. Ducaale	30. Yuusuf	30. Xirsi
31. Maxamed	31. Haaruun	31. Loeox	31. Cali
32. Cali		32. Ibrahim	32. Maxamud
33. Yuusuf		33. Sh. Maxamed	33. Cabdullhi
34. Maxamed			
35. Yuusuf			
36. Cali (Keenediid)			
37. Yuusuf			
38. Cusmaan			
39. Yaasiin			

Fig. 6b: The fusion of Islamic and non-Islamic names (Hawiye clan family).

1. HAWIYE

Karanle	2. Gugundhabe	2. Gorgaarte	2. Gorgaarte
Wadaare	3. Iibade	3. Daame	3. Daame
MURUSADE	4. Molkaal	4. Sariir	4. Sariir
Kliibaar	5. BAADACADE	5. Sacmaal	5. Sacmaal
Wacayle	6. Digaale	6. Baradle	6. Baradle
Makahaan	7. Warable	7. Abkaal	7. Abkaal
Ximyar	8. Jiir	8. Madable	8. Madable
Xayle	9. Kuxeebeen	9. Hiraab	9. Hiraab
). Warwaaq	10. Qulubeen	10. Mudulood	10. Madarkicis (H/Gidir)
1. Sabti	11. Ciise	11. Darandodle	11. SACAD
2. Majabe	12. Gacal	12. Cusmaan	12. Cawireere
3. Abokor	13. Odaale	13. ABGAAL	13. Daa'uud
4. Codweyne	14. Ilkajar	14. Wacbuudhan	14. Culus
5. Maxamud	15. Illaabe	15. Daanweyne	15. Muuse
3. Xashane	16. Muuse	16. Yuunis	16. Nimcaad
7. Cigalle	17. Faarax	17. Galmaax	17. Cali
3. Maxamed	18. Walaal	18. Yuusuf	18. Afrax
9. Cismaan	19. Xasan	19 Cali	19. Afdheere
). Yuusuf	20. Culus	20. Cosoble	20. Sahal
1. Aaadan	21. Colow	21. Maxamed	21. Axmed
2. Wardheer	22. Caalin	22. Madaxweyne	22. Aadan
3. Jimcaale	23. Xasan	23. Macallin Salid	
4. Dhiblaawe	24. Cilmi	24. Xasan	
5. Casayr	25. Deerow	25. Abiibakar	
3. Faarax	26. Xussen	26. Idriis	
7. Cabdullahi	27. Cali	27. Cali	
		28. Daa'uud	
		29. Sh. Maxamed	
		30. Sh. Cumar	
		31. Cabduraxman	
		32. Sh. Maxamed	

Fig. 6c: The fusion of Islamic and non-Islamic names (of the other Somalis).

1. DIR	1. MAYLE	1. DIGIL	1. MIRIFLE
2. Maha	2. Urmidig	2. Maad	2. Madoobe
3. Surre	3. Kasheenle	3. Talamador	3. Dherganow
4. Lafaqaab	4. Lo'doon	4. Kalamagod	4. Xariiq
5. Sinji	5. Wacwacle	5. Sifir	5. LUWAAY
6. QUBEYS	6. Hiyood	6. Maad	6. Dumaala (?)
7. Reer Toonlle	7. XAWAADLE	7. Aleemow	7. Dooyo
8. Weceyeen	8. Samatalis	8. GELEDI	8. Kulmis
9. Abtiudug	9. Dige	9. Cumar Diin	9. Baarleeli
10. Waqantiile	10. Ciise	10. Dhiig	10. Buubow
11. Ciise	11. Madaxweynw	11. Dub	11. Abow
12. Buraale	12. Agoon	12. Subug	12. Maad (Max'e
13. Xussen	13. Caddow	13. Warantoble	13. Iidle
14. F. Cumar	14. Irib	14. Yarafle	14. Geedda
15. Yabar Cadde	15. Macow (Baadi)	15. Jarmaxumo	15. Fijiray
16. Mahad Alle	16. Gadiid	16. Cellquod	16. Awle
17. Adeer	17. Cumar	17. Limaan	17. Mudub
18. F. Walaal	18. Maxamuud	18. Warcadde	18. Reegow
19. Ay Bakar		19. Cali	19. Eymow
20. Khalif		20. Aadan	20. Ibrahim
21. Maxamuud		21. Cabdullahi	21. Cabdi
22. Cabdi		22. Cumar	22. Xasan
23. Cali		23. Ibarahim	23. Aadan
24. Xasan		24. Maxamed	24. Ibraahim
25. Cali		25. Cumar F.	25. Cali
26. Ibraahim		26. Abiikarow	
27. C/irsaaq		27. Cali	

Fig. 7

HAWIYE			SAMAALE	
Karanle	2. Gugundhabe	2. Gorgaate	2. Mayle	2. Gardheere
Wadaarre	3. JIDLE	3. Daame	3. Uurmidig	3. Maataay
MURUSADE	4. Weyteen	4. Sariir	4. Kasheente	4. Riidhe
Kliibaar	5. Delcatire	5. Sacmaal	5. Lo'doon	5. Garjeen
Wacayle	6. Cadde	6. Baradle	6. Wacwacle	6. Saransoor
Makahaan	7. Samakaab	7. Abkaal	7. Hiyood	7. GAALJECEL
Ximyar	8. Gumashole	8. Madoble	8. Xawaadle	8. Sooraante
Xayle	9. Waaqmahadle	9. Hiraab	9. Lo'doon	9. Abturaale
). WarWaaq	10. Quman-hale	10. Madkicis	10. DiintiWaaq	10. DoorWaaq
1. Sabti	11. BiddeWaaq	11. SACAD		11. Lahado
2. Cabdalla	12. Saleebaan	12. Cawareere		12. Cumar
3. Naxriis Waaq	13. Aadan	13. WaaqJire		13. Maxamud
		14. CiqWaaq		
		15. Cali		
	1. Aji			
	2. Dangalo			
	3. DAAROOD (C/raxman)		1. DIR	1. DIGIL
			2. Maha	2. Maad
			3. Surre	3. Caleemo
Kablalax	4. kabalax	4. Sade	4. Lafagaab	4. GELEDI
Kuumade	5. Koombe	5. MAREEXAAN	5. Sinji	5. Caah+CumarD
Absame	6. Amlaalo	6. Awsame	6. Qubays	6. Dhiig
OGAADEEN	7. Hantaale	7. Baalyare	7. Reer Tonlle	7. Qarsin
Tagalle Waaq	8. Harti	8. Hedambari	8. Wacayeeen	8. Naaraq
BarWaaq	9. Morrosanto	9. Geashireedle	9. Abtiudug	9. DalWaaq
). Miyir	10. WARSANGELI	10. Reer Xasan	10. Waqatile	10. Xasan
1. Kaante	11. Mame'eke	11. Ibrahim Waaq	11. Ciise	11. Waaqdoor
2. Yuusuf	12. Kooge	12. Gaabane	12. Buraale	
3. Muuse	13. Maxamed		13. Xussen	
4. Siciid	14. Xasan		14. F. Cumar	
5. Talamuge	15. Dubays		15. Yabar Cadde	
6. Cabdi	16. JidWaaq			
7. SiinWaaq				

131

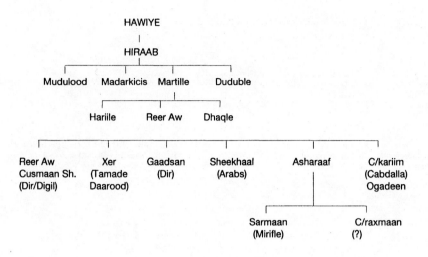

Fig. 8a: People from different origin associated to form part of a clanic structure

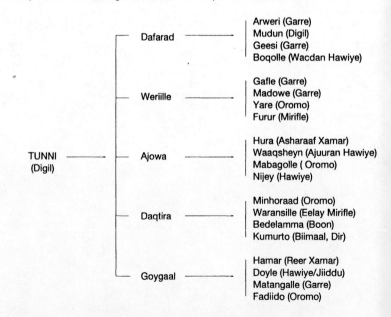

Fig. 8: People from different origin associated to form an autonomous group.

Fig. 9: Several folktales talk about fission and fusion
of subclans like these controversies.

CONTROVERSIES

Cali Geri (Dhulbahante)	←——————→	Duduble (Hawiye)
Macalin Dhiblaawe (Abgaal)	←——————→	Baaba Xasan (Sheekhaal Gendershe)
Macallin Dhiblaawe (Abgaal)	←——————→	M. Dhiblaawe (Siwaaqroon)
Cawrmae (Warsangeli)	←——————→	Cawrmale (Gardheere Samaale)
Wagardhac (Marexaan)	←——————→	Qayad (Dhulbahante)
Tagalla Waaq (Ogaadeen)	←——————→	Habar Awal . . . (Isaaq)
Ayaanle (Cayr)	←——————→	Faqashinni (Ajuuraan)
Warsangeli (Harti Abgaal)	←——————→	Warsangeli (Harti Daarood)
Hinjiile (Mirifle)	←——————→	Hinjiile (Dhulbahante)
Lelkase (Xawaadle)	←——————→	Lelkase (Darood)
Cumar Dheer (Habargidir)	←——————→	Mareexaan
Cali Ganuun (Gadabursi)	←——————→	Bartire (Daarood)
Xeebjire (Gadabursi)	←——————→	Sheekhaal (Hawiye)
Sacad (Habargedir)	←——————→	Amuudaan (Ogaadeen)

Etc.......

Fig. 10: The modernization of Somali clan system with false labels.

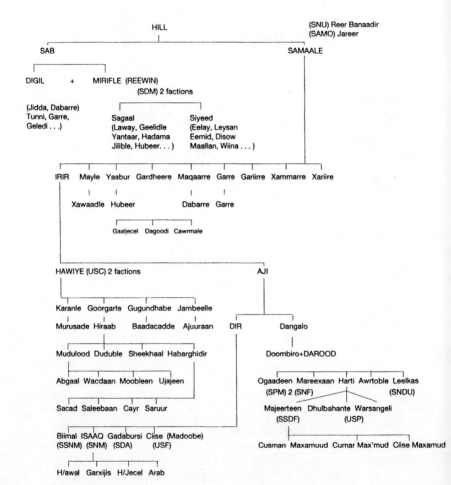

"Daybreak Is Near, Won't You Become Sour?"[1]

Going Beyond the Current Rhetoric in Somali Studies

∽

Ali Jimale Ahmed

Somali society ought to be regarded as the product of interactions among small groups of herdsmen, farmers, itinerant Shaykhs, and townsmen who came together under diverse circumstances in the past and whose modern sense of national identity derives less from primordial sentiments than from a set of shared historical experiences.

— Lee Cassanelli, *The Shaping of Somali Society*

'Nation' as a term is radically connected with 'native'. We are born into relationships which are typically settled in a place. The form of primary and 'placeable' bonding is of quite fundamental human and natural importance. Yet the jump from that to anything like the modern nation-state is entirely 'artificial'.

— Raymond Williams, *The Year 2000*

> Where explanation and interpretation 'come to an end',
> surely is... when we arrive at a certain interpretative log-
> jam or sticking place and recognize that we shall not get
> any further until we transform the practical forms of life
> in which our interpretations are inscribed.
>   —Terry Eagleton, "Ineluctable Options"

Let me start with an anecdote, one whose punchline is central to situating the locus of the Somali negative dialectic. In
the town of Afgoye (in southern Somalia), they say, there was
a man who was seen one day beating the waters of the river
with his stick. The residents of the town were amazed. They
then asked the man, "Why are you beating the waters of the
river since you know that water is innocent and that it sustains
life?" To which the man answered: "Once in awhile, there is
a crocodile down there." There is always a tendency among
Somali intellectuals to hunt for crocodiles, real or imagined,
rather than examining things and ideas on merit. For me,
therefore, an intellectual (of any sort) is the person who, to
quote from Gramsci, "assume[s] that the purpose of discussion is the pursuit of truth...."[2]

Such an intellectual is one who attempts to identify problems, reflects on them, and does not shy away from asking
hard and unpleasant questions, and who suggests, not impos-
es, some type of solution to the problem under his/her scrutiny. An intellectual is also one who understands the validity of
Somali poet Qamman Bulhan's words: *"Maashaan la saarin
waa dambey, sare kacaantaaye"* ("Pus that is not tended to and
cared for timely, will eventually suppurate with devastating
consequences"). On the basis of this practical, albeit crude
definition, it is not hard to see why I had earlier suggested
elsewhere that Somalia has never had that many intellectuals. Instead, I argue, we had university or college "graduates."
For, "education which does not bring about a transformation
in the consciousness of the 'educated' is hardly beneficial to
the individual, let alone to society.... For, as a Chinese adage
has it, 'To know and not to act is not to know.'"[3] Implicit in
the proverb is the notion that action prefigures and is

inscribed in theory. The two complement one another; thus, the importance of praxis — "the action and reflection of men and women upon their world in order to transform it."[4]

The trouble with Somali intellectuals emanates from what Hisham Sharabi calls "a fetishized consciousness" which manifests itself in both imitation and passivity.[5] In the case of the traditional intellectual, this form of consciousness shows itself in most of our playwrights' inability to reflect in their works the modus vivendi of the urban dweller who constitutes the largest group of theatergoers in towns. This is why much of our literary production which employed too much of pastoralist imagery did not fare well among town dwellers. Lest we play down the importance of town dwellers, we should remember that all regimes in Africa, one-city nation-states that they are, work towards contentment and, at the same time, containment of this group of people.[6] Thus, one could argue that literary production which uses imagery and techniques that ignore or do not reflect the town dweller's mode of living merely upholds the status quo. This point will be clarified later in the discussion when we talk about Abdi Muhumed's play *Muufo*. Suffice it to say that undue valorization of the pastoralist ethos in modern Somali literature only contributes to the perpetuation of certain values that impede any real development.

Also, this fetishized consciousness is one that Somali intellectuals share with their Western counterparts. There are two reasons for this: first, the prevalent tendency among intellectuals to tow the line — not so much a party line as fear of the established scholar; secondly, this consciousness is indicative of sheer laziness. In other words, it is much easier to glean information from existing sources than to break new ground and be taken to task. The consequences of this servile imitation and passivity have been devastating for Somalia, while the rest of the world has found itself in utter amazement. Nothing they had read about Somalia could have prepared them for this shock. This prompted the former American Assistant Secretary of State for Africa, Herman Cohen, to say: "Perhaps we did not really know that much about Somalia."[7]

The actions of the following four important groups have contributed to this "misrepresentation."

1. *The historians' (both Somali and non-Somali) reconstruction of the past:* Clan narratives and genealogies were accorded undue importance. In the process the genealogist gave legitimacy to what I call the "dervishization" of the Somali state.[8] By dervishization is meant a conscious effort on the part of successive Somali regimes and their intellectual acolytes to monumentalize, to the exclusion of other groups, the dervish experience in Somali history. The denial of recognition to other Somali freedom fighters and their movements has to be seen as public denial that is directed against the clansmen of the spurned martyrs. Since the spoils of independence are too few to spread around, the scions of Sayyid Mohamed Abdulle Hassan and his Dervishes saw to it that no other comparable figure will ever emerge in the annals of Somali historiography. This was done in Somalia by securing the mass media and other industries of cultural production in the hands of Dervish sympathizers.

To get its point across, the new Somali state created an elite police force called *Daraawiishta* — the dervishes. The dual purpose of the name was not lost on Somalis, especially northerners (Isaaqs), who read the appellation as a political affront against them. In essence, the revisitation of the dervish wars was meant not only to pay homage to a group of warriors in the "nationalist anti-imperialist struggle," but more ominously to remind Somalis whose fathers had fought clan wars against the Dervishes that they indeed have now lost the war. The Isaaqs were not the only Somali group that had an ax to grind against the dervishization of the state. The Hawiyes and the Reewin (mistakenly called 'Rahanweyn') were later outraged by the construction of a monument for the Sayyid. The site was equally laden with political symbolism. The erection of the monument in front of the People's Hall (Parliament & Party Headquarters) was an allusion to a contested idea that the Sayyid was the father of the modern Somali state. The construction of the monument unilaterally accentuated the Sayyid's stature as a national hero, irrespective of the fact that some of his poetical diatribes and his raids against other clans were motivated and shaped by a clannish world view. It is no wonder, therefore, that the monument was immediately destroyed by the masses after Barre's overthrow. The destruction of the monument does not only symbolize the overthrow of Barre, but it also brings to an end the political supremacy of the Dervish followers.

2. *The colonial anthropologist's warped method of sifting through the raw and the cooked in developing countries*: And while the logocentric privileging of 'modernity' as opposed to 'tradition' paves the way for a "geopolitics [that] has its ideological foundations in chronopolitics,"[9] making some forms of anthropology vulnerable to what Levi-Strauss calls "the hand-maiden of colonialism,"[10] the perversity of the Somali scene is seen through hilarious ethnographic accounts that relay to other Somalis and to the rest of the world intra-Somali squabbles with the ethnographer as the arena/space for the working-out of Somali contradictions.[11]

3. *Our unscrupulous politicians*— not so much through writing as through actions, off-the-record comments, and interviews given to equally unscrupulous Western and non-Western journalists. The mediocrity of the Somali political scene is perhaps unparalleled in East Africa.

4. And finally, *Somali orature, especially the oral poet*: Poetry in the Somali context is important in that much of their experience is kept in the bardic memory. In the last 30 to 40 years, however, the nation has made use of only the dervishized poetry. In this sense, by focusing on the *Gabay*— the poetry of a section of the society (and only *one* form of poetry at that) — and masquerading it as universal, Somali poetry has been robbed of its most salient contour: engaging dialogue with tradition and subcultures. This statement bespeaks the need to "detribalize" Somali poetry. To compound the problem, the poet's localized utterances find a wider audience through the noble endeavors of Somali and non-Somali transcribers. The latter cultivate a lasting friendship with poets and/or reciters. Based on these encounters, the non-Somali writer and critic especially relays to the rest of the world his or her

understanding of Somali culture as gleaned from such oral (or written) texts as are available to him/her. The mode of their contributions is in essence "narrative and descriptive."[12] Their informants' voices are inscribed in the narrative aspect of their contributions. Hence the importance of the problematic of the informant/interlocutor who is aware of his/her importance in shaping the consciousness of the ethnographer/critic.[13] The descriptive aspect of the latter's contributions focuses on the elucidation and exegesis of the narrative. In short, absent from their contributions is oppositional (i.e., unofficial) narrative, hidden in women's and other groups' subcultural poetry. By conferring a mantle akin to what Levin calls "an institution of literature"[14] onto a form of poetry that is panegyric of the "dervishes," these writers failed to anticipate the day when the unofficial narrative would be written in blood. Thus, the words of Mr. Cohen, whose knowledge of the Somali as a construction of "a textual attitude"[15] (to use Edward Said's words) came from the persona in the official/ethnographic narrative.

These four sources, *inter alia,* are mainly responsible for the myths about Somalia that we read in books. It is therefore incumbent upon the *contemporary* intellectual to sift through these myths and half-truths. The task is daunting, to say the least.

Here are some of the myths that need an urgent reevaluation before we could even attempt to reconstitute the deconstructed fragments of the old Somalia. First, that Somalis are Arabs with a tan. Early writers, especially some British anthropologists, unable to situate the origin of the Somali opted for the easy way out and concocted the Arab factor in Somali history. This went well with the 19th-century European obsession with "origin." The Somali in the ensuing enigmatic paradigm became endowed with European physical features. Fiction writers caught onto the idea. This is what Marjorie Perham wrote in *Major Dane's Garden:*

> They were a striking couple: the woman, Khedichu, was the most beautiful Somali I have ever seen. She stood

as straight as a spear and had regular features, a European profile.[16]

Senghor, writing the preface to William Siyad's collection of poems, *Khamsine*, calls Siyad "a marginal negro" (whatever that means).

Jack Mapanje's poem "At the Metro: Old Irrelevant Images" is the first conscious effort by an African poet to understand the myth for what it is:

> They are still so anthropologically tall here
> Still treating you in irrelevant metaphors:
> Somalis have softer skins, they drink milk, they say
> And yours is cracking, you drink Kachasu.[17]

These perceptions have contributed to the creation of a Somalia that is *in* Africa, but not *of* Africa. The tragedy emanating from these perceptions need not be catalogued here. Suffice it to say, in the words of one *Washington Post* reporter: "Poor Somalia — not enough Arab and not enough African." The fate of the proverbial person attempting to straddle two horses needs no further comment. The Somalis are also aware of the consequences of such an attempt. As the lyrics of a popular Somali song have it, the endeavors of the straddler are compared to a she-camel that likes to rest in shade simultaneously under two different trees. The outcome of such an endeavor is tragic for the camel as she is killed by a hyena somewhere in between the two trees. Thus, the aptness of the reporter's insightful remark about the fate of a Somalia that does not identify itself with one or the other — African or Arab.

Of the dozen or so movements in Somalia today, only one — SAMO (Somali African Mukay Organisation) seems to be ready to confront the issue of the Somali as an Arab with a tan. By including "African" in its name, the organization bares a hidden secret in Somali society. Supporters of the movement belong to that segment of Somali society who are often given the derogatory epithet of *jareer* (kinky hair). The organization's name therefore is indicative of their subtle refutation of the Arabization of the Somali. In this sense, political considerations are not absent. SAMO supporters have attracted the attention of the world as a group that has among other reasons been victimized for its physical features. The *Mukay* in the organization's name underlines the democratic ideals of the group. *Mukay* — like Tagore's famous *Banyan* — is a type of a tree in Somalia under whose shade Somali elders (usually men) sit to adjudicate cases.

Second, the myth of the homogenous Somali, which is based on the 19th-century European view of the nation-state — same race/ethnicity, language, religion, etc. — needs an examination. We forgot that there is unity in diversity; that the Reewin (in the riverine area) with their Maay language are as Somali as those who speak Maxaatiri (the official language of the state); that persons speaking in Chimbalazi or Chizigula are also authentic Somalis. This is not to discount the relevance and importance of myths in — to use Nietzcheian terms — rounding off a social or national movement to unity.

Third, the question of what is meant by "nomadic Somalis" also needs a reappraisal. Is the concept connected to region? Clan? Mode of living? How, for example, are the nomads in Hoddur (Reewin) different from those in Gedo (Barre's birthplace)? Are the nomadic Hodduri camel herders who live in contiguity with their counterparts in Gedo less nomadic because of their clan background?

Fourth, what constitutes Somali culture — particularly literature — also begs for reexamination. I remember literary discussions I had with some members of the Somali Academy of Arts and Sciences in the early 1980s. Some of these "intellectuals" were of the opinion that certain parts of the country did not have literature. In relation to this we have to redefine the role and function a future Somali Academy is to play in a new Somalia. This is important. The Academy played a central role in shaping, facilitating, and/or distributing the findings of some of the groups mentioned above. It is not accidental that none of the Academy's past presidents came from outside the Dervishized circle. This assertion does not suggest or imply that all past presidents of the institution were part of the conspiracy to institute the primacy of the Sayyid and of tribalized poetry in Somali culture. What it does assert, however, is that Barre and his close associates did not appoint a president for the Academy solely on the basis of merit. To put it bluntly, the overriding qualification for the post was that one had to come from (i.e., be born into) the circle. The elites at the Academy did not and could not object to the structuring of the institution in such a way that it had to serve the interests of the Barre regime. This is partly so because these elites had a vested interest in the production and dissemination of "operative tropes" that were reflective of the regime's goals.

Thus, the need to overhaul and redefine the objectives of the institution is apparent. Such a redefinition, of necessity, calls for the creation of a new type of intellectual, one who is aware of the magnitude and gravity of his/her historical responsibility at this juncture of Somali history. If we are to avoid a repetition of the mistakes of the 1940s, 50s, and 60s, we must take note of what Farah Seefey, a traditional intellectual living in the 50s, called "Beware of a hollow liberty midwifed by travellers." The allusion is to the Somali concept of *"Nimaan Kuu Fureyn, Yuu Kuu Rarin"* ("Make sure that he who helps you with the packing will also be there for the unpacking"). This traditional intellectual could discern a hidden compromise between the moderates of the SYL (Somali Youth League) and the Italian colonial administration in the South. Farah Seefey's keen analysis of the dynamics and dialectics of the colonial enterprise led him to believe that the latter's departure was not due to a sudden epiphany, nor impelled by an altruistic reason. Rather, such a compromise could be explained in the words of a Punjabi adage: "When halter and heel-ropes are cut, don't give chase with sticks, but with grain." Frantz Fanon, in *The Wretched of the Earth*, came to a similar conclusion in 1961:

> This idea of compromise is very important in the phenomenon of decolonization, for it is very far from being

143

a simple one. The partisans of the colonial system discover that the masses may destroy everything....As a general rule, colonialism welcomes this godsend with open arms, transforms these 'blind mouths' into spokesmen, and in two minutes endows them with independence, on condition they restore order.[18]

Farah Seefey's prediction of a hollow liberty turned out to be true, for the old order in Somalia came to a standstill in 1969. Again, Fanon:

That is why in certain underdeveloped countries
the masses forge ahead very quickly, and realize
two or three years [nine years in the Somali case]
after independence that they have been frustrated,
that 'it wasn't worthwhile' fighting
and that nothing could really change.[19]

Reminiscent of Langston Hughes' "A Dream Deferred" and Hugh MacDiarmid's "Reflections in a Slum," Somali poet Mohamud S. Togane succinctly sums up the frustrations associated with dashed hopes. In a poem called "When I Considered," Togane writes:

When I considered
in lucid drunken anger
the freaks of Africa
I hollered: UHURU, a whore!
A shout shook me shuddering the shack bar:
Come back! Come back, white man! Come back to Africa!
EVERYTHING FORGIVEN!

We share some of the poet's concerns, but a critical approach is in order here. We cannot throw our hands up in the air and holler in exasperation, "Uhuru, a whore!" As the poet himself suggests in the second stanza, this is announced in a drunken stupor. A sober analysis will yield some positive results. This is intimated by the poet who is elevated from his drunken stupor by Malcolm X's words which remind him among other things, that "Every shut eye ain't sleep/ Every good-bye ain't gone."[20]

It was against that background of disillusionment that Siyad Barre came to power. Yet he was initially conceived as a stopgap. The 1969 coup was unanimously received with a great deal of enthusiasm and encomium. Even the skies were generous to the coup makers: long awaited rains fell in abundance. Only a week before, the late President Abdirashid Ali Sharmarke was in Las Anood in the North, encouraging people to pray for rains that were long overdue. It was a strange coincidence that the brutal assassination of the President "triggered" a heavy downpour. The ideologues of the new regime quickly utilized the event to their advantage and interpreted it as a divinely symbolic act. The coup was interpreted as a good omen. With the exception of a few individuals who realized the impending danger now that the reins of the country had fallen into the hands of some of the colonialist-trained soldiers, the majority seemed ignorant of the past histories of some of the coup makers.[21]

Siyad Barre immediately put to good use the traditional intellectuals and artists. It seemed that someone well versed in Gramscian ideology gave Barre a crucial piece of advice. Gramsci had written: "One of the most important characteristics of every class which develops towards power is its struggle to assimilate and conquer 'ideologically' the traditional intellectuals."[22] The Somali intellectual came up with moral justifications from the lore of the people for Barre's ascendancy to power. Songs like *Geediga wadaay* ("Lead the track"); *Guulwade Siyad aabihii garashada* ("Siyad the victory-bearer, and the father of knowledge"), and *Caynaanka haay* ("May you hold onto the reins of power forever") became the hue-and-cry of the traditional intellectual. These traditional intellectuals seemed to confer legitimacy to Barre by delving into the lore of the people. Barre's actions were justified through an elaborate system that showed how his brand of leadership not only had affinities with but also emanated from the deep recesses of Somali tradition.

This Somali obsession with finding a putative genealogy

for one's actions is close to what Alioum Fantoure describes in his brilliant novel, *Tropical Circle*. The concepts of *koi* ("reserved for the aristocracy of the central power, ministers, chief counsellors, provincial governors" in the old Mandinga Empire) and its derivative *koism* are now employed for political expediency by rulers of the newly independent country of "South-Majiland" to simulate a farcical return to tradition. The strategies used to legitimize such a return to tradition ironically unveil the hidden underbelly of the rhetoric, for they suggest, as cogently explained in the introduction by Aliko Songolo, how "the modern power structure misuses tradition and history to mystify the people and justify the violence it perpetrates upon them."[23] Therefore, the words — *koi* in the case of Fantoure's fictional country; *caynaanka* in the case of Siyad Barre's Somalia — betray their user's intentions. Such intentions are best captured in Ellul's categories of propaganda, viz., political, vertical, and integration.[24] In the case of Somalia, the poet's attempt to connect Barre's style of leadership to the pastoral concept of the trailblazer not only reveals the inadequacy of the pastoralist language to capture the essence of the new nation-state, but it demystifies the widely-held notion of Somali egalitarianism. Absent in the idiomatic use of *caynaanka* (reins) is the notion of collective leadership, flaunted at the time by Barre, whose official title was *"Guddoomiyaha Golaha Sare ee Kacaanka"* (Chairman of the Supreme Revolutionary Council). The implication in the *"caynaanka"* is that the country is like a camel or horse: the leader is the one with the reins. This is reflective of a Confucian ideology in which the leader of the country is like the wind, the subjects are the grass; and the grass bends where the wind pushes it. Laden in the imagery of the reins is the existence of a stubborn/untrustworthy animal that responds and is prodded to progress only by brute force.

Also absent in this kind of logic is the concept of consensus. Embedded in the first absence is yet another, viz., our inability to "reinvent the language of culture so as to get out of this crisis."[25] The importance of reinventing the language of culture could be demonstrated through the creative use of a cultural concept called the *paidatra*, still extant in the Indian subcontinent. Bernard S. Cohn writes: "The Indian pilgrimage was adapted to politics in the form of Gandhi's marches, and the idea of the *paidatra* (the walking of the politician amongst the people) is still part of the political rituals of India."[26]

The Somali masses were duped by some well-meaning poets. One such intellectual is the great poet, Abdi Muhumed. Abdi, however, found out that he had been had. His play (performance piece) *Muufo* was more than an atonement. It was a classic case of *mar i dage* ("once bitten, twice shy"). Once the poet finds the locus of his weakness, a whole new vista opens for him. The keen perspicacity of his actions crystalizes in the manipulation of language. As Fanon explains, "By losing its characteristics of despair..., [Abdi's play] becomes part of the common lot of the people and forms part of an action in preparation or already in progress."[27] Here, the poet breaks with the past, both in terms of content and form. In this sense, "He will note unusual forms of expression and themes which are fresh and imbued with a power which is no longer that of invocation but rather of the assembling of the people, a summoning together for a precise purpose."[28]

Muufo was the first performance piece that began to speak in the language and idiom — to borrow from Gramsci — of the people. *Mandeeq* (the pastoralist image of the she-camel) now became *Muufo* (bread). The allusion is to the widening gap that now exists between the rich and the poor in urban centers. The poor are represented by the workers and the city lumpen proletariat. Reminiscent of Bertolt Brecht's poems, "The Zinc Coffin" and especially "A Worker Reads History," *Xoogsato* (workers), one of the poems in the play, attempts to defetishize the reified helplessness induced in the worker. The poet asks questions that prick the conscience of any worker: Who builds castles? Who produces both industrial and agricultural goods? At first glance, the questions sound naive, as we must assume that any producer knows the product of his/her sweat. On closer examination, however, Abdi's questions echo those of the Brazilian educator, Paulo Freire. Freire conducted research among the Brazilian peasants who were reluctant to answer certain questions, even some that were related to their own work. They intimated that the feudal lord, presumably somewhere in the city, knew more about farming than they. This led Freire to write in his book, *The Pedagogy of the Oppressed,* that docility is not an inherent characteristic, but the result of a long socio-political indoctrination. Cognizant of this fact/reality, Abdi's role now becomes similar to that of the "problem-posing educator" who "is to create, together with the [audience] the conditions under which knowledge at the level of doxa is superseded by true knowledge, at the level of the logos."[29] The old invocation of the nomadic trailblazer (read "the inculcation/imposition of a personality cult") through such doxologies as *Guulwade* and *Aabe* ("Victory Bearer; Father") now give way to reasoned analysis of the lot of the workers. Consequently, the old panegyric songs are now replaced by *ilowsho dhowinaa innagu Soomaaliyey* ("O Somalis, how prone we are to forgetfulness"). The allusion is to the circumstances that brought Barre to power in 1969. He came to power ostensibly to restore hope and revamp a decadent system. *Muufo* in this sense becomes for the poet/playwright what Helen Cixous hoped writing to be: *anti-oubli*[30] It was not unexpected therefore that the piece infuriated Barre who was in the audience. Barre's anger is similar to that of the necrophilous person who "can relate to an object....only if he possesses it; hence a threat to his possession is a threat to himself...."[31] Abdi's play was a daring attack on the sacrosanct edifice of Barre's hegemony.

Latent in the song *Xoogsato* ("Workers") is also an intention on the part of the poet to reveal a tragic flaw in the Somali nomad's character: his disdain for all sorts of manual labor. Needless to say, this character lingers on in the Somali nomad now in the diaspora. *Muufo*, the play, marks the beginning of the end for Barre's hegemonic hold on the Somali cultural scene. In one of the poems of this writer, this hegemony is traced to the initial successes of the coup which made a lot of people complacent about "a curse lifted/But never put to rest."[32] The curse is the original one that made Farah Seefey and Frantz Fanon unfortunate Cassandras.

One does not need to catalogue the various manifestations of the curse. By 1976, with the founding of the Somali Socialist Revolutionary Party, it became apparent that Barre had run out of most of his tricks. This fact was not lost on many commentators on the Somali political scene. I.M. Lewis, in "The Politics of the 1969 Somali Coup," writes: "It seems to me significant, however, that Somalia's shift from multi-party democracy to one-party rule and finally to military control coincides with a general movement from wide-ranging national solidarity to extreme lineage particularism."[33] Fanon captures this period succinctly:

> This party which of its own will proclaims that it is a national party, and which claims to speak in the name of the totality of the people, secretly, sometimes even openly, organizes an authentic ethnic [clan] dictatorship.... The ministers, the members of the cabinet, the ambassadors and local commissioners are chosen from the same ethnological group as the leader, sometimes directly from his own family....[Heads of government like Barre] are the true traitors in Africa, for they sell their country to the most terrifying of all its enemies: stupidity.[34]

This enemy has inflicted on Somalis what no other enemy had ever succeeded in doing: the disintegration of the country into a mosaic of fiefdoms. The ensuing events of the last four years could perhaps be understood through the following proverbs:

1. *Ayax teg, elna reb.* ("Don't be fooled by the migration of the locusts. They leave their larvae behind.")
2. *Waxaad i baday waxaa iiga daran, waxaad ibartay.* ("What you made me go through, i.e., your brutal persecutions and oppression, is less innocous than that which I learned from you, i.e., the possibility of having my way through the barrel of a gun.")

The mindset that was created under the reign of that "stupidity" still haunts the nation. Under Barre's autocratic rule, all attempts were made to create an infantile public. His paternalistic condescensions were all geared to stifling all forms of creativity; people were denied the opportunity to solve their problems and/or initiate new programs that were relevant to their lives and surroundings. Barre became the "father of the nation." Freire writes: "When their [people's] efforts to act responsibly are frustrated, when they find themselves unable to use their faculties, people suffer."[35] "'This suffering due to impotence is rooted in the very fact that the human equilibrium has been disturbed.'"[36] In short, the Somali people were denied the opportunity to solve their problems and/or initiate new programs. In the case of the North, the Hargeysa group (named after the second largest town in the country) were incarcerated for initiating self-help projects in Hargeysa. Young professionals started organizing the townspeople to rely on their own labor. The government saw in these projects a subtle desire on the part of the townspeople to dispense with Barre's handouts. Ironically, *iskaa wax u qabso* ("self-help schemes") was part of Barre's revolutionary rhetoric of creating a self-reliant Somalia. The incarceration of the professionals was to pave the way for the destruction of the human spirit. Such a spirit would explode with a great force when it experienced "freedom."

In the absence of legitimate forums to express their opinions, the people who are caught in a highly compartmentalized clan system organize themselves along the lines that they know the best: clan. The clandestine aspect of their association leads to more fragmentation within the society, as everyone comes to trust and rely on only those of his/her clan. Hence the clan character of all pre-Barre movements. The movements, in this sense, fell into Barre's trap of divide-and-rule. The clan in this respect plays and performs the function of what Somalis call *"awr kacsi"*— code words uttered to cajole a stubborn camel to stand on its feet. In this sense the movements' pending failure was already woven into the loom of their fate. They used the same tactics used before by Barre.

The alternative they envisioned for the country "is itself a repetition of the structure it seems to displace. In fact, it is perhaps the most seductive variation on that pattern and perhaps even more dangerous."[37] If Barre's ascendancy to power was tragic, what has happened since his overthrow is farcical. This is important to note, so that Barre does not become a footnote to this misery. The civil war is prefigured in Barre's actions. This shows the need to read Barre as an authentic expression of the Somali culture, granted that such culture is characteristically a hybrid and cosmopolitan by design. To be fair to Siyad Barre, he was only the last piece of a puzzle that has taken more than 50 years to unravel.

The curse is still with us. And this is where it becomes important for the Somali intellectual to muster courage and to tell his people that it is impossible in this age to run a "tribal" government or regime. All trials in this direction have come to nothing. All attempts to institute a clan government have failed miserably, with devastating consequences for all who tried it. What we need instead is the construction of a new ethic. The new ethic must reflect "the mode of existence of the new intellectual [which] can no longer consist of eloquence, the external and momentary arousing of sentiments and passions, but must consist of being actively involved in political life, as a builder, an organizer, 'permanently persuasive'."[38] The intellectual can be the lightning rod for the implementation of this new ethic. We must teach our people by example. We must by the same token learn from them. We must install and strengthen, wherever it exists, the importance of tolerance and of accommodating the views of others. We must understand with Gramsci that: "In the formulation of the historico-critical problems it is wrong to conceive of scientific discussion as a process at law in which there is an accused and a public prosecutor whose professional duty is to demonstrate that the accused is guilty and has to be put out of circulation."[39] Nothing is to be gained from that type of discourse, thus, the importance of avoiding any pretense which claims to possess the "last word." Such a presumption is indicative of what Fanon calls "childish stupidity."[40] The only way to break out of this vicious cycle is to initiate a politics of emancipation in which the combatants go through the clan system but emerge on the other side[41] ready and empowered to imagine a just society. History will judge us according to the sincerity and integrity of our actions.

Coda

I would like to end with a poem. Endings, as Edward Said tells us, are also beginnings.[42]

"Of Nations and Narratives"

Happy endings are
not concocted
Nor delivered in
a C section
They must germinate in
The belly of the narrative
And have their fate
Woven,
exquisitely
In the loom of the plot.

Notes

1. The title is a translation of a pastoral work song in which a lady pleads with the churn: *"Haanyahay, dhigdhigo dhabaryar, Waagii dharaarowyee sow maad dhanaanaatid?"* By employing a title that is reflective of the very thing I am going against is not meant as what Umberto Eco calls "guerilla tactics." Rather, it serves two related purposes: first, the call to transcend pastoralist language in the depiction of the city and of the nation-state is not a call to do away with all forms of pastoralist imagery in the parlance of the poet (in short, the baby should not be thrown away with the bath water); secondly, the use of such title indeed signals an intention to revamp and restructure the Somali language.
2. Antonio Gramsci, *Selections from the Prison Notebooks*, trans. & ed. Quintin Hoare and Geoffrey N. Smith (London: Lawrence and Wishart, 1971), p. 344.

3. "Editorial," *Ufahamu*, 17, no. 2 (1989):2. This does not negate the role of traditional and organic intellectuals such as Hadraawi, Saada Ali, and Abdi Muhumed who, through thick and thin, stood by their people against the corrosive and corrupt system of Siyad Barre. As Edward Said writes in *The World, The Text and the Critic*, (Cambridge, Mass: Harvard University Press, 1983), "there is some compelling truth to Julien Benda's contention that in one way or the other it has often been the intellectual, the *clerk*, who stood for values, ideas, and activities that transcend and deliberately interfere with the collective weight imposed by the nation-state and the national culture." (1983: 14).

4. Paulo Freire, *Pedagogy of the Oppressed*, trans. Myra Bergman Ramos (1970; rprt. New York: Continuum, 1993), p. 60.

5. Hisham Sharabi, *Neo-Patriarchy: A Theory of Distorted Change in Arab Society* (New York & Oxford: Oxford University Press, 1988), p. 24.Cf., Talal Asad's critique of Ernest Gellner's "Concepts and Society": "How is it that the approach exemplified by Gellner's paper remains attractive to so many academics in spite of its being demonstrably faulty? Is it perhaps because they are intimidated by a *style*? We know, of course, that anthropologists, like other academics, learn not merely to use a scholarly language, but to fear it, to admire it, to be captivated by it. Yet this does not quite answer the question because it does not tell us *why* such a scholarly style should capture so many intelligent people." — see: Talal Asad, (from "The Concept of Cultural Translation in British Social Anthropology," in James Clifford and George E. Marcus, eds., *Writing Culture: The Poetics and Politics of Ethnography* (Berkeley & Los Angeles: University of California Press,1986), pp.163f.

6. "For this reason, development strategy was never people-oriented, and this is the crux of the matter. Development strategies were urban-biased, oriented to elitist consumption and outward-looking." — Ahmad Abubakar, *Africa and the Challenge of Development*, (New York: Praeger Publishers, 1989), pp. 2-3.
This harps on a familiar universal theme — the inequities that exist between the city and the countryside. See also Raymond Williams' excellent book *The Country and the City*.

7. Herman Cohen, "Opening (Oral) Remarks," at a roundtable discussion on Somalia, organized by the U.S. State Dept., Washington D.C., January 21-22, 1992. This writer was one of the invited participants.

8. This argument does not deny a role for the Sayyid and his dervishes in, to use Edward Said's words, the "nationalist anti-imperialist struggle" or what T. O. Ranger terms "primary resistance." What it attempts to get across is that the nationalist anti-imperialist strug-

gle was spearheaded by `Prophets and Priests,' among them poets and visionaries, versions perhaps of Hobsbawm's precapitalist protest and dissent." — (see E. Said, "Yeats in Decolonization" in Eagleton, Jameson, and Said, intro. Seamus Deane, *Nationalism, Colonialism and Literature* (Minneapolis: University of Minnesota Press, 1990), pp. 69-95.

The Sayyid, contrary to what his supporters had argued in the state-controlled media while stifling all oppositional voices, was not the only priest/poet who took up the cudgels against colonialism. See Sheikh Abdi Elli (1954); Harlow (1960); G. B. Martin (1969); Christine Ahmed (1989 & 1993); and Said Samatar, the leading Somali authority on the Sayyid (1992).

9.   Johannes Fabian, *Time and the Other: How Anthropology Makes Its Object* (New York: Columbia University Press, 1983), p. 151.

10   Quoted by Edward Said in *Culture and Imperialism* (New York: Knopf, 1993), p. 152.

11. See, among others: F. L. James, Esq., "A Journey through the Somali Country to the Webbe Shebeyli," in *Proceedings of the Royal Geographical Society* 7(1885):625-646; see also, I. M. Lewis, *Peoples of the Horn of Africa* (London: International African Institute, 1955) especially pp. 18, 38.

12. Said, *Culture and Imperialism*, p. 64.

13. This is not a flimsy remark that can easily be brushed aside. Sophistications of all sorts are no guarantee that an ethnographer will not be duped. Even some modern "television" ethnographers such as Oprah Winfrey and Phil Donahue, with all the intricate systems they have installed against fraudulent guests/interlocutors, are occasionally taken for a ride.

14. Quoted by Said, *Culture and Imperialism*, p. 73.

15. Quoted in Olivier Richon, "Representation, The Despot and The Harem: Some Questions around the Academic Orientalist Painting by Lecomte-Du-Nouy (1885)" in Francis Barker, et al. eds. *Europe and Its Others*, Vol. 1, (Colchester: University of Essex Press, 1985), p. 8.

16. Marjorie Perham, *Major Dane's Garden* (New York: Africana Publishers, 1970), p. 90.

17. Jack Mapanje, *Of Chameleons and Gods* (London: Heinemann, 1981).

18. Frantz Fanon, *The Wretched of the Earth*, trans. by Constance Farrington, Preface by Jean-Paul Sartre (New York: Grove Weidenfeld, 1991), p. 73.

19. *Ibid.*, p. 74f.

20. Mohamud S. Togane, *The Bottle and the Bushman: Poems of The Prodigal Son* (Quebec: The Muse's Co., 1986), p. 37.

21. See: Ali A. Mazrui, *Soldiers and Kinsmen: The Making of a Military Ethnocracy* (London, 1975).
22. Antonio Gramsci, *The Modern Prince and Other Writings* (New York: International Publishers, 1980), p. 122.
23. Aliko Songolo, "Introduction" in Alioum Fantoure, *Tropical Circle*, trans. Dorothy S. Blair (Charlottesville: University of Virginia Press, 1989), p. xxiv.
24. Jacques Ellul, *Propaganda: The Formation of Men's Attitudes*, trans. Konrad Kellen & Jean Lerner (New York: Vintage Books, 1973), pp. 61-87; also quoted by A. P. Foulkes, *Literature and Propaganda* (London & New York: Methuen, 1983), pp. 10f.
25. Quoted in Miriam Cooke, *War's Other Voices: Women Writers on the Lebanese Civil War* (Cambridge & New York: Cambridge University Press, 1988), p.43.
26. Bernard S. Cohn, "Representing Authority in Victorian India," in Eric Hobsbawm & Terence Ranger, eds., *The Invention of Tradition*, (Cambridge: Cambridge University Press, 1983), p. 209.
27. Fanon, *Wretched of the Earth*, p. 241.
28. *Ibid.*, p. 243.
29. Freire, *Pedagogy of the Oppressed*, p. 62.
30. Helen Cixous, "From the Scene of the Unconscious to the Scene of the History," trans. Deborah W. Carpenter, in Ralph Cohen, ed., *The Future of Literary Theory*, (New York & London: Routledge, 1989), p. 7.
31. Erich Fromm, *The Heart of Man* (1966:41); quoted by Freire, *Pedegogy of the Oppressed*, p. 58.
32. "Premonition," *Ufahamu* 18,2 (1990):84.
33. I. M. Lewis, "The Politics of the 1969 Somali Coup," in *Journal of Modern African Studies* 10,3 (October 1972):408.
34. Fanon, *Wretched of the Earth*, p. 183.
35. Freire, *Pedagogy of the Oppressed*, p. 59.
36. Quoted by Freire, *Ibid.*
37. Paul Bove, *Intellectuals in Power* (New York: Columbia University Press, 1986), p. 5.
38. Gramsci, *The Modern Prince and Other Writings*, p. 122.
39. Gramsci, *Notebooks*, p. 343.
40. Fanon, *Wretched of the Earth*, p. 47.
41. See Terry Eagleton, "Nationalism, Irony and Commitment," in Eagleton, et al., *Nationalism, Colonialism and Literature*, pp.23-39.
42. Edward Said, *Beginnings: Intention and Method* (New York: Columbia University Press, 1985).

Finely Etched Chattel:
The Invention of
a Somali Woman

∞

Christine Choi Ahmed

Iman, the Somali superstar, marries David Bowie in a much publicized event and uses the occasion to splatter her well-shaped body, naked, across the pages of international magazines, wrapped in fur and posing with assorted Zulu warriors. A few months later we watch women thinner than Paris runway models holding dying children in the streets of Baidoa. For most people in the Western world, the latter is the Somali woman. Unfortunately, the historical and anthropological writings concerning Somali women, as limited as they are, do little to change this perception.

This paper will attempt to do two things. First, to critique the historical and anthropological literature in English on gender and women in Somalia; and second, to propose several different ways to recapture gender relations and the role of women in Somali history.

Much of the research on gender — and, in particular, women — in Somalia, with notable exceptions (to be discussed later), suffer from some very serious flaws. The discussion in this paper will not add substantial unknown or unknowable factors, but will attempt to peel away the layers of colonial anthropology, orientalism, and androcentric

Western scholarship in order to more clearly see gender relations and the participation of Somali women in their history. As Martin Bernal states in his epic work *Black Athena:*

> All cultures have some degree of prejudice for, or more often against, people whose appearance is unusual. However, the intensity and pervasiveness of northern European, American and other colonial racism since the 17th century have been so much greater than the norm. . .[1]

For this reason, we open with an examination of the works in the English language on Somali women. First, of course, is Richard Burton, who, in *First Footsteps in East Africa* (the title itself is blatantly ethnocentric), contributed much to orientalist scholarship and directly included Somalia as a part of the Orient. Orientalism, Bernal remarked,

> has served to distance and objectify non-European cultures, lumping their very different characteristics into a general category of "oriental" merely because they are not European. These have been seen as "exotic," and viewed as inert or passive in the face of European dynamism.[2]

Burton's observations concerning Somali women follows this orientalist approach.

> Daughters, as usual in Oriental countries, do not "count" as part of the family: they are however utilized by the father, who disposes of them to those who can increase his wealth and importance.[3]

He describes the Somali woman as follows:

> Generally, [they] are of cold temperament, the result of artificial as well as natural causes: like the Kafirs, they are very prolific, but peculiarly bad mothers, neither loved nor respected by their children. The fair sex lasts longer in Eastern Africa than in India and Arabia: at thirty, how-

ever, the charms are on the wane and when old age comes
on they are no exceptions to the hideous decrepitude of
the East.[4]

The following image of a wedding night in northern Somalia
is another example of Burton's "love of the exotic":

On first entering the nuptial hut, the bridegroom draws
forth his horsewhip and inflicts memorable chastisement
upon the fair person of his bride with the view of taming
any lurking propensity to shrewishness. This is carrying
out with a will the Arab proverb, 'The slave girl from her
capture, the wife from her wedding.'[5]

Several scholars have relied on the foregoing quote to indicate the status of women in Somali society, including the illus-
trious British anthropologist, I. M. Lewis. One could excuse,
to a certain degree, Burton's orientalist approach, given the
historical period in which he was writing — the 1850s. While
Burton's limitations are understood, the much more recent
work of I. M. Lewis — who above all others in the English language has defined Somalia and Somali women — disap-
pointingly follows a similar vein. Even younger scholars like
Bernhard Helander have taken up the orientalist torch. They
not only do not criticize Burton's approach, but they impute
the semblance of science to his observations on Somali
women and his so-called objective analysis of their role and
position in Somali society. Orientalism coupled with a patriarchal view of African women has yielded the systemized
anthropological studies of I. M. Lewis and other colonial
anthropologists, which have created the myth of the Somali
woman as chattel, commodity, and a creature with little power.
Anthropology, a genre of research that is supposedly scientific but is often ahistoric in its categorizations of culture and
human social behavior, is a natural child of orientalism. And
the institutional rise of orientalism is associated with the
expansion of colonialism. Edward Said and R. Rasid write that
within the orientalist scholarship,

> Not only was a systematic understanding of non-
> European peoples and their spoken languages needed to
> control these peoples, but a knowledge of their civiliza-
> tion, by seizing and categorizing their cultures, ensured
> that the natives [future elites] themselves could learn
> about their own civilizations only through European
> scholarship.[6]

Orientalism is a term usually applied to Asiatic cultures,
but Somalia and Ethiopia have often been lumped together
with "oriental" societies, in opposition to their "Black" or
"Bantu" African neighbors. The obsession with Somali lineage systems, classifying who is noble and who is commoner,
slave, or caste is found in I. M. Lewis' work and that of his disciples, Virginia Luling and Bernhard Helander. Just as divide
and conquer has always been a vital aspect of colonial policy,
so too have dissection, redivision, inventory taking, and classification of Somali society been the mainstay of research on
Somalia, and have, in effect, defined Somalia.

To criticize I. M. Lewis may seem like attacking a "straw
man." After all, are not the "new" anthropologists much too
sophisticated to fall into the trap of orientalism? And haven't
they much more progressive attitudes towards gender and the
role of women? Perhaps. Yet the fact remains that younger
anthropologists and historians of Somalia — with the notable
exceptions of Francesca Declich, Amina Adan, Lee Cassanelli,
and Edward Alpers — are still working with models and concepts about Somalia set up by I. M. Lewis.

It is not accidental that scholarship of Lewis' type is coupled with strong androcentric analysis. The godfather of kinship studies in structuralist anthropology, Claude Levi-Strauss,
takes the asymmetry between the sexes in the male mode of
circulating women as a universal characteristic of human society. This theory is based on the assumptions that ultimate
authority is concentrated in the hands of men, that groups of
men exchange women like objects or livestock, and most
importantly that women follow the dictates of men.[7] I. M.
Lewis, in *A Pastoral Democracy*, states:

For marriage involves the temporary surrender of a woman's fertility (genetricial rights as well as uxorial rights) by her natal lineage to the lineage group of the husband. Divorce which is frequent breaks marriage and the wife's genetricial and uxorial rights revert to her lineage to be transferred anew in successive marriages and payment of bridewealth.[8]

First, one must wonder how Lewis can define the role of women as only a "womb for rent" passed from lineage to lineage upon receipt of brideswealth, and then describe Somali society as democratic. Women comprise 51% of the population; yet, apparently, the disenfranchisement of the majority of the population does not seem to contradict Lewis' definition of democracy. The unimportance he attributes to women may be more a byproduct of his Western androcentric scholarship than a true reflection of Somali society. (We will examine this later.) In his ethnographic study *The Peoples of the Horn of Africa*, Lewis writes that "Somali women . . . are outside the agnatic lineage structure of Somali society. When they appear in social relations involving segmentary groups, they do so as clients attached to agnatic units, never directly or *sui juris* [in their own right]."[9] In these remarks, Lewis combines his orientalism and patriarchal ideology in comparing the status of women to that of a client in Somali culture. His thesis is that the male in Somali society is like the "noble" Somali, while the woman is the "commoner," "slave," or "low caste person." (We will find this theme reappearing in more recent research.) He does concede, however, that there are some obvious contradictions in his analysis of Somali gender relations :

> While many people are influenced by the patriarchal character of Somali society, [and] have drawn the obvious inference that women are of little account, more careful observers assure us that beneath the agnatic facade, they are quite as influential as men. Drake Brockman writes, 'In the *rer* a clever woman will frequently rule the roost, and her husband will seldom dare to scold her. I have more than once heard a Somali woman severely rep-

rimand her husband, who has slunk away in a most shamefaced sort of way to escape her bitter remarks. No Somali will admit this, but it is none the less a fact.' It would probably be true to say that the Somali woman has low rank but may have considerable standing.[10]

Yet he continues:

Associated with a woman's subordinate structural position are the following customary practices. Neither the birth of a daughter nor the death of a woman is an occasion for ceremonial. A husband has the right to enforce his authority by striking his wife with his horse-whip, and this is an essential gesture before the consummation of marriage. When the *rer* is on the move the women carry the family property on their backs while their husbands ride on horses if they have them.[11]

How can Lewis characterize these conditions as "considerable standing"? His observations have not changed with time, as is apparent in his 1989 description of a Somali husband's reaction to the *zar* possession of his wife: "If a good beating will not do the trick (and it often seems very effective), there is always the threat of divorce."[12]

The importance of Lewis' contribution to the invention of Somalia and Somali women can not be overstated. He is the first and best-known scholar to examine Somali society in English. Besides his orientalist and androcentric approach, Lewis' writing on Somalia suffers from two additional weaknesses. First, almost all of his field work was done in northern Somaliland, while his writings on the southern Somali region appear to be based on the Italian archives and writings of explorers, and the scholarly work of the Italian colonialists.[13] Second, as a result in part of his orientalist approach to Somalia, he either is unaware of or ignores the similarities in kinship and gender relations between Somalia and the rest of East Africa.

Lewis (in 1955) indicated a Somali woman's "low rank" by observing that "she cannot own substantial property."[14] In a more recent (1989) work, he tells the story of a Somali woman who spent her husband's fifty pounds for a *zar* ceremony — in retaliation for which he sold her sewing machine and jewelry for a similar ceremony with religious men. Lewis tells this story to illustrate the male attitude towards *zar,* but has in fact contradicted his own analysis that women do not own substantial property on their own: the husband tried to teach his wife a lesson by selling *her* property — *her* jewelry, *her* savings account.[15] The story shows that both spouses owned significant property on their own, and the fact that neither the wife nor the husband's property is considered joint property indicates a particular type of economic relationship in which the woman has independent resources. The actual point of the story seems to be that each spouse should not spend the other's funds. How she obtained the property is unclear, but at least part of the jewelry must have been either gifts at her wedding or inherited from her mother or grandmother.

While I. M. Lewis sat with the northern male Somali pastoralists and wrote how the women had no access to wealth, Somali women surely came into his view wearing much assorted jewelry. *Somalia in Word and Image*[16] is a photo book showing material and decorative art from Somalia. There are articles on woodworking, house building, oral literature, and one by Lewis himself on Islam in Somalia. Also there are ten pages of pictures of Somali women's jewelry, but no chapter on the jewelry itself, only interesting "tidbits" written under many of the pictures. An 18th-century silver wedding necklace, for instance, bears the following commentary :

> Given to a bride by her husband, a wedding necklace remains her property for life. In the instance of a divorce, if a husband would ask for the return of the necklace, he would be frowned upon by the community. In one Somali poem, a mother says that she will give up her necklace to aid her daughter in trouble."[17]

A Biimaal silver bracelet with a large red stone is accompanied by this caption:

> This bracelet is worn on the upper arm during a dance
> performed on the last day of healing rites in a women's
> society.[18]

An 18th century silver comb is described as follows:

> [The] type of comb. . . usually given to a bride by her
> mother or grandmother. It is called *saqaf* in the north and
> *shanleh* in the south."[19]

And from Xamar Weyn in Mogadishu there is a silver 18th-
century kohl pot with lid and stick in an old saddle bag design
with bangle bells:

> Kohl pots are usually a gift to the bride from her mother
> or grandmother.[20]

According to this book and oral testimony, jewelry is women's
property, it is often passed on from mother and grandmother (on the maternal side), and women seem to receive a great
deal of wealth at their weddings; the jewelry is in fact their
property and asset.

I. M. Lewis was formally educated during the colonial peri-
od, when African women were silenced, but even younger
scholars tend to analyze the role of Somali women similarly.
A younger anthropologist from Scandinavia, Bernhard
Helander, for example, wrote in 1987 a short monograph,
*Gender and Gender Characteristics as a Folk Model in Southern
Somali Social Classification and Symbolism,* based on his work
among the Maay-speaking people of the interriverine area.
In his monograph, Helander perpetuates and builds upon
Lewis' hypotheses as follows:

> Above all I shall show that gender distinctions also entail
> a distinction of values. Thus male and female are not just
> a complementary pair, male characteristics are the hier-
> archically superior.... It will be seen that there are areas
> where male and female threaten to shade into one anoth-

er and this becomes the subject for both direct action and sharply phrased commentary.[21]

Helander then proceeds to create a whole gender mythology:

> Thus woman and man in one sense form complementary parts of the same whole, but in another sense they are hierarchically ranked and assigned distinct qualities. Men are strong and hard (*lab, adag*). Whatever contribution a man makes at conception is also hard and all the parts of the body that are hard — bone, teeth, reason, genitals — are acquired patrilaterally and therefore male. Above all, bone (*laf*) is hard and lineage called "bone" or "testicle" (*ray*), are hard too. Women are weak and soft (*nugul, jileec-san*). The female blood, which is the chief element that a woman contributes at conception, will develop into the soft parts of the foetus. All the soft parts of the body — blood, hair, skin, flesh, veins, nails and muscles — come from the mother and are therefore female. "Veins" and "roots," i.e., *xidid* or matrilateral relations which the term also means, are thus also "soft."[22]

It is unclear how nails and muscles can be considered soft, and (excuse the Freudian implication) how genitals can be classified as primarily hard. To shore up his thesis that women are considered weak, he states that there are more illnesses associated with women than with men (surprising since women do give birth). He identifies certain other cultural manifestations of the weakness of the female sex, such as the fact that women are more easily influenced by emotions, are more often victims of spirit possession, and react more rapidly to visual impressions. He quotes the following proverb in support of this contention:

Caqli: xoolo dhego baa galey
dugaag san baa galey
raga habad baa galey
naago indho baa galey

Intelligence (knowledge): for domestic animals
it enters through the ears
for wild animals it enters through the nose
for men it enters their chest
for women it enters their eyes.[23]

Which he interprets as follows:

whereas domestic animals follow the calls from humans
and the sound made by the bells on cows and camels,
wild animals rely on their sense of smell. Men are constantly preoccupied with the worries of providing for
their families' daily expense (*Masruuf*) and they carry that
worry in their hearts, but women are only bothered by
whatever their eyes catch a glimpse of. This is said to be
exemplified by the fact that women prefer to dress in
bright colours whereas men usually stick with less conspicuous dress.[24]

I showed this proverb to several Somali scholars who special-
ize in linguistics and oral literature. None interpret it as in
any way derogatory to women. (One, Professor Abdallah
Mansur, states that the proverb refers to a Somali saying
among *Maay*-speakers that the elders have eyes all over their
bodies, meaning that they can see and understand everything.) With this dubiously constructed gender hierarchy as
a base, Helander continues, "[t]he argument of this paper is
that gender and gender characteristics provide a clear cut
model onto which other social categories of the southern
Somali are mapped."[25] Yet, he admits, there is one slight problem with his whole paradigm: "Although the ideological
frame of women's roles appears extremely confining, few
Somali women will readily admit that men are their superi-
ors. Women constantly question the authority of men."[26]

If more than half of the population questions the ideology, can it be a tenet of that society? Of course, one could
accept this if women's belief systems have little value in comparison to men's, and Helander readily admits, "The fact that
real women deviate from the way they should be, is a fact of

great concern to many a Somali man." He then lists the
derogatory names men have for women [27] (I wonder, did he
ask women for the derogatory names they have for men?) and
adds that, even though such misogynistic names exist, "I have
only rarely heard these terms directed at or used about a particular woman one is close to. Rather, they are used for talking about women in general or, exceptionally, a woman with
whom one has no relations."[28] Interestingly, this echoes a
comment made by Burton:

> The [female] sex indeed has by no means a good name;
> here, as elsewhere, those who degrade it are the first to
> abuse it for degradation.... Perhaps, however, by these gen-
> eralisms of abuse the sex gains: they prevent personal and
> individual details; and no society of French gentlemen
> avoids mentioning in public the name of a woman more
> scrupulously than do the misogynist Moslems[Somalis].[29]

According to western scholars, then, Somali men are more
than willing to relate their own negative perceptions of
women to foreigners, but seem more reluctant to relate those
perceptions to the women themselves. This reluctance does
not conjure images of downtrodden women without power
in their own society, whose menfolk are too polite to point
out their failures.

Helander admits, in *Death and the End of Society: Official
Ideology and Ritual Communication in Somali Funeral* (1986), that
when puzzled by the actions of some women he asked a man
to explain the behavior.[30] It is rather clear that he constructed a whole mythology of gender relations on the basis of evidence obtained solely from men. In addition, throughout the
work he quotes Lewis' research in the north to make points
about gender among the Maay-speaking, agricultural, and
agropastoralists of the south. The bottom line to all these
mental gymnastics is support for Lewis' theory that the relationship between male and female in Somali society is the
same as between "noble" Somali and *"boon"* or "slave." He
argues that the reason *"boon"* children are denigrated for their

hard hair is because their hair "should be" soft like the female role they play in society.[31] I would argue that this rather reflects well-known prejudice in Somali society against those with so-called Bantu blood, or "hard-hair" people.

There are, of course, others who have written on women in Somalia. A former British colonial official, Major H. Rayne, wrote the book *From Sun, Sand, and Somals,* which has added, in spite of itself, some interesting insights into the depiction of women in northern Somalia. In the anecdotal manner in which he wrote this book, Rayne recounts a court proceeding in Berbera as follows:

> Then comes a "grievous hurt" case. Husband, wife and the other man. How the wife fights to save her reputation. She is prepared to sacrifice her husband if only that can be spared. But facts are too strong for her. One after the other they are uncovered, and shred by shred the woman's reputation goes, until only rags are left. Yesterday how highly she held her head, and how disdainfully she scorned her more unfortunate sisters whose ranks she joins today. But she fights on, as no queen ever fought for her crown, until she is forcibly removed. Her morals have nothing to do with the present case beyond having provided a provocation for her husband's offense. And yet, serious as is the matter for her, she is no worse than hundreds of the other townswomen. She has only committed the unpardonable offence of having been found out.[32]

And in another court case between a former and present wife of the same man, who were fighting over the public affront each had inflicted on the other, the Somali interpreter certainly gives us a graphic description of the intensity of Somali women. The British colonial officer tells his interpreter to shut a woman up who has been ranting and yelling for quite a long time. The interpreter replies, "No, Sahib, who can stop a Somal[i] woman? Drown her. Murder her — yes, but as long as she has breath in her body she'll talk."[33]

In relating these stories, factoring out the racism and

paternalism of the writer, Rayne clearly depicts independent women with a strong sense of self. Both cases also demonstrate that a Somali woman finds that her relationship to her community is of more importance to her than her marriage, and as a woman she is able to act for herself (*sui juris*). The confidence and ability with which these women are able to present their positions in court belies Lewis' description of Somali women having no traditional means to represent themselves. (Considering the ideological constraints of British colonialism, this role of Somali women can hardly be a creation of the *colonial* court system!)

Unfortunately, the three most important historical works in English on Somalia have included nothing on women or gender dynamics. The first study is Ali Hersi's UCLA dissertation, "The Arab Factor in Somali Society: The Origins and Development of Arab Enterprise and Cultural Influences in the Somali Peninsula." Another is Mohamed Nuuh Ali's dissertation, "History in the Horn of Africa, 1000 B.C. to 1500 A.D.," also from UCLA, reconstructing 2,500 years of history in Somalia from the linguistic evidence. Finally, of course, is Lee Cassanelli's seminal work on southern Somali history, *The Shaping of Somali Society*. Cassanelli has significantly changed the historical perceptions of southern Somalia and challenged I. M. Lewis' version of Somalia. Still, however, in all three historical works, women have been excluded from both the analysis and the data-gathering process.[34]

Thus, in current significant histories written about Somalia, women and gender dynamics are excluded; and when one looks at the few bibliographies on African women, one finds that more than 60% of the entries under Somalia deal with infibulation, another 20% discuss *zar* or spirit possession, and the rest, current health issues. Thus, 80% of the articles on Somali women discuss the exotic: either infibulation or spirit possession. It seems that the subject of Somali women has been the convergent point for orientalism and the androcentrism towards Africa. Any historical or ethnographic data these works may contain is just a rehashing of Lewis' analysis.

From Burton's writings in the 1850s to the 1987 work of Bernhard Helander, there is a distinct and unbroken thread. The Somali woman is portrayed as a non-person in her own society, albeit at times a loud, nagging, or complaining one. What began as Burton's ethnocentric observations became Lewis' anthropological bible on Somalia. Helander makes a few appropriate revisions to render the "religious text" more palatable in a postcolonial or neocolonial world. In the following section of this paper, the words of these men will be adduced to show both the internal contradictions and the ideological constraints within their work. Then, after freeing ourselves from the canon of Lewis et al, we will examine the available historical data in a fresh manner.

Before discussing alternative approaches to recapturing gender in the history of Somalia, it is important to note some writings that are exceptions to the rule. Works by two women contradict the view of Somali women as oppressed and without political or economic power. One by a Somali woman, Amina Adan, "Women and Words,"[35] discusses the independent role of Somali women in northern Somalia on the evidence of women's poems and songs. One of the more interesting poems in Adan's article could be termed a Somali variation on the theme "Diamonds are a Girl's Best Friend": older Somali women sing this to younger women, warning them that words of love from a man may be fine, but get gold instead — it lasts longer. Instead of conjuring images of "a downtrodden female," Adan's article reveals strong women with an opportunistic approach to romance. Our second author, the Italian scholar Francesca Declich, wrote her doctoral dissertation on "The Significance of Marital Gift Exchange Among Women in Southern Somali Riverine Communities on the Juba River"[36] based on her two years' living in Gosha. Declich documents a complicated exchange of surplus controlled entirely by women and redistributed at the time of weddings. She also has observed and discusses the relationship between women, especially mother and daughter in this region and the various ways women are able to maintain their economic independence. Her work clearly challenges the brideswealth exchange theory, showing that in fact women maintain a great deal of power and can obtain a significant amount of wealth within the marriage exchange. Declich's work on the independent role of Somali women in this region parallels some of the oral histories I have recently collected from Somali women who were born and raised in the Shabelle River agricultural region. One other work that has clearly described an independent economic role for Somali women in an historical context is Edward Alpers' paper on the Somali population in the late 19th century in Aden, showing the economic independence of Somali women working as street vendors and prostitutes.[37]

It is, of course, self-evident that if women are not included or interviewed or even considered part of the history or society, their presences will be lacking. It is not just a question of placing women into the history, but calls into question the actual historiography and ethnographies so far written. Somali society, like most in Africa, has clear and specific gender roles, often parallel gender organizations. So far a very incomplete history has been written because these important aspects have been excluded. In general, Western scholars are conditioned by two important ideological constraints. The first is that in European/American society a woman's legal or jural definition is primarily that of wife; her roles of mother and sister are considered less important. The family unit is defined as nuclear: a man and his wife and his children (or, when extended to places such as Africa, husband, *wives,* and *his* children). This clearly excludes the woman's relationship to her own lineage, which is often a source of great support. In Somalia there is a well-told story about a young, pregnant wife whose own clan was feuding with her husband's clan. Her brother comes, the young wife does not tell her husband. The brother kills her husband and she returns to her family. The story represents the threat to the nuclear family found in a society where one's blood ties are so strong. Unlike Eastern Asia, the African woman does not become a member of her husband's lineage or change her name as she does in much of Western Europe and the

United States. In addition, marriage is often brittle and easily broken in Somalia, a fact readily testified to by Burton and Lewis.[38] Therefore, to concentrate one's research on the Somali woman as wife negates her larger and much more significant relationships as mother and sister. Karen Sacks' book, *Sisters and Wives,* argues convincingly that within a patrilineal-kin corporate-structured society, a woman loses power as a wife with her husband's kin, but retains power as a sister in her own lineage. This, I think it can be argued, is true of Somali society as well. As mother she has a great deal of control over her daughters on a day-to-day basis[39] and can exert informal power over her son especially at the time of raising brideswealth for a wedding. A mother's brother, after the mother, is often the most important person in a Somali child's life. Therefore there is clearly a strong link through the mother's line.

The other major problem is that of interpretation. If one assumes, *a priori,* male domination, then all the observations are placed within that context, limited by that assumption. An example is the oft-quoted "wife beating on the wedding night" scene recorded by Burton. Even if we accept that this is a tradition in northern Somalia, then its significance could actually be interpreted in an exactly opposite way: in a society where men are confidently in control, there would be no need to beat a bride into submission, even in a ceremonial manner. Instead, this custom could well indicate the independent behavior of women, a behavior the men are having a difficult time controlling.

An additional barrier to understanding the role of gender in Somali history is that the subject is studied primarily by anthropologists who usually look at gender from an ahistorical perspective. This is a problem not just in Somali historiography, but also in much of the work on women in East African history generally. It is acknowledged that the 19th century was a time of turmoil and radical change in East Africa and that this transformation occurred well before the colonial expansion into the area. Cassanelli chronicles the radical changes in southern Somalia with the incorporation of the Shabelle and Jubba River areas into the sphere of influnce of the Omani empire, the beginning of slave and plantation cultivation in the area, and, finally, the incorporation of the region into the world economy. In a limited manner, northern Somalia was also experiencing an economic transformation via the increased livestock trade with British-dominated Aden. Recently there have been several important works documenting the extreme change in gender relations and the role of women during the precolonial 19th-century convulsions in East and Central East Africa.[40] Therefore it seems quite incorrect to look at even precolonial 19th-century gender relations (i.e., the role of women) as exemplary of the traditional African role. This leads us to a very basic problem. How does one go about understanding gender in an earlier period of time, before the writings of the colonialists and the 19th-century gender transformation in Somalia and the rest of East Africa?

The second and primary purpose of this paper is to attempt to find new ways and tools to reconstruct a social history of Somalia that, as accurately as possible, reflects past Somali society and the role of gender in that society. I will discuss five methods employing gender to analyze Somali history : (1) the applying of historical linguistics to gender issues in Somali history; (2) analyzing and further collecting oral histories from women and oral literature and oral traditions from and about women in all regions of Somalia; (3) constructing a jewelry history; (4) an examining of the slaveholding records from the late 19th and early 20th centuries; and (5) reevaluating kinship studies done on Somali society.

The work of Mohamed Nuuh Ali and Christopher Ehret has laid the basis for understanding migrations and basic economic trends in the early history of Somalia using linguistic analysis, while applying historical linguistics to cultural questions has been done quite successfully by Ehret in "The Antiquity of Agriculture in Ethiopia" and "Cushitic Prehistory."[41] To actually apply linguistics to these cultural questions in some historical depth, it is necessary to gather words that are tied to gender specific concepts. This could include ritual words, kinship terms, tools and objects used only by women today, female body parts, and religious words. Kinship imagery in matrilineal and patrilineal societies are quite different. Societies that tend to be matrifocal link kinship terms to female body parts, the breast, the womb, etc. Audrey Richards states that in matrilineal kinship relations, "[t]he metaphors of kinship stress the ties between people from the same womb or suckled at the same breasts."[42]

An example of what kind of evidence could be uncovered for Somalia using historical linguistics is the reconstructed word *min* (from proto-Eastern Cushitic which meant "house.")[43] In Standard Somali, which is heavily influenced by northern Somali, one of the meanings of *min* is "uterus," yet it remains "house" in Maay and other southern Somali dialects. Evidently Maay has retained the original meaning, whereas in standard Somali the meaning has now become something directly related to females and possibly a female-kinship image: the uterus. On the evidence of one word it is not possible to make definite statements about kinship and the role of women in earlier Somali or even proto-Eastern Cushitic society. But it does at least raise some interesting possibilities. Is it an indication of an earlier, more matrifocal society, or is it just a reflection of the fact that women build the houses in Somali society and that, as in other East African societies, a wife in a polygynous marriage has her own house?

I. M. Lewis writes that the word *Abti* ("mother's brother") is used to construct other words in Somali as diverse as "judges," "elders," "referendum," and "recent immigrant," "ability," and "to run away from danger." An examination of his data by linguists shows that he has used any word that had the element *abti* in it to arbitrarily establish connections between words that have no genetic connection. But in fact the word *abti* raises some very interesting questions about kinship terms in Somali. *Ab* in Somali means "ancestor," yet forms of this word are used to indicate "relatives on the mother's side." When examining other Eastern Cushitic languages we find the same word in Rendille, Burgi, Dullay, and Afar meaning "mother's brother" or "relatives on the maternal side."[44] Paul David Black in his dissertaion reconstructs *ab as the proto-lowland Eastern Cushitic word for "maternal uncle."[45] Why has Somali used the word to indicate ancestor in general when other Eastern Cushitic languages use the word to indicate "maternal relatives" or often more specifically "mother's brother"? There is not enough evidence to draw any conclusions from this example, but *ab* together with *min* raises questions about the "established" tenet of eternal Somali patrilineality.

Other Somali words like *inanlayaal* (the period in which a young wife stays with her own family and her husband does not officially reside with her until the birth of her first child) or *garoomey* and *gashaanti* (the words for a woman who has reached puberty but is still unmarried) also need to be analyzed. *Inanlayaal* is a period of matrilocal residence, and the custom parallels a similar tradition in the matrilineal belt of Tanzania, where "[the] husband will first move and stay with the parents-in-law where he will cultivate for a period from one to several years, basically until the birth of the first child."[46] Whether inanlayaal once included brideservice is a subject for further investigation. The term *garoomey* in the south and *gashaan(ti)* in the north are acknowledgements that a woman has entered a very particular stage of life, a stage of life that in East Africa, especially among the matrilineal and formerly matrilineal people, is marked by important celebrations. An examination of these words and any changes in meaning in an earlier form or interesting relationships to other words might help shed some light on whether these are remnants of a more matrifocal period in Somali history.

A second important source for understanding the role of women in Somali society is the collection of oral tradition and oral histories from women. An acknowledged problem in collecting oral histories and traditions in Somalia is that each person interviewed attempts to present his clan in the most favorable light. Almost no oral traditions have been taken from women; therefore we do not know if there will be the same problem with women.

There is also a great deal of potential history in the gathering of oral literature, since poetry is the form in which much of Somali history is preserved. Amina Adan, as stated above, has been collecting songs, poems, and stories from women of northern Somalia, and I have been collecting some from the southern region.[47] There can be important social elements in a poem or song that people may not necessarily feel is significant enough to include in their oral histories.

"An interesting characteristic feature of Somali folk tales is that most of the principal characters in them are females, rather than males," observes Ahmed Artan Hanghe in his book *Sheekoxariirooyin Soomaaliyeed (Folktales from Somalia)*.[48] Unlike the the Western anthropologists, he writes that:

> The predominance of female characters in Somali lore is perhaps due to the theory that in earlier centuries matriarchal lineage was the base upon which Somali family life rested in earlier periods.....The matriarchal lineage did not wholly lose its historical identity in Modern Somalia; for there are clans still bearing the names of their ancestral mothers, such as, for instance, reer-Cambaro, reer-Maryan.[49]

An origin myth of the Somalis, "Daldaloole," is about Daldaloole, the sky, who hung so low that women pounding grain would punch holes in him with their pounding sticks. One day a girl, who the people believe was a cloud, spilled her bucket of water and she cried to Daldaloole to hold the water for her. He replies, "How can I with these holes made in me by the women?" And this is how humans and animals received water, the source of life. And the story concludes :"A woman is a source of life, as well as the instrument of its destruction."[50] This story shows the centrality of women to Somali life.

In the tale *"Wiil Adoogiis Talo Guur Weydiistey"* (A Father's Advice), a father tells his son: "Remember, the Somalis say that your son needs your help but once; and this is when you are choosing his mother."[51] This tale contradicts Helander's contention of the Somali belief in the limited contributions of a mother to the creation of a child. There are also many folk tales that show women outsmarting men and men outsmarting women. The key element of the story is the intelligence of the individual, not his or her particular gender traits. If, in fact, as Helander states, Somali women are considered incapable of rational thought, then the folk tales would have fewer women heroines who outsmart men and other women with their wits.[52] In the tale *"Dhagar Dumar"* (Feminine Deception),[53] an unfaithful wife composes a song while she is pounding to warn her lover that her husband has arrived, and she successfully hides her unfaithfulness. The moral of this story is not that she is punished for her infidelity, but that if she is smart enough she can have a lover and a husband with no dire consequences.

The most important characters in Somali folk tales are two women, both of whom started out as young lovely girls. One, Dhegdheer, is a cannibal woman whose fantastic adventures are told in many regions of Somalia. She is a woman who gave birth only to daughters and during a severe drought became a cannibal and terrorized everyone. She is finally killed by her youngest daughter and two young girls. The other is Arraweelo, a queen of Somalia, who castrated all the men and ruled with an iron hand. While some of the tales of the queen are obviously myths, other stories seem to indicate that Arraweelo did actually live and rule most, if not all of Somali territory. These semi-biographical tales, which give us many details of this fabulous queen, are among the well-known Arraweelo stories. For instance, Arraweelo's mother was said to have been called Haramaanyo, but no mention is made in the tales about who her father was.[54]

Scholars of Somali history dismiss her as a historical figure, even though several of her stories indicate the names of two villages in which she resided, Hawraartiro (a place-name in the Nugal valley in northeastern Somalia) and Ceelaayo (a village on the Red Sea Coast in northeastern Somalia).[55] The lack of historical research on Arraweelo is, I believe, the result of an unquestioning acceptance of I. M. Lewis' s definition of Somali women: a Somali queen from northern Somalia is considered just some fairy tale.

Even if Arraweelo turns out to be entirely a fable, her stories could well represent some drastic change in gender and social relations in Somalia. There are various tales throughout East Africa about a period of time when women ruled, and then were overthrown. A good example is the Kikuyu myth related by Jomo Kenyatta in *Facing Mount Kenya*. The first man and first woman, Gikuyu and Moombi, had nine daughters and no sons. Each daughter became the head of a clan. The women ruled, they practiced polyandry, and men were put to death for committing adultery and other minor offenses. But, as the women were physically stronger than the men of that time and also better fighters, the men came together in order to find a way to overthrow female rule. They decided to seduce all the leading women by flattery and get them pregnant. After six months, when the women were too big to fight, the men sucessfully rebelled. The first thing the men did was to abolish polyandry and establish polygyny. But when they tried to change the names of the female genitors to males, the women prevented this by saying they would bear no more children for the men. The men, fearing this, gave in and this is why in patrilineal Kikuyu society each clan is descended from a female ancestor. Here the myth marks a significant social change in Kikuyu society; the story of Arraweelo could well have a similar meaning in Somali history.

Arraweelo has the men castrated because in that condition they cannot challenge her. There is one man who escapes her knife and begins to advise the men around the queen, and eventually fathers Arraweelo's grandson, the grandson who later kills her. The theme that men without their sexual organ are incapable of being a threat to women is repeated often in these stories. This corresponds to a significant component of matrilineal ideology in that a man should not, in any way, be an object of exclusive emotional investment nor the focus of attention. Instead, women are socialized to invest their emotions and material wealth in their respective matrilineage. Poewe observes in the matrilineal society of Luapula in Zambia that "so strong is [a man's] sexual power that she is in danger of giving into his attraction. Hence, the pressure on women, indeed, their systematic socialization, is not to become intimately dependent on men."[56]

Whether there ever was a Queen Arraweelo of Somalia or not, in the village of Ceelaayo in northern Somalia there exists a stone mound that the people believe is Arraweelo's tomb. Men throw stones every time they pass. But, "[i]n contrast, Somali women place green branches and fresh flowers onto the supposed Arraweelo's grave as a sign of respect for the greatest woman-ruler in Somali oral literature."[57]

The custom of infibulation or female circumcision in Somali society is perceived as almost the antithesis of matri-lineal or matrifocal behavior. But this may need further exam-ination since in almost all of my interviews Somali women would describe their mothers as good and discuss in great detail how a mother worked hard for the daughter's future. Yet when these women described their own infibulations, their good mother is quoted as telling the midwife perform-ing the operation:

> Make sure you do a good job. Cut the whole thing out.
> I don't want my girl to go to a man. If they cut it off
> she won't go to a man.[58]

Now, the standard way to analyze the above statement is that Somali women are so brainwashed into believing in the sanc-tity of virginity that they will have their daughters mutilated. I think there could be another way to analyze the role this surgical procedure plays in women's lives. First, the relation-ship between the Somali mother and daughter is extremely strong. Mothers weep and cry for the loss of their daughter at the wedding[59] and the long period of *inanlayaal* or living with the bride's family may be necessary, in part, to help ease this. In Somali society, like most of African society, men and women feel they have different interests. The solidarity of Somali women as testified to by various scholars could well be the envy of Western feminists, as the following description by Lewis indicates:

> Somali women have a strong and explicit sense of sexual solidarity and feelings of grievance and antagonism towards men, who in turn, regard the opposite sex as possessing a unique endowment of guile and treachery.[60]

A few young Somali men, refugees in Rome, told me that they were opposed to infibulation because they felt that the procedure caused Somali women to lack respect for them. "They just want children, but are not interested in the man himself."[61] As the stories of Arraweelo and many of the folk tales indicate, both sexes see a real danger in being sexually controlled by the other. Somali mothers might see infibulation as a way to insure that their daughters will not fall under the "spell" of some man and become unable to rationally control their own lives. Admittedly, these observations about infibulation are based on anecdotal discussions with small groups of people; but they may help explain why this procedure is still so widespread in Somalia and, even more importantly, why the practice of infibulation, in and of itself, should not be used as a gauge for determining the role Somali women play in their society today or in history.

Another tool that could be used to recapture the history of Somali women is jewelry history. As discussed above, there is considerable evidence, including testimony from various Somali women, that a woman's jewelry constitutes that woman's assets. Bracelets, necklaces, and earrings are often sold at times of drought, and collections are expanded at times of surplus. A mother's jewelry is often wealth passed on through the woman's side. Many women know the history of the jewelry that they wear — a history of drought and famine and plenty that could well add to our knowledge of Somali history. Whether jewelry history will be effective prior to the colonial period is still unclear, but, by the dates of the jewelry collection photographed in *Somalia and Image,* the importance of women's jewelry dates at least to the 1700s in Somalia.

Recently, both African and Middle Eastern historians have discovered a much more significant role of women in the economics of precolonial societies by examining the land-sale records.[62] Land-sale records are effective evidence for parts of the Sudan, feudal Ethiopia, and Egypt. But in East Africa, and Somalia in particular, where individual land ownership was not significant, there are few land-ownership documents. But from the late 19th century, Robecchi-Brichetti, an avid Italian abolitionist, collected data on manumitted slaves. There are lists of manumitted slaves for three major coastal cities: Barawa, Mogadishu, and Merca.[63]

Interestingly, many women are indicated as owners of slaves, often owning more than just one. This is particularly significant since it is believed that Islam was much stricter in the coastal cities, and it would be expected than many women from the upper classes would have a brother or father file any official documents concerning the disposal of their property. Whether slave ownership at that time was an exclusively urban phenomenon is unclear right now, but it certainly calls into question the belief that women had no access to property.

The significance of gender relations in understanding African society, in particular the early period, has been skillfully addressed by a number of female anthropologists.[64] Using their theoretical work, it will be possible to understand gender dynamics in precolonial Somalia. Today Somali society is organized into patrilineal kinship organizations, but this does not necessarily mean that Somalis have always been patrilineal. Lewis and other Somalists have insisted that Somali society is structured on a strictly patrilineal basis, yet even Lewis describes the following matrilineal access to land rights:

> [C]ultivating settlements often contain extraneous aliens who have married into the land-holding lineage of a village and who share in its blood compensation agreements. But, marriage to a landed lineage confers upon a man cultivating rights only for his children by his wife of that lineage. His rights, and the rights of his children, lapse if he divorces the woman and marries again outside the settlement. Such matrilateraly entitled rights moreover cannot be disposed of without the consent of the

elders of the land- holding lineage. In fact, if matrilateral
male heirs to land wish to dispose of their holdings, they
have often to surrender them and receive scant compensation.[65]

Helander also observed the giving of kinship rights through
the mother's line among the Raxanweyn:

> A mother's brother just visiting the area will be
> QARAABO (general relative) of his sister's son and
> regarded as SHISHEEYE (unrelated and unknown) by
> most of the people. Should he, however, decide to settle
> with his niece and "apply" for membership in his niece's
> lineage, he will become a member of his niece's Tol and
> related or known (SOKEEYE) to most other people of the
> area.
> He will retain links of origin and people will know that
> he and his children are part of clan X, but over time will
> be integrated.[66]

Whether these are just aberrations in a strictly patrilineal society or remnants of an earlier form of descent needs more
investigation. The significance of a gender-specific descent is
not just a question of who inherits from whom, but, as Poewe
argues, persuasively, "any system of distribution and control
over resources has an associated ideology about the worth of
categories of persons."[67] Accordingly, evidence of a more
matrifocal precolonial Somali society could indicate a much
more central role of Somali women in Somali history than
previously has been recognized.

Other evidence of a more female-centered past is found
at a Somali funeral: when a person is buried, their name is
not recited with their father's and grandfather's name, but
with their mother's.[68] When Somalis are asked why, "They
answer that when one enters heaven it is important that one
is named correctly and only the mother's side do we know for
sure." This is often the ideology behind matrilineal kinship
relations. *Burji* is believed to be the the basic personality of
a person in the southern Somali belief system, and there are

twelve *burjis* with equal numbers of male and female ; and in calculating one's *burji,*

> It is important to mention that in the procedures where the name of a person is used as a basis to determine the *burji* this is not the normal, patrilineally transmitted name. Instead, to the first name is added that of the mother of the person.[69]

Another contradiction to the "strict" patrilineality of Somali society is that various clans have divisions that are started by women. In the Mijertein sultanate only children descended from a Dir mother can become sultan, therefore the mother's line determines the successor.[70] *Inanlayaal,* the previously discussed period of matrilocal residence, is reminiscent of the period of brideservice found in matrilineal societies. Even when there are indications of a more female-centered Somali past, Somalists like Lewis dismiss them, as exampled by the following quote:

> I[t] is important to add here that the concept uterine family *(bah)* is well developed and connections through women, derived from common uterine origin, provide important points of unity and distinction within the ramifying agnatic lineage system as it proliferates over time. Lineages whose ancestors were sons of the same mother cleave together in opposition to those from other wives. Hence terms (such as *bah* and also *habar* — literally, 'mother', 'woman,' etc), denoting uterine maternal origin and affiliation, form an important part of lineage terminology. They are most emphatically not survivals, pointing to an earlier 'matrilineal stage', etc. Quite the contrary: they are part and parcel of the plural marriage practices noted above carried out in a strongly patrilineal kinship ambience.[71]

There are several sub-clans that are named either *Bah* or *Habar,* as stated above, but also there are two interesting uses of the word *habar:* the first is *habar dugaag,* which is translated "the wild animal kingdom" — *habar* is used in this context to denote a large group of carnivores; the second, *habar-wacasho*, is a verb used to call a whole clan together for a mobilization — in this case, *habar* is the term used to refer to the whole immediate clan, not just a small section related through a single mother. More study needs to be done on these and other words that use terms for the mother's lineage in broader terms and see whether in fact they are residuals of a matrilineal past. These matrifocal Somali customs could be just the effects of matrilineal influences on Somalia, but it is impossible to rule out an earlier matrilineal past without more research. Finally, a colonial officer in Berbera collected the following tradition:

> The Sheikh[Somali] married a woman from the Dowa people who lived between the Danakils and the Abyssinians. When he was killed his progeny found their way back to their mother's town, where their descendants are still to be found. This town of Dowa or Daoua has, according to my informant, a custom or law that forbids any unmarried Mahomedan man to sleep within its precincts for even one night. Immediately on arrival the stranger is provided with a wife who remains with him as long as he lives in the town. Should he leave he may take neither wife or children.[72]

Whether this is just a myth or represents a matrilineal, matrilocal crack in the supposed patrilineal monolith of Somali society is unclear.

I am not in any way arguing for some evolutionary theory that there had to have been a matrilineal past in Somalia, but I am suggesting that there is evidence of some rather different kinship relations historically than the situation observed by Lewis in the 1940s and 50s. In conclusion, the purpose of this paper is not to say that Somali society isn't patriarchal or oppressive to Somali women, but to urge that whatever form the oppression takes must be understood in the Somali context, and, that Somali gender relations must be analyzed historically.

Notes

1. Martin Bernal, *Black Athena The Afroasiatic Roots of Classical Civilization* (London: Vantage, 1987),p.201.
2. *Ibid.*, p.236.
3. Richard Burton, *First Footsteps in East Africa or, An Exploration of Harar (1854-1856)* (London, 1856), p.86.
4. *Ibid.*
5. *Ibid.*, p.85.
6. Cited in Bernal, *Black Athena*, p. 236.
7. Karla Poewe, *Matrilineal Ideology* (London: Acadmic Press, 1981), p.61.
8. I. M. Lewis, *A Pastoral Democracy* (London: Oxford University Press, 1961), p.139.
9. I.M.Lewis, *The Peoples of the Horn of Africa* (London: International African Institute, 1955), p.128.
10. *Ibid.*
11. *Ibid.*, p.129. Burton's wedding night story has now been generalized to an "essential" Somali custom.
12. Lewis, *Ecstatic Religion* (New York & London: Routledge, 1989), p.68.
13. Enrico Cerulli, *Somalia: Scritti vari, editi ed inediti.* (Rome, 1959);Massimo Colucci, *Principi di diritto consuetudinario della Somali italiana meridionale* (Firenze: Soc. Editrice la Voce, 1924);Luigi Robecchi-Bricchetti, *Lettre dal Benadir* (Milan: Societa Editrice la Polografica,1904); Vittorio Bottego, "L'Esplorazione del Giuba," *Bollettino della Societa Geografica Italiana* 31 (1893); V. Puccioni, *Antropologia ed etnografica delle genti della Somalia*, 3 vols. (Bolonga,1931-36).
14. Lewis, *Peoples of the Horn*, p.129.
15. Lewis, *Ecstatic Religion*, p.69.
16. Edited by Katheryne S. Loughran, John L. Loughran, John William Johnson, and Said Sheikh Samatar; published by the Foundation for Cross Cultural Understanding, Washington D.C., in cooperation with University of Indiana, Bloomington, 1986.
17. *Ibid.*, p.156.
18. *Ibid.*, p.158.
19. *Ibid.*, p. 159.
20. *Ibid.*, p.167.
21. *Working Papers in African Studies*, no.33 (University of Uppsala, 1987), p.5.
22. *Ibid.*, p.6.
23. *Ibid.*, p.27.
24. *Ibid.*
25. *Ibid.*,p.37.

26. *Ibid.*, p.7.
27. *Ibid.*, pp.7-8; *guumays* = a woman that gets old without being married; *arrajo* = a woman that cooks badly; *areebo* = a woman with dirty appearance; *garaafo* = a disorganized woman; *iddoogaa toor iyoow* = a woman that scratches her body in public places; *ilkooga maliintoow* = a woman that fights and bites; *dumaalishee naderujaayto* = a woman that acts disrespectfully toward the brothers of her husband or the husbands of her sisters; *dugoow dugow walki aanto* = a woman that can't control her hunger, but eats wherever she may be; *dawo kar liinguntiyi* = "a fox without clothes", a bony woman whose dress is not properly tied and drags on the ground after her; *sallaq* = a woman that eats before her husband and children; *suruun kinnaar* = "makes hell standingly," a woman that eats things while standing in teashops; *sarriibiyeey*—a woman that does not respect her husband and children but eats before them if she gets hungry; *karaa kiigubudi* = "with burning clothes," a careless woman that gets tired while cooking and whose dress may catch fire due to her not tending the fire properly.
28. *Ibid.*, p.8.
29. Burton, *First Footsteps*, vol. 1, p.42.
30. Bernhard Helander, *Death and the End of Society* (Uppsala: University of Uppsala, 1987), p.20, n.15.
31. *Ibid.*, p. 38.
32. Rayne, *From Sun, Sand and Somals*, (London: London & Witherby, 1921), p.46.
33. *Ibid.*, p. 55.
34. There is a whole chapter on his informants in which he lists their names, and there are no women listed. Women are not even included as an entry in the index.
35. Amina Adan, "Women and Words," *Ufahamu* 10, no.3 (Spring, 1981). Also personal communication with Dr. Adan, December, 1991.
36. Francesca Declich, "Processo di formazione della identita culturale dei gruppi Bantu della Somalia meridionale," Ph.D. diss., University of Naples, 1992. Contributo allo Studio sull'Organizzazione Femminile in Rapporto alla Divisione del Laboro tra gli Vagoscia Tradizione e Mutamento, il Caso di Mareerey e Zone Limitrofe nel Distretto di Jilib in Somalia"; cf., "Identity, Dance and Islam among People with Bantu Origins in Southern Somalia," paper presented to the A.S.A., Seattle, Washington,November,1992.
37. Edward Alpers, "The Somali Community at Aden in the Nineteenth Century," presented to the Fourth Michigan State University conference on Northeast African Studies, East Lansing, Michigan, May 1–3, 1986 (unpublished).

38. Lewis,*Ecstatic Religion*,p.68. "[she is] always menaced by the precariousness of marriage ... divorce is frequent and easily obtained by men." B.Helander, "Death and the End of Society: Official Ideology and Ritual Communication in the Somali Funeral," *Working papers in African Studies*, no. 26 (1986), p.6: "it is evident that for many women a lover may provide a support of a more enduring kind than that of a husband, in an environment where almost half of the women have been divorced at least once." F.Declich, "The Significance of Marital Gift Exchange among Women in Some Somali Riverine Communities on the Juba River," London School of Economics and Political Science, 1990, p.11: "When a woman wants a divorce, she makes life unpleasant for the husband by neither cooking on time nor minding her husband's guidelines....If she can afford it, she can also "buy" [her] divorce."

39. "One should recall that mothers have almost absolute rights over their daughters until they marry, because daughters are more than their right hands." See Declich, "Significance of Marital Gift Exchange," p.23; also, my interview with Asha Osman Biikar, 37, Rome, 1992.

40. See, in Claire C. Robertson and Martin Klein, eds., *Women and Slavery* (Wisconsin: University of Wisconsin Press, 1983): M. Stobel, "Slavery and Reproductive Labor in Mombasa" (p.111); Edward Alpers,"The Story of Swema: Female Vulnerability in 19th century East Africa" (p.185).

41. *Journal of African History* 20 (1979): 161–177; and L. Bender, ed., *The Non-Semitic Languages of Ethiopia* (E. Lansing: Michigan State University, 1976), p.85-96.

42. Audrey Richards, "Some Types of Family Structures Among the Central Bantu" in A.R.Radcliffe-Brown and Daryll Forde, eds. *African System of Kinship and Marriage*,(London: International African Institute/Oxford University Press, 1975), p. 205.

43. Abdallah Mansur, "A Lexical Aspect of Somali and East Cushitic Languages," in Annarita Puglielli, ed., *The Proceedings of the Third International Congress of Somali Studies* (Rome:Il Pensiero Scientifico Editore, 1988), p.14. "House" in proto-Eastern Cushitic is *man/*min; in southern Somali Dialects Maay, *man/min;* in Dabarre, *min*, in Jiddu, *min;* in Banaadir, *minan;* in Standard Somali, *guri;* (Harar gar?), *aqal* (?cf. Am. Ge'ez saqala 'tenda' Reinisch), *min*=uterus. *Minyaro* = wife married for last, *minfiiq/mafiiq* = sweep, house cleaning.

44. Afar: *abu* = maternal descendants, male kin on mother's side, E.M.Parke, and R.J.Hayward, *An Afar-English-French Dictionary* (London: School of Oriental and African Studies, 1985), Burji: *ab*=mother's brother; Dullay: *apiyya*=mother's brother; Highland

Eastern Cushitic: *abo*=maternal uncle — Grover Hudson, *Highland Eastern Cushitic Dicitonary* (Hamburg: Helmut Buske Verlag, 1989), Rendille: *abiyo*=mother's brother or member of one's mother's tribe — Gunther Schlee, *Sprachliche Studien zum Rendille* (Hamburg: Helmut Buske Verlag, 1978), Abore: *Pa'w*=mother's brother — Lionel M. Bender, *Non-Semetic Languages of Ethiopia* (E. Lansing: Michigan State University, 1976). Dr. Giorgio Banti, University of Rome, La Sapienza, helped me with the linguistic evidence.

45. Paul David Black, "Lowland East Cushitic Sub-grouping and Reconstruction," diss., Yale University, 1984, p. 174.

46. Ulla Vuorela, *The Women's Question and the Modes of Human Reproduction: An Analysis of a Tanzanian Village* (Finland: The Scandinavian Institute of African Studies, 1969),p.99: "Helander, 1986 [p.6] in describing this custom in Southern Somalia.....the ideal of a period of uxori-local residence (*inanlayaal*) that places the children of a woman under temporary authority of her brother although the latter lack formal means of sanctioning this authority."

47. I have collected women's poetry, stories, and oral histories from Somali women from Shalombod, Merca, and the rural areas outside of Merca.

48. Ahmed Artan Hanghe, *Sheekoxariirooyin Soomaaliyeed (Folktales from Somalia)* (Uppsala, Sweden: Somali Academy of Science and Arts/ Scandinavian Institute of African Studies, 1988).

49. *Ibid.*, p.131.

50. *Ibid.*, p. 111.

51. *Ibid.*, p. 152.

52. Examples are "Talo Haween" (p.153), "Huryo iyo Kabacalaf" (p.157), "Naago Yaraan ma leh" (p.159), "Saddexdii Maanlaawe" (p.175).

53. *Ibid.*, p. 154.

54. *Ibid.*, p. 132.

55. *Ibid.*

56. Poewe, *Matrilineal Ideology*, p.68. This is clearly the opposite of Islamic ideology, in which the female is the one with the strong sexual power.

57. Hanghe, *Folktales from Somalia*, p.132.

58 Interview, Rome, August 1992, Asha Osman Biikar, 37 years old, born and raised in Shalombod.

59. Cf., the author's interviews with Somali women in Rome, 1992; personal conversation with Dr. Declich; and Dr. Declich's video tapes of Somali weddings in Gosha. Dr. Declich elsewhere comments: "the relationship of companionship between a mother and her daughter... involves a great emotional investment, [while] the

husband is expected to come home regularly to sleep with his wife, and to provide her with maintenance, none expect him to enjoy his time alone with his wife. A woman passes most of her time alone with her children. Herein daughters play a predominant role..." (Declich, "Significance of Marital Gift Exchange," p.23).

60. Lewis, *Ecstatic Religion*, p.69.
61. Personal conversations with several young Somali men, September, 1992, Termi Train Station, Rome.
62. Margret Jean Hay and Marcia Wright, eds., *African Women and the Law: Historical Perspectives*: "The Misfortunes of Some — The Advantages of Others: Land Sales by Women in Sinner" by Jay Spalding ,(pp. 3-18) and "Women Property and Litigation Among the Bagemder Amhara 1750's to 1850's" by Donald Crummey (pp. 19-32); also manuscript of a forthcoming book by Dr. Afaf Marsot on 17th- and 18th-century land sales by upper class women in Egypt.
63. Luigi Robecchi-Briccheti, *Lettre dal Benadir* (Milan: Societa Editrice la Polografica, 1904), p.68.
64. S. Coontz and P. Henderson, *Women's Work Men's Property* (London: Verso, 1986); K. Poewe, *Matrilineal Ideology*; K. Sacks, *Sisters and Wives* (Westport, Conn.: Greenwood Press, 1981); P. Sanday, *Female Power and Male Dominance* (Cambridge: Cambridge University Press, 1981).
65. Lewis, *Pastoral Democracy*, p.122.
66. B. Helander, "The Social Dynamics of Southern Somali Agro-pastoralism: A Regional Approach" in P. Conze and T. Labahn,eds., *Somalia: Agriculture in the Winds of Change* (Saarbrucken-Schafbruucke: Epi Verlag,1986),p.7.
67. Poewe, *Matrilineal Ideology*, p. 55.
68. B. Helander, "Death and the End of Society: Official Ideology and Ritual Communication in the Somali Funeral," *Working Papers in African Studies*, 26 (1986): 12.
69. B. Helander, "The Concept of Burji," in Puglielli, ed.,*Proceedings of the Third International Congress of Somali Studies*, p.172.
70. Dr. Abdallah Mansur, Rome, 1992.
71. I. M. Lewis,"The Child Is the Father of the Man: Some Problems of Somali Kinship Terminology," in: Thomas Labahan, ed., *Proceedings of the Second International Congress of Somali Studies*, (Hamburg: Helmut Buske Verlag,1983), p.3.
72. Rayne, *From Sun, Sand and Somals*, p.13.

IDENTITY, DANCE AND ISLAM AMONG PEOPLE WITH BANTU ORIGINS IN RIVERINE AREAS OF SOMALIA[1]

∞

Francesca Declich

Introduction

It is widely recognized[2] that accounts of a country's customs, history, and people not only influence its public image but may also have retrospective effects on the way its people perceive and describe themselves. When constructing an image of Somalia, therefore, it must be borne in mind that the process of categorizing people by describing them is part of this construction.

The impression that Somalis are closer to an Arab cultural context than an African one is reflected by the common characterization of Somali studies as distinct from other East African literature. From the point of view of someone who has lived in Somalia, however, it is apparent that large numbers of Somali people of Bantu-speaking ancestry who practice agriculture as their main economic activity and share cultural traditions with other East Africans have been omitted from description, for they do not fit this characterization.

In this paper I do not analyze the historical and political reasons why this is the case. Hersi[3] has shown how under British colonial rule Somalis preferred an identity associated with the higher status ascribed to "Asians" over that associated with "Africans."[4] Nor did Italians provide a better context during the colonial period.[5]

Because many dances are perceived as being part of a monolithic "African" heritage,[6] this paper shall attempt to reveal the conflicting and interacting identities underlying dance performances in rural areas of Somalia. Much of what is related to dance in the rural area covered by this study is usually designated religious conflict between Islam and tradition; in an Islamic cultural context, this controversial matter is dealt with within the ritual dimensions of the law *(ibadat)*.[7] In fact, dance performance conceals various aspects concerning the identity of the people and is related to the internal dynamics within social strata in Somalia. Finally, this paper will illuminate what is at stake in dance performances and how they become political statements.

In the Gosha area, belonging to a dance society or other dance group is equivalent to belonging to a kin grouping: people share a network of relationships, incest rules, and ancestors by dance group. The dances are closely related to initiation into adulthood and their performance is closely related to control and, therefore, political power.

In Somalia, being a Muslim is a matter of group identity; so is the way in which Islamic religiosity is expressed. In the southern areas of the country, this trend has been characterized by specific features. Belonging to Islam, as witnessed since the beginning of the 20th century along the Jubba River, was a major factor distinguishing free people from slaves.[8] A person who could prove he/she was a Muslim could claim freedom more easily than someone who could not so prove. This is evidenced in oral sources by a cliche[9] recounted about powerful leaders[10] and most saints who came to Islamicize the Gosha area: such people are said to have gained their freedom from slavery through "working hard at a Mosque well" — i.e., their masters freed them because they had become very religious and pious.[11] Thus, in those times, being considered pious was a route to freedom. It is therefore not surprising that to this day any ritual performance, whether Islamic or traditional, is an indicator of ethnic identity and a distinguishing characteristic between groups, especially for those with ex-slaves among their ancestors. The further south one goes in Somalia, the more relevant this aspect becomes because of the plurality of ritual practices and dances.

This paper is based on field data gathered along the Jubba River between 1985 and 1988.[12] Today (1994), the situation has changed because of four years of civil war. At the time of fieldwork, however, the area was populated mainly by people with Bantu-language speakers among their ancestors and who, depending on the area in which they were living, called themselves either the Shanbara or the Zigula.[13] Most were Somali-speakers, although Chizigula was the main spoken language in about fifteen villages.

The Gosha area is noted for its abundance of traditional dances and rituals. Certain dynamics observed in the Gosha area, resulting from continuous intermingling of people swept onto the Benadir coast from different African countries during the 19th century (mostly through the slave trade), could indicate a more general interplay of traditions,[14] statuses, and power relations between rich and poor in southern Somalia. These dynamics highlight some features of the interplay between group and individual identities among Bantu and Cushitic speakers in southern Somalia.

This interplay will be demonstrated through an analysis of attitudes towards both Sufistic celebrations (dikri)[15] and traditional rituals which involve drum (durbaan) playing. The latter, locally categorized as "to play the drum" rituals, are mainly mviko[16] and spirit-possession performances. Although mviko and spirit-possession rituals differ in performance, aim, and meaning (as will be described later on), both entail "playing the drums" and are locally forbidden by the Islamic saints. Dikri, on the other hand, are held weekly at a village level and performed on a massive scale at pilgrimages (siyaaro) to the communities (jamaac) of the local Islamic sheekhs. Visits are made to the early saints' graves in these holy villages; vows are made and advice sought from the saints' main descendants.

In principle, *dikri* and celebrations that entail "playing the drums" are seen as contradictory because Islam prohibits dancing and singing while praying;[17] spirit worship and/or ancestor worship[18] are similarly proscribed because of the threat they pose to the main precept of monotheism. However, many people do participate in both celebrations, even though such participation implies a moral conflict that most people have to face during their life. I shall attempt to analyze some of the mechanisms underlying this conflict from both an individual and a communal point of view.

Some Features of Belonging to Islam:

The significance of belonging to Islam in riverine southern Somalia needs to be emphasized. Belonging to Islam was connected with the legitimation of free status and thus was not only a matter of status within a generic social hierarchy, but also was related to people's control over their own lives.

Slaves have the lowest status in Somali society; slave status is associated with people who used to eat unclean and/or forbidden meat.[19] At the beginning of the 20th century, Father Leandro Dell'Addolorata (1906) argued that most people living in the Jilib area declared themselves Muslim in order to strengthen their free status.[20] Italian colonialists[21] asserted that the little Islamic education ex-slaves had received during their slavery vanished as soon as they achieved their freedom. Colonialists ascribe ex-slaves' unwillingness to work in their fields, their taste for games and dances, and their amazing sexual freedom to a lack of basic and religious ethics among people of Bantu origins.[22]

For several years, the Trinitarian Fathers, an order dedicated to the defense of slaves, were prevented from entering Somalia by the Italian government, which feared that their activities would lead the Muslim population to rise in revolt. This prohibition adds weight to Father Dell'Addolorata's suggestion[23] that the people living along the Jubba River were not Muslim; he endorsed the idea that evangelization was feasible. Chiesi,[24] on the other hand, sided with Somali ex-masters when expressing disapproval of most of the ex-slaves' customs; he claimed there was a need for more Islamic education. Despite their opposing points of view, both sources highlight political tension relating to Muslim status; they suggest the existence of dynamics of social mobility underlying this status rather than giving data about the Islamic religious practices of the social actors involved.

The early Italian policy of supporting Islamic brotherhoods (tariqas) reinforced the political importance of being considered Muslim in Somalia.[25] Through membership in Muslim brotherhood settlements, one could evade colonial justice.[26] Later, during Fascist Italian rule, people with lower status, especially if they had slaves among their ancestors, were the first to be conscripted into forced labor.[27]

A small digression is necessary here concerning local definitions of Islam and related status. Lewis suggests adopting an operational (and tautological) definition that "those are Muslims who call and regard themselves such"[28]; using his definition, then, everyone in the Gosha area is a Muslim. In fact, the five pillars, which are the main precepts for Muslims, are "best regarded [as] ideals to which all professing Muslims subscribe and seek to honor with varying degrees of determination and success." Putting this definition in the dynamic of the interacting identities within the Somali context, the fact of regarding themselves as Muslims does not prevent groups of people from being seen as nonorthodox by other Muslims and hence not only of lower status but also needing to attain a stricter constraining religious behavior in order to prove their Islamic identity. This dynamic results in control over individuals, groups, and sections within Somali society.

The minimum requirement for becoming Muslim in Somalia, as anywhere else, is to publicly proclaim oneself Muslim; this entails being able to recite the *shahaado* or *kalimah*, the profession of faith, which is a formula entailing the recognition of God to the exclusion of all other deities and Muhammed as his Prophet. Many of the remaining Islamic practices and precepts remain an arena for claims of legitimacy by groups or individuals over others. In fact, although some practices such as the five pillars should be applied by every Muslim, many nuances of the way one should behave and deal with traditional customs continue to be the basis for claims of distinction within more or less strict ranges of Islamic "orthodoxy."

Nowadays, when speaking to people who live in different villages in the area, it is evident that concepts of "orthodoxy" are locally constructed and result from the process of creating labels to distinguish different degrees of status within a community. This process is common in the Kenyan Swahili culture, where such degrees are expressed in higher and lower social statuses, rich and poor, higher and lower echelons of Muslims.[29] In southern Somalia, these kinds of distinctive features have not been studied recently.

Theological issues which are disputed at a level of the Islamic intelligentsia easily become a means of fostering certain constraining behaviors in the name of an orthodoxy at a grassroots level. The following are only a few examples of the struggle over the legitimacy of groups and individuals that seem to underlie such distinctive features. They show what kind of interactions within groups revolve around a claim of orthodoxy.

Informants from Isaaq nomadic families, who recently came from the North, reject the practice of visiting area saints during pilgrimages *(siyaaro)*. They see this practice as approaching the worship of saints; according to them, the people in the Jubba River area consider some *sheekhs* more important than the Prophet Muhammed. Their attitude can be seen as reflecting the old dispute between Salihiya and Qadiriyia brotherhoods, despite the fact that the *siyaaro* in question was for a *sheekh* of the Ahmediyia brotherhood (see footnote no.18.) The same informants also regard dances performed during *mviko* and spirit-possession rituals as repugnant: they consider the obvious sexual metaphor often expressed in these performances as improper behavior. However, it is impossible to recognize a universally accepted Islamic prohibition in the revulsion shown by these informants to these dances which they nevertheless dismissed as non-Muslim behavior. Thus, characterizing some people as nonorthodox may become a pretext for rejecting aspects of their behavior which appear in any way unacceptable.

Yet the local categories of "orthodoxy" in Islamic rules do not coincide neatly with lines of ethnic or lineage differences, nor with brotherhood affiliation. Northern Somali Mijurteen families that have been living in Jilib since the turn of the century do not show the same dismissive attitude towards the communities of the saints and their massive pilgrimages. They participate in them, bringing offerings to the communities' saints, and are aware of the institutional power held by such saints in the area. Nor do they reject *mviko* and spirit-possession rituals so resolutely; rather, they see *mviko* and spirit possession dances as spectacles one can enjoy watching although they are not part of a proper Muslim behavior. Significantly, the higher status these Somali enjoy is not related to different ways of expressing Islam but to the quantity of land they own around Jilib town.

Local concepts of "orthodoxy" are sometimes constructed according to different features of the Sufistic Islamic rituals that occur in a given area. Some litanies *(qasiido)* performed in the Somali Rahanweyn language[30] instead of in Arabic are considered by Somalis with Mijurteen origins living in Mogadishu as pertaining to "peasants"[31] and therefore as practices to be dismissed.[32] As only a small percentage of the Somali population speak Arabic, the claim to orthodoxy in this instance primarily expresses urban dwellers' rejection of peasants.

However, questions concerning what is really at stake in the debate in the Gosha area about the different kinds of religious performance and related communal dances remain unanswered.

Metaphor of "playing the drums" and Islamicization

Oral accounts of the mechanism used to Islamicize the Gosha area provide the key to the opposition between "playing the drums" rituals and *dikri* in local categorization.

Sheekhs[33] used to attract people to "dance" their *dikri*. Although *sheekhs* considered *dikri* as incompatible with dances involving drum playing, the way the Muslim saints caught the Goshas' attention is locally represented as though the *sheekhs* had established a competition between the different kinds of dances. The *sheekhs* had apparently persuaded people to alternate daily between the *dikri* and dances involving drum playing. Having convinced people to dance the *dikri* a few times, the *sheekhs* progressively established a foothold.[34] The continuing existence of competition between dances can be readily observed when one is invited to *"giocare"* ("play") a *dikri* rather than participate *(aan dikriinaya)* in it.

Dikri consist of litanies *(qasiido)*[35] sung mainly in single-sex groups. All participants sing and the litanies can be sung repeatedly for hours. They are usually accompanied by rhythmic movements *(xadrayn)* of the body and swingings which are performed simultaneously by a circle of participants. Often, some participants fall into a trance *(jadbo)* and thereafter are helped by the others. Songs and rhythmic movements attain a certain peak of excitement which decreases progressively. Participants usually withdraw from their trances once the excitement of the songs has subsided. Very rarely, *dikri* are accompanied by musical instruments, generally a tambourine.[36] Although the *sheekhs* considered *dikri* incompatible with dances entailing drum playing, originally they used the tactic of persuading Gosha people to alternate daily between the two dances: those which entailed drum play, and the *dikri*. Participating in "playing the drum" rituals is not considered appropriate, let alone correct, Islamic behavior, although most people do it at various times on special occasions.

Islamic *sheekhs* in the Gosha area forbid the performance of "playing the drums" rituals in their own and neighboring villages. Despite this prohibition, rituals of this kind are widely performed, especially in villages whose elders have expert knowledge of the dances and songs. Performing "playing the drums" rituals, particularly those involving public dances is, however, strictly forbidden by Islamic *sheekhs* during the month of Ramadan. *Sheekhs* do, however, turn a blind eye to the dances celebrating the end of Ramadan, the *Ciid* festival. This begins after sunset on the last day of Ramadan and lasts for three days. People, especially young adults, dance as much as possible. All the specialist dance groups, including spirit-possession dance groups, involve themselves in organizing their performance. The dances at the end of Ramadan are usually cited as the most enjoyable of the year.

The category of "playing the drums" includes performances entailing both dances and songs accompanied by the rhythm of the drums. This is called *kuvina ngoma* in Chizigula and *tun durbanka* or *tuma ayarta* in the Somali language. Sometimes the linguistically incorrect Italianized form "giocare i tamburi"[37] is used.

The local concept of "playing the drums" rituals, as opposed to *dikri* celebrations, functions to unite several realities which are otherwise historically and actually well separated. This incorporates *mviko* and *jin*-spirit-possession rituals as well as other songs and dances accompanied by the rhythm of the drums. *Mviko* rituals relate to the basic matrifocal kin unit and, as such, are a crucial feature of the identity of people in the Gosha area because they lie at the base of kinship structures. A person inherits rituals and related dances from both parents although those inherited through the mother are the most important. These rituals, each entailing specific dances, are believed to relate to one's fortune or misfortune in life, so no one willingly abandons them. Among Somali Chizigula speakers, people belonging to the same *mviko* cannot marry each other: *mviko* members behave as an exogamous group. During the past two centuries, the *mviko* unit, which is based on the sharing of common kin, ancestors, rituals, and dances, was the core tradition which provided newly free ex-slaves arriving in the Gosha area with a communal sense of the self.[38]

Jin-spirit-possession rituals and dances, on the other hand, have been imported into the area more recently.[39] Performances are said to have become progressively more frequent in the last forty years, reflecting the progressive hold of the institutional organization underpinning them (the hierarchical structure which is at the base of the performances). Old Zigula say that in their youth being possessed by a *jin* was a rare and sad event; now, people celebrate the occasion with dancing and feasting. They say that *jin*-possession rituals have come from outside the Gosha area: some rituals are said to come from the Kenyan and Tanzanian coast, some from other parts of the southern Somali interior. Some of these rituals are performed in Mogadishu (the *numbi* and *aw daare*,[40] for example), whereas others, like the *jin kitimiri*[41] or *manyika*, certainly originated from more southern East African coastal areas.

Of other "playing the drums" rituals, those relating to *dabshid* are the most important. *Dabshid* is a feast organized at the beginning of the harvest period and entails different rituals according to where in Somalia it is performed.[42] However, it always includes a dance that is considered "most improper" by Muslims and colonialists alike.[43] Both men and women participate in the dance; however, some men are dressed as women[44] and mime sexual intercourse with other male dancers. Yet despite involving "indecent" behavior (in the eyes of people born outside the Gosha area), this feast is tolerated; in fact, government officers are included among the officiants. The last time I participated in a *dabshid* feast (in the Mareerey village in 1988), the festival ended with the communal recitation of the *fatiha*[45] and the sprinkling of *tahli-il* (water over which saints have spoken a few words from the Koran) over those present.

We now turn to the local Gosha concept of "playing the drums" rituals and examine the contexts to which it relates.

Firstly, the idea of playing the drums in the Gosha area is associated with the arrival of powerful and holy saints *(awliyo)* — not characterized as Islamic — who brought a powerful dance with special songs and drums with them. The most well known of these was Au Geddu, who was of Yao origin: he is always associated with his little drum and his dance. Au Shongoro Geddu Thes, to give him his full title, is also reputed to have been the first chief of the Gosha area, i.e., before

Nassib Bundo,[46] who was still alive circa 1850. People visit his descendants and place offerings under his old *mukui* tree;[47] if their petition is successful, they return to his grave[48] to perform the *makoko* dance to break their vows. Au Geddu is still considered a very potent saint and is believed to cure pilgrims' infertility problems. Another powerful saint is Au Kalandima, who was of Ngindo origins. His *dengere* dance is performed annually in the village where he lived. Prophecies about the future are made by his oldest descendants during this overnight performance.[49] A special drum is preserved for the occasion.

The metaphor of "playing the drums" in the Gosha area has become almost a cliché often reported in oral historical sources. Similarities can be found in the various accounts people with Bantu-speaking ancestors give of their arrival in the Gosha area. The basic story is that they spread from their original East African countries because of a famine precipitated by an invasion of locusts. This event had been forecast through the divination of certain signs (thunderbolts) given by the mountains overshadowing their territories. Drum play was prohibited because of the coming famine, but people did not believe the signs and danced regardless. This behavior brought ruin, causing them to leave their homes and be captured as slaves along the coast.[50]

Chizigula speakers explained this famine (which is called *gumbo chidja nchingo* in the local dialect) as the period when people were forced to eat boiled "hides of drums."[51] In Tanzania, *kidyakingo* is translated as the drought of the "cattle hide" because they had no other food to eat.[52] Thus a metaphor commonly used in northeastern Tanzania to indicate the worst possible starvation[53] assumes new connotations in Somalia, relating the famine to a "playing the drums" context.

"Playing the drums" is sometimes perceived as a cardinal fault: playing the drums at an inappropriate time can cause disorder and misfortune. Playing the drums when expressly advised not to brought the biggest disaster, enslavement. This does not mean that dances with drums should not be performed at all but rather that the drums are very powerful; they must be handled very carefully so that they do not become dangerous.

Dances with drums are also remembered as playing a very powerful role during the escape from slavery. One version of the flight relates that a great feast with wonderful dances was organized; several spells were prepared for the occasion. The Arab slave masters were fascinated by the dances and gave the group of dancers permission to visit several villages over a period of some days. A large number of Zigula from other villages joined the company because they enjoyed performing *mviko* together and remembering their land. By the end of the dances, among which were *uganga* (strengthening spells), the group was large and strong enough to escape towards the South.

Proper times for "playing the drums" are determined according to purpose. The timing of *mviko* rituals is usually determined by divination and dreams; *dabshid* is determined by the solar calendar; spirit-possession rituals are said to be determined by the will of the *jins*.

"Playing the drums" is often considered necessary in order to avoid misfortune and to keep a clear conscience with regard to the dead, who may appear in dreams asking for certain performances; they are said to be refreshed in their graves by the rituals.

One should not think, however, that the people keep a clear conscience towards the ancestors only by "playing the drums." A person must also offer annual *duco*[54] to the dead during which *dikri* celebrations are often performed and a communal *fatiha* is recited, led by a local *sheekh*.[55] In fact, the particular circumstances and kin preference determine which of the two celebrations is given most attention.

"Playing the drums" is an enjoyable activity; even the Islamic holy month of Ramadan may not be an obstacle to playing. For instance, when I complained (in 1986) that I would not be able to attend any dances during Ramadan, I was mocked by an official who told me I should wait until the end of the month. However, a woman friend spoke to him angrily in a broad local dialect in the hope that I would not understand: "As if we would not forget Ramadan when there is a need to 'play the drums'."

By now it should be clear that, despite appearances, the worship of the dead or of the spirits[56] or opposition to these practices, as well as to any form of polytheism *(shirki)*, is not really what is at stake in the local dualistic contradiction between "playing the drums" and *dikri* performances. Taking Lewis' suggestion[57] that sacrifices at the tombs of ancestors are deeply rooted in Somali society (because they recall Cushitic beliefs), the important point is *which* dead or *whose* ancestors are revered; tension exists regarding how ancestors are invoked, i.e., through which performance. Both traditional and Islamic ancestors are considered sources of power, and having one's own ancestors invoked by many people also conveys power.[58] Among the Gosha, no single ancestor has supremacy and few if any traditional ancestors are absorbed into Islamic ancestors, as happens with Sufism in other parts of Somalia.[59]

That drums and related performances involve power is indicated in the Somali proverb *"Ninki durbaanka [or ushaada] aad kaqadan karto aya loo dhiibta"* which means "Do not give the drums [or the stick] to somebody from whom you cannot have them back."[60]

Dance and Identity

Along the Jubba River an individual usually belongs to several dance groups. Belonging to a dance group can be acquired through inheritance (this particularly applies to *mviko* and some spirit-possession dances) or according to taste, skill, age, and residence. A person who is especially gifted or likes dancing can belong to many dance groups. Belonging to *mviko* dance groups, however, is inherited from kin groupings and is related to the educational process; most *mviko* dances are taught formally during initiation to the people who inherit them. Some *mviko* dances are very exclusive and are only taught to gifted youngsters under sixteen years of age.

A whole social organization carrying its own hierarchical

structure underpins dancing. Big celebrations called *esfel*[61] are held in which groups of dancers compete against each other. One *mviko* group competes in dances and masks against another, married people compete against unmarried (*minli* and *manjar*), sections of a village against each other, groups of villages against others. There can also be *esfel* of spirit-possession dance groups. Each group shows the best dances and masks it can possibly perform in *esfel* competitions. Victory in *esfel* competitions rewards the winning group with a rise in prestige.

A crucial point is that in the Gosha area sharing dances may be seen as sharing a whole kin grouping, including dead kin. This can be associated with the *mviko* ritual groups in that in performing certain dances, sharing is essential to please the ancestors. Similarly, sharing *dikri* "dances" can be considered as providing the kind of support one could expect from a kin grouping.

The following case shows how *dikri* Muslim celebrations may provide a whole set of individual precepts and communal dances for people who are uncomfortable with the matri-centred kin incest rules.

I met a Zigula woman who was very enthusiastic about female *dikri* celebration because, she said, of her father's devotion to Islam. Later, she told me of the event which prompted her decision to follow female *dikri* celebrations and to abandon "drum play" rituals. At the age of fifteen, she took part in a *chidede,* a public Zigula dance in which boys and girls dance in couples and recite poetry but never touch each other. When it was her turn to dance, she came out of the girls' group in order to dance with a member of the young men's group. Unfortunately, she had not realized that her maternal cousin was coming out of the boys' group in order to dance while she was performing. This experience made her feel extremely ashamed because maternal kin are not only not allowed to marry but cannot even dance together (maternal cousins are considered siblings). Ever since, she had felt too shy to dance "drum play" and became a fervent "*dikri* player." Her new attachment to the "*dikri* players" provided her with dances and religious precepts which she could cope with; dances such as the *dikri,* which can be used to please the ancestors, were made available to her. Moreover, because dances including the *dikri* are usually performed according to very rigid rules governing gender roles, she felt safe from any possible (if only metaphorical) future fear of incest.[62] The example also shows how dances in this area are tightly knitted together with the specific understanding of attitudes towards matri- and patri-focal incest rules and to a cultural construction of gender. This probably results from the widespread use of dances during initiation rituals into adulthood which strictly bind certain performances to the expression of an adult sexuality in the participants' lives.

Dances are closely related to both individual and group identities. To be a supporter of dance groups, or of *dikri* celebration groups, can be a matter of group or individual pride.

In the village of Moofi, I witnessed a competition between supporters of different "dance" groups. Sitei had worked with me for a while and was a supporter of the Qadiriya Sufistic group related to the village religious community of *Sheekh* Murjan. I had not visited her for a few months when I happened to see her in the street. I was in the company of Isha, a woman experienced in traditional *mviko* dances, who was introducing me to the dances of secret societies at that time. Sitei used to tease me because I was joining dance groups other than *dikri.* However, she invited me to a *dikri* celebration which she was holding the following night as a *duco* for her father's death. One needs to offer such *duco* to deceased parents, as otherwise they are believed to feel forgotten. I accepted and went to the celebration together with Isha. At midnight, having joined a *dikri* "swaying" for a few hours and having eaten after dancing, Isha and I decided we had better go home. Sitei did not want to let me go and she justified herself for having stopped the *dikri:* she would push the group to start dancing again soon, instead of resting for half an hour, if I would stay.

At an individual level, however, the conflict caused by participating in both Muslim and traditional dances is not always easy to resolve and some people do not choose exclusively one or the other group. Some people may experience an identity conflict; others may not. During *anyago*[63] performances (a traditional dance related to *mviko* kin units), I frequently met a man who would avoid me, refusing to speak to me. He finally revealed how guilty he felt about participating in a dance which was prohibited by Islam. However, he said he could not stop himself participating because he had entered the secret society of dance when he was a boy.

The reasons given for participating in "drum play" dances suggest that they have a powerful attraction for people who have participated in them since puberty and feel a strong obligation towards them. The choice does not follow an *a priori* moral decision; rather, it is deeply rooted in the education received at an early age.[64] The moral injunction not "to play the drums," as fostered by local Islamic saints, may mean that individuals are deprived of a support group which shares the same dance and is constituted by a whole kin grouping, especially including the dead.

My hypothesis that dancing is an expression of shared kin groupings can be further developed and may be one reason why "playing the drums" is so strongly prohibited by the *sheekhs*. For *mviko* dancers or supporters of other dance groups such as spirit-possession dances, this would mean abandoning old or deceased relatives. Separating oneself from these groups entails transferring allegiance from one's own, well-known group of ancestors to an entity whose forerunners are said to be the Prophet Muhammed and, after him, the saints who have some intercessory power — Faadumo,[65] Awo[66] and other women mentioned in the Koran. However, it is not easy to transfer allegiance and people often say they dream of their ancestors who ask them to perform a traditional dance in order to rid the community of the misfortune which has befallen it. Although in northern Somalia *sheekhs* and *wadaad*[67] are included in lineages' hierarchies and ancestors are likewise considered *sheekhs*,[68] this is not always the situation in southern Somalia. Rather, both kinds of "groupings," Islamic and traditional, exist side by side and the attention people pay to one or the other varies according to the circumstances and the context.

Dance in an Historical Context

If at a "micro" level some mechanisms of identity construction through dance can be described as above, the relevance of dances to the identity of people in Somalia is not a recent problem nor one localized along the Jubba River.

In southern Somalia, the alternation of power among different groups was often described in colonial records as a moral matter pertaining to what people could or could not dance. Prohibitions on certain kinds of dance accompany accounts both of tensions between groups vying for power and of the overthrow of rulers. The famous 19th-century mystic and holy man *Sheekh* Suufi, "who is remembered as the 'Guardian of Mogadishu'... discouraged bad sorts of dances like Maduundi,[69] Beeba[70] and Luunbi,[71] which had its origins in Kenya. These dances were to propitiate devils... Sheekh Suufi spared no efforts to guard the town against everything he thought was harmful."[72] This is evidence of underlying conflicts between people with servile origins and Muslim Somali society in the 19th century in Mogadishu.

Southern Somali people from the coastal town of Brava are reported to have greatly enjoyed drum playing; around 1840, the sultan of Bardera, by proclaiming an Islamic orthodoxy, tried to force them to give up these dances.[73] People from Brava town sought and obtained an alliance with the Geledi sultan, Yussuf bin Mahmud, to restore their traditional customs.[74] The sultan of Bardera had attempted to impose moral rules: women's arms and faces were to be covered by the veil; men were not to chew tobacco; both sexes were to cease dancing "fantasie."[75]

What may appear in some written sources to be just a metaphor proves to be a concrete, and recent, imposition regarding people's customs. Italian colonialists of the early 20th century describe dances performed by supposedly Swahili-speaking groups and ex-slaves as "obscene," "ruleless," and "wasteful."[76] It was thought that should these groups become better Muslims and, therefore, "moralized," they would take a further step towards "civilization." This seems to suggest that it was thought that the people of the Gosha area should be ruled by the "Muslim" Somali speakers. Other attempts to "civilize" the people included prohibiting dancing after a certain hour,[77] apparently because fighting often occurred on such occasions. During the 1970s, the Ogaden mayor of Jilib town obliged secret societies of dancers with East African ancestors to perform during the day. The traditional rule was to perform these dances on moonless nights. Spirit possession rituals as well as other kinds of dances were banned in Somalia during Barre's rule.

Along the Jubba River people complained that nowadays one could not dance as much as before. They claimed that several years ago they would play most nights whereas now it was difficult. There were continuous raids by the police, who were impressing people to be sent to the war in Hargeisa in northern Somalia; the newly resettled nomads would often disrupt performances. Young boys threw stones at the dancers, the Security Service would stop some of the dances, and police often prohibited people from playing overnight.

Although reasons for the prohibition of dances have differed over time, the fact that this idiom recurs in the historical accounts shows that dance performance can be considered a key aspect with regard to social change in Somalia. I would suggest that the idiom reveals real clashes of relational identities among groups of people and, perhaps, the right of legitimacy for the role models existing among the people who perform such dances. In other words, the way people dance in public reflects different ways of conceiving relations between and within gender; this aspect becomes an issue to be controlled through prohibitions of dances.

The ethnographic data can be looked at from another perspective. Unlike the *dikri, mviko* and spirit-possession cults as well as other "to play the drums" rituals share dance performances which involve enjoying bodily freedom, sexual metaphor — behaviors which are not considered proper for public display — and sometimes specific sets of incest rules.

Dances involving drums are danced according to different rules from the *dikri*. Men and women dance *(ayar)* together, often in couples; people publicly court members of the other sex and compete with people of the same sex[78] by showing their agility and their graceful movements. Meetings for dancing, often held at night, provide occasion for love and sexual encounters.[79] On the other hand, *dikri* are strictly performed by people of the same sex; this separation is operated deliberately in order to avoid transferring attention from prayers to sexual thoughts. Moreover, movements performed during *dikri* are very repetitive swingings; they are supposed to be performed by everybody together and leave little space for individual creativity. Individual bodily freedom only appears to be allowed to people who fall into a trance during the performance of litanies and swingings.[80] It is difficult to see any sexual metaphors in *dikri* dance movements, especially when compared to most of the other dances performed in this area by people who claim East African ancestors. In fact, the public display of sexual metaphors in dance is considered absolutely improper by people from northern Somali nomadic backgrounds although many other Somalis who have settled in the area do not reject them; yet, among people with Bantu speakers among their ancestors, such display is widespread and enjoyable. As a result, dance performance has become a relevant distinguishing aspect, defining local categories of orthodoxy.

In Somalia, being allowed to perform certain dances and music of a particular kind legitimizes the identity of the people who participate in them. This became obvious to me when I was asked by a Security Service officer to erase some of the film I had shot of *dabshid* dances (including the representation of coitus) performed by people from Baidoa. I was told that these dances showed the wrong image of Somalia. I erased the film although I was surprised because similar dances are quite common in other parts of Africa. However, the reaction of the officer, who was of nomadic origins and had apparently had little education, cannot merely be seen as intolerance. His attitude towards such dance was not so different from what Lewis[81] had observed in the 1950s: the amazing decency of the dances organized during the *gu* (rainy) season among Somali nomad boys and girls. In contrast with many other African countries, the idea that dances could be followed by any kind of sexual relationship, even if only metaphorically, was abhorred.

Conclusions

Two decades ago Terence Ranger in his forerunner book wrote about Beni dance societies in Mombasa that this was "not essentially an oppositionist phenomenon. It was profoundly assimilated into African societies for it was exclusively or even mainly concerned with the externalities of opposition."[82] Nevertheless, the Beni dance revealed significant tensions within African societies, and significant aspirations. Almost contemporaneously Margaret Stroebel[83] presented a similar picture, but from a feminine point of view: in Mombasa, feminine dances fostered an integration within different social strata.

Certainly, conflicts and competitions in dances conceal significant tensions within Somali people of the riverine areas. The political issue about whose ancestors or spirits should be pleased obviously relates to power. When people are forbidden to dance certain dances, they are also denied the means of expressing their sharing of the basic kin unit, the *mviko*. This entails being deprived of the opportunity of visiting one's ancestors in order to avoid misfortune, which further involves being deprived of access to this type of traditional power. Moreover, the *mviko* key unit had constituted a basic principle of aggregation for many different people coming from different parts of East Africa after the sad experience of slavery.

The aspect of competition and opposition between types of rituals, Sufistic and traditional, however, remains alive despite the relevance of the traditional ones for the people.

The fact that Islam for a long time represented a flag of freedom, especially in the southern riverine areas, seems to explain the importance of maintaining both conflicting and interacting aspects of the Somali identity, the Islamic practices and the traditional ones. Moreover, as Islam is a major feature of the attainment of the highest status possible among Somalis, the striving towards reaching ideally perfect Islamic manners operates in tension with the desire of people to be legitimized as equals in the Somali society.

However, competition in dances should not be seen only as a sign of tensions and aspirations residing outside the dances themselves. Tensions are somehow inherent in the very structure underlying the two competing kind of "dances" which reflect different moral codes concerning gender roles. These moral codes are an integral part of the ritual performances that are used in order to pray to the ancestors. Each of the performances entails a different way of expressing sexuality through the metaphor of the dance. Most of the people who "play the drums" enjoy it and do not wish to stop, whatever prohibitions may appear at various times.

In the specific context of the people who live in the Gosha area, the metaphor of "playing the drums" — often mentioned in historical accounts — can be viewed from the perspective of a more general tension that exists historically between Islamic and traditional "dances," between less and more constrictive moral codes, and, ultimately, between freedom and slavery.

Notes

1. Comments on early or more complete versions of this paper from Dr. Ali Jimale Ahmed, Prof. Ioan M. Lewis, Dr. Virginia Luling, Dr. Wendy James, Dr. Douglas Johnson, Dr. Henrietta Moore, Dr. Luisa Elvira Belaunde Olschewski and Prof. David Parkin (who kindly gave me some of his unpublished paper), Dr. Paul Spencer, Prof. Terence Ranger and Awes Mohamed Wasuge were all very stimulating. Comments of the participants to seminars at the African Studies Association meeting in Seattle, at the Department of Anthropology in Oxford and at the School of Oriental and African Studies in London greatly helped me to shape in a final form these ideas. Many discussions with Christine Ahmed in Rome helped me to collate and further develop my argument on the relevance of dances to the identity of people in Southern Somalia. The responsability for what I wrote, however, remains

entirely mine. I welcomed finances from the Accademia dei Lincei in Rome that allowed me time to think and write.

2. See,e.g. V.Mudimbe, *The Invention of Africa. Gnosis, Philosophy, and the Order of Knowledge* (Bloomington: Indiana University Press,1988); T.O.Ranger, *The Invention of Tribalism in Zimbabwe* (Gwern: Mambo Press, 1985); and M. Vaughan, "Theory of African History," seminar given at the History of Africa Seminars, School of Oriental and African Studies, London, January 1993.

3. See: Ali Abdirahman Hersi, "The Arab Factor in Somali History: The Origins and the Development of Arab Enterprise and Cultural Influence in the Somali Peninsula," ph.D. diss., University of California, Los Angeles, 1977.

4. It is worth saying, however, that written narratives result not only from writers' intentions but also from the image their informants gave of Somalia. Similarly, different kinds of narrative may result from the selection made of sources available. For example, Ali Abdirahman Hersi wonders "how Somalis came to assume an Arabo-Islamic identity in preference to their African heritage" ("The Arab Factor," p.110); yet, when reconstructing the process of Islamicization of Somalia, he selects mostly Arabic written sources.

5. Francesca Declich, "La Somalia Coloniale alle Garesa," in *L'Africa in Vetrina*, ed. La Banca (Milan: Ed. Pagus, 1992).

6. Following Independence, the dances were included as part of Somalia's artistic patrimony; many have been reconstructed and re-elaborated in an artistic form by the National Theatre in Mogadishu dance company. Dances from the riverine areas, especially the *kabeebey*, used to be shown by national groups in theatres all over the country. They were often used in theatre to connote peasant agriculturalists as opposed to urban people. Behind this urban phenomenon of assimilation, most dances I mention are still performed at a grass roots level in rural areas by people living in the riverine areas of Southern Somalia. They are performed by specific groups of people and reflect local social relations.
See: Sheekh Abdi Abdullahi, "Danze folkloristiche somale," in *Proceedings of the Third International Congress of Somali Studies*, ed. A. Puglielli (Rome: Il Pensiero Scientifico, 1986).

7. See: Muhammad b. Bazi Ibn Waddeh, *Kitab al-bida: (tratado contra las innovaciones)*, Nueva edicion, traduccion, estudio e indices por M. Isabel Fierro (Madrid: Instituto de Filologia, Departamento de Estudios Arabes, 1988),p.101.

8. See: Leandro Dell'Addolorata, "Lettera al rev.mo padre provinciale," Stazione Issa Kristos, Gelib, 17/4/1906.

9. See: D. Henige, *Oral Historiography* (London: Longman, 1982), pp. 87-90.
10. I refer here to *Sheekh* Murjan who is said to have come to Islamicize the Gosha area during the second half of the nineteenth century. However, I have also found a similar cliché referring to the chief Nassib Bundo. An Italian written source reports that he was freed because, having found a hidden store of tusks, he informed his master of his find; freedom was his reward for his fidelity.
11. To be pious meant observing the five daily prayers, being faithful to one's master, and hard working.
12. Fieldwork was carried out in three phases from 1985 to 1988 in the area between the towns of Jilib (Middle Jubba region) and Jamame (Lower Jubba region). I wish to thank for this opportunity the following persons and institutions: Prof. Bernardo Bernardi, the Italian National Research Council (C.N.R.), the Comitato Internazionale per lo Sviluppo dei Popoli, the Somali National Academy for Sciences and Arts (Miryam Warsame and Abdullahi Ahmed Hombooy), the Faculty of Languages at the Somali National University (Dahabo Farax Hassan and Ciise Maxamed Siyaad). For financing several periods I spent writing up I thank the Accademia dei Lincei and the Italian National Research Council (C.N.R).
13. Most colonial records refer to them as Gosha. For more details about this issue, see: Lee V. Cassanelli, "Bantu Former Slaves Communities (Somali)," in *The African Frontier: The Reproduction of Traditional African Societies* (Bloomington & Indianapolis: Indiana University Press,1987); Francesca Declich, "I Goscia della regione del Medio Giuba, Un gruppo etnico di origine bantu," in *Africa*; 42(4) 1987: 570-599 and her *Il processo di formazione della identita' culturale dei Bantu della Somalia meridionale*, tesi di Dott.Ric., Istituto Universitario Orientale, Naples, 1992; and K. Menkhaus, "Rural Transformation and the Roots of Underdevelopment in Somalia's Lower Jubba Valley," Ph.D. diss., University of South Carolina, 1989.
14. See: E.A. Alpers, "Dance and Society in Nineteenth Century Mogadishu," in Thomas Labahn, ed., *Proceedings of the Second International Congress of Somali Studies*, vol. 2, (Hamburg: Helmut Burke Verlag, 1983).
15. Literally, *dikri* means "mentioning" the name of God or some of His attributes. A *dikri* is one of the most important liturgical acts and is distinct from the *duco* (personal prayer for petition) and from canonical prayers (A. Bausani, *L'Islam* [Milan: Garzanti, 1987], p.85). *Dikri* is commonly practised within Islamic brotherhoods.

16. *Mviko* are traditional rituals performed by matri-kin lines. Most of them entail dances and songs with drum play and usually include metaphorical and secret meanings. The performance of *mviko* dances is thought of as being strictly tied to one's chances in life. *Mviko* duties are unavoidable if one wants to avoid serious problems or misfortune in life; they are also especially relevant to the fertility of both men and women. *Mviko* membership is inherited on the maternal side but, when misfortune occurs, divination may suggest the performance of *mviko* rituals of the paternal side. Chizigula speakers usually recognize a female ancestor as the founder of a particular *mviko*, whereas among other Shanbara such ancestors are generally male. The performance of *mviko*-connected rituals is generally prescribed after divination or dreams and people belonging to the same *mviko* are called to participate.

17. The chanted recitation of the Koran, the celebration of non-Islamic feasts, raising the voice or hands during invocations, are innovations which, when deemed loans from other rites, are prohibited by the *hawadit* (Ibn Waddah, *Kitab al-bida'*, pp.105-116). *Hawadit* are traditions about the Prophet's sayings and deeds which complemented the Koran in the codification of the Islamic canonic law. Innovations of this kind are forbidden in the name of the Prophet's exhortation to differentiate Muslims from followers of other rites such as the Christian and Jewish religions (ibid:106, 108). However, the chanting of litanies and the body movements in *dikri* were spread through Sufistic brotherhoods and therefore, at least in Somalia, were not considered unorthodox until recently. During the government of Siyaad Barre (1969-1991), however, new Islamic trends imported into Somalia from South Arabia have tended to dismiss some Sufistic practices.

18. I. M. Lewis points out that in the Somali context, ancestors have long been formally incorporated into Islamic beliefs by converting them into saints. (See the following works by Lewis: "Sufism in Somaliland: A Study in Tribal Islam. I," in *Bulletin of the School of Oriental and African Studies*, 1955, pp.145-160; "Shaikhs and Warriors in Somaliland," in M. Fortes and G. Dieterlain, eds., *African Systems of Thought* [London: International African Institute & Oxford Univ. Press,1965],pp.206-216; *Democrazia pastorale* [Milan: Franco Angeli, 1983],p.252; and "Syncretism and Survival in African Islam," in *Convegno su Aspetti dell'Islam "Marginale"*, (Rome: Academia Nazionale dei Lincei,1983],p.252.) This inclusion is so important to Somali society that most lineages claim the Prophet Mohammed among the relatives of their founding ancestors (see: Lewis, *Democrazia pastorale*, p,258; "Syncretism and Survival," p.258; and "Sufism in Somaliland...I," p.582). However,

belief in the powers of the dead over the living is the kind of ancestor worship that is a matter of controversy in the Gosha area, regardless of whether the ancestors in question were Muslim or traditionalist.

This controversial matter is also reflected in an old theological dispute. Whether deceased saints have intercessory powers *(tawasul)* or blessing validity to the living was debated by the Salihiya and Qadiriya brotherhoods (see: G.B.Martin,"Muslim Politics and Resistance to Colonial Rule: Sheikh Uways b. Muhammad al-Barawi and the Qadiriyya Brotherhood in East Africa," *Journal of African History*; 10[3] 1969 :492). Said S. Samatar reports (see his "Sheikh Uways Muhammad of Baraawa,1847-1909. Mystic and Reformer in East Africa," in S.S.Samatar,ed., *In the Shadow of Conquest: Islam in Colonial Northeast Africa* (Trenton: Red Sea Press, 1992),pp.54-55) that "Veneration of deceased saints, pilgrimages to their tombs, offering sacrifices on their behalf, ecstatic trances — practices Qaadiriya regularly engaged in — were viewed with horror by members of Saalihiya as polytheistic *(shirk)*." E. Cerulli, however (in his *Somalia* I (Rome: Istituto Poligrafico dello Stato,1957, p.195), claims that no substantial reasons divided the two movements other than political competition.

In the Gosha area, the best known communities of the Sufistic saints are still named for their founders such as *Sheekh* Murjan and *Sheekh* Nuur; the former died about a century ago. When people visit the communities, they usually say they are visiting the saints rather than their living descendants. This suggests that it is the power of the deceased saints which is popularly considered to operate through their descendants, regardless of any theological affiliation.

19. See: F. Declich, *Il processo di formazione,* pp.138-139; and I.M.Lewis, "Sufism in Somaliland: A Study in Tribal Islam. II," in *Bulletin of the School of Oriental and African Studies,* 1956:153.
20. See: Dell'Addolorata, "Lettera al rev.mo provinciale."
21. See: G. Chiesi, *La colonizzazione europea nell'Est Africa* (Torino:Unione Tipografica Editrice Torinese, 1909); and G. Pantano, *Nel Benadir, La citta di Merca e la regione Bimaal* (Livorno: Belforte Editori, 1910).
22. Chiesi, *La colonizzazione europea.*
23. Dell 'Addolorata, "Lettera al rev.mo padre provinciale."
24. Chiesi, *La colonizzazione europea.*
25. Cerulli (*Somalia* I, p. 202) suggests that during the early Italian occupation, members of Islamic brotherhoods were used as mediators with the clans; members gained religious and political prestige from this activity. This policy initially legitimized the authority of the dominant class of Arab and Somali traders, whose

political and economic power was otherwise jeopardized by anti-slavery trends (Chiesi, *La colonizzazione europea*, p. 292). At the beginning of the 20th century, it was becoming increasingly difficult for the dominant classes to keep their slaves at work, especially after the antislavery acts of 1903-1904 (see: Lee Cassanelli, "The Ending of Slavery in Italian Somalia: Liberty and the Control of Labor, 1890–1935," in S. Miers and R. Roberts, eds., *The End of Slavery in Africa* [Madison: University of Wisconsin Press, 1988], p.316). I suggest that the Italians' early support for the Islamic religion stemmed from the tension between themselves and Locals over the slavery issue. The early Italian policy against the presence of the Trinitarian Fathers' mission along the Jubba River supports this hypothesis (see: E. De Albertis, *Victoria, Nyanza e Benadir* [Bergamo: Istituto di Arti Grafiche, 1909], p.112).

26. Cassanelli ("Ending of Slavery," p.321) suggests membership could be claimed in order to gain exemption from corvée labor during the Italian colonial period. See also: Cerulli, *Somalia* vol. I, p.203.

27. Cassanelli, "Ending of Slavery," pp.321-327-329; and A.Del Boca, *Gli Italiani in Africa orientale. La conquista dell'impero* (Milan: Laterza, 1986), p.204.

28. I. M. Lewis, *A Modern History of Somalia: Nation and State in the Horn of Africa* (Boulder: Westview Press, 1988),pp.58-59.

29. D. Parkin, "Islam, Symbolism and the Problem of Bodily Expression," in A. De Luz and S. Heald, eds., *Anthropology and Ethnopsychoanalysis* (London: Routledge, 1992).

30. Some *qasiido* are in Rahanweyn language which is sometimes referred in Gosha as the Eelay language, though this has derogatory connotations in some contexts.

31. *Sheekh* Uways Mohamed translated mystic songs into several Somali dialects in order to spread the Qadiryia doctrine among the rural people of Southern Somalia (Cerulli, *Somalia* I, pp.187-188).

32. This attitude, which I observed in 1988, was most probably related to the more traditionalist trend which was being imported from Saudi Arabia at the time; it was widely enforced by the major *sheekhs* of Mogadishu mosques.

33. This refers particularly to *Sheekh* Murjan who came to Islamicize Gosha around the second half of the 19th century. *Sheekh* Nuur, who appeared along the Jubba River more recently in the sixties, is also said to have adopted the same tactics. This may reflect acceptance and accommodation of other religious practices. The Somali have a proverb regarding such behavior, *"Meel sey utaal ayaa loola yaal,"* which corresponds to the English "When in Rome do as the Romans do."

34. A similar mechanism is said to have been adopted by Muslim saints to gain entry among the Yao of Lake Nyasa (see: E.A. Alpers, "Towards a History of the Expansion of Islam in East Africa: The Matrilineal People of the Southern Interior," in T.O.Ranger and I.N. Kimambo,eds., *The Historical Study of African Religion* [Berkeley & Los Angeles: University of California Press,1972], p.188). It should be noted, however, that among the central African Yao, Muslim practices were soon included in initiation rituals to an adult age (ibid:180). This did not happen in the Gosha area despite most people's Yao origins.

35. All other types of non-Islamic songs are referred to as *hees*.

36. This applies to both Ahmediyia and Qadiriyia *dikri* I observed (the most common in the Gosha area). This fact gives prominence to the local avoidance of drums in Muslim celebrations, which is probably related to the special relevance of playing drums in traditional rituals. In other areas, drums are not so strictly avoided. I.M. Lewis (personal communication, 1992) points out that in the Northwest, Qadiriyia *dikri* including drums are very common, although the drums in this case are probably tambourines. Moreover, several writers call attention to the drums used during *dikri* performed by followers of *Sheekh* Uways (who was initially a Qadiriyia affiliate) (C. Ahmed, "God, Anti-Colonialism, and Drums: Sheikh Uways and the Uwaysiyya," in *Ufahamu* [1989] 17[2]: 107; G.B. Martin, "Muslim Politics and Resistance," p.474). Ahmed (ibid., p.111) suggests that the use of drums and banners has helped "the massive conversion to Islam" of Somalis of Bantu origins. Virginia Luling told me that there is a Somali commoner lineage in Afgooye which claims to be an especially holy group despite using tambourines with their prayers; they are most particular, however, to differentiate themselves from people who "play the drums."

37. In Italian, one can either say "*suonare* (to play) *i tamburi*" or "*danzare* (to dance) *alla musica dei tamburi*" or "*cantare* (to sing) *alla musica dei tamburi.*" The etymology of such an odd Italianized linguistic form is not clear. It is likely to be a translation from the Somali *ayar* which also means "children's play" or a tentative translation from the Kiswahili *kucheza ngoma* which means "dancing or playing with drums" and is associated with the rhythmical movement made by drummers when beating the drums.

It is not clear, however, why locals use the Italian word *giocare*, which refers to children's play. Is the use of the word *giocare* part of local tactics of connoting for outsiders that "playing the drums" is a simple, almost childish activity (supposedly for the early colonial Italians who expected such a childish behavior, as epitomized in Pantano, *Nel Benadir*, p. 91)? Yet, in colonial literature, Italians referred to the dances as *fantasie,* an even odder and more archaic word: *fantasia* means "fantasy" which is again a feature of children's play. Noticeably, the word "fantasia" took in Italian also a specific connotation indicating the indigenous dances of the Italian colonies; this highlights a facet of the colonialists' perception of those countries.

38. The basic matrifocal kin unit, the *mviko,* and the way it became an organizing principle in reconstructing the identities of people arriving in the Gosha area from different parts of East Africa, is ethnographic evidence which could be included in Christine Ahmed's analysis of the relevance of matrilineal principles in early African history (see: C. Ahmed, "Not from a Rib: The Use of Gender and Gender Dynamics to Unlock Early African History," in *Journal of African History* 1992:11; cf., Declich, *Il processo di formazione,* pp. 147-183).

39. Many different spirit-possession rituals are widespread in Somalia. Each relates to a specific cosmology; each has its own songs, dances, and procedures to heal the spirits' presence. They are also said to originate from different geographical areas.

40. According to Alpers ("Dance and Society," p.134) spirit-possession rituals called *luunbi* and *aw deere* were performed in Mogadishu during the 19th century.

41. I have been unable to ascertain whether or not this spirit-possession ritual is performed outside the Gosha area. However, the old man who brought it along the Jubba River is said to have come from Tanzania. Alpers reports that in the mid-19th century at Zanzibar a spirit-possession cult was dedicated to a spirit named *kitimiri* (E.A. Alpers, "'Ordinary Household Chores': Ritual and Power in a 18th-century Swahili Women's Spirit Possession Cult," in *IJAHS;* 17/4 1984: 677-702).

42. The feast of *dabshid* is widely mentioned in literature about Somalia (see: P.Barile, *La colonizzazione fascista nella Somalia meridionale* [Rome: SIAG,1935],p.128; Cerulli, *Somalia* I, p.187 and *Somalia* II, pp.162–163; Lewis, *A Modern History of Somalia,* p.72; V. Luling, "The Social Structure of Southern Somali Tribes," Ph.D. thesis, University of London, pp.311-352). The date for *dabshid* is fixed according to the solar year (24 July), unlike Islamic festivities which are held according to the lunar year. The *dabshid* feast is sometimes called *neyruus.* The Persian *neyruus* festival is mentioned in the Islamic book against innovations, the *Kitab al-bidac* (Ibn Waddah, *Kitab al-bidac,* p.106), because it had become confused with some Christian festivals in al-Andalus; the prohibition on celebrating the *neyruus* relates to the Prophet's warning that Muslim religious worship was to be strictly differentiated from Christian and Jewish cults. There is evidence that very

"orthodox" Muslims in Somalia disapproved of the *dabshid* feast (Barile, *La colonizzazione fascista*, p.128); however, as neither Christianity nor Judaism present any imminent danger for Islam in Somalia, other fears are likely to be related to a disapproval of *dabshid*.

43. It is interesting to note the moral support the Italian Barile (loc.cit.) gave to this attitude. He considers the *dabshid* (which in this instance he calls *neyruus*) improper, defining it as much more "licentious than our carnival".

44. The idea of men playing women's roles is abhorred by the *sheekhs* who consider it un-Islamic. The injunction goes back to disdain of the *muxannat* (effeminate singer) (Ali Jimale Ahmed,"Of Poets and Sheikhs: Somali Literature," in Kenneth Harrow,ed., *Faces of Islam in African Literature* [Portsmouth & London: Heinemann & James Currey, 1991], p.84). The story of Ciisa pastoral man epitomizes such horror in a Somali context: Ciisa heard of the existence of a homosexual man (khanis) in Djibouti and killed himself saying this meant the end of the world.

45. *Fatiha* — the name given to the opening *sura* of the Koran.

46. Declich, "I Goscia della regione del Medio Giuba," p.589.

47. The *mukui* tree is seen to be suitable for ritual purposes.

48. The grave was originally sited close to Kamtande village. Following flooding from the Jubba River, Au Geddu is said to have appeared in several people's dreams, asking for his grave to be relocated. It has recently been moved close to Buulo Manyassa.

49. Declich, *Il processo di formazione*, p.171.

50. Fieldnotes, 1988:m/sto 35–37.

51. Ibid., p.93.

52. J. Giblin, "*Famine, Authority and the Impact of Foreign Capital in Handnei District, Tanzania, 1840–1940,*" Ph.D. thesis, University of Wisconsin, Madison, 1986, p.77; and J. Giblin, personal communication, 1992.

53. Giblin, *Famine, Authority and Foreign Capital*, p.77.

54. *Duco* are blessings. All over Somalia they often include celebrations during which *suras* from the Koran are recited; usually, animals are sacrificed and eaten communally.

55. This is a widespread practice in many Somali areas.

56. One could interpret the prohibition of dancing *jin*-spirit-possession rituals as an attempt to avoid addressing attention to the *jin*. In Muslim theology, *jin* are those "rebellious spirits created similarly to man, but of fire in place of earth... who seek to lead man astray and to subvert the teaching of the prophet" (Lewis, "Sufism in Somaliland II," p.152). Certainly, in some cases, spirit-possession rituals may offer accommodations to an inclusion of earlier

spiritual entities into an Islamic context. In the Gosha case, however, *jin*-possession rituals are not condoned by either the supporters of traditional rituals or the Islamic saints.

57. Lewis, "Sufism in Somaliland I," p.583.

58. For a wider discussion about struggle for power over ancestor veneration in the Gosha area, see Declich, *Il processo di formazione*, pp.120–122; 176–178.

59. Lewis, "Sufism in Somaliland I," p.583; "Sufism in Somaliland II," p.156.

60. I thank Seinab Jama and Rashid Hassan for telling me this proverb.

61. An interesting etymology of this word has been suggested to me by a Somali linguist who remembered that in the Baidoa region, the word *esfel* was used because of its assonance with the Italian word *"sveglia,"* "to wake up." The word was used to refer to groups of singers and dancers of the *kabeebey* dance, who, during Ramadan, used to perform at three o'clock in the morning and compete with one another in keeping the villagers awake. Ostensibly, this was done to provide people with a better way of staying awake until the last Islamic prayer of the night. During Independence (1960–1969) this kind of competition increased, but was stopped almost completely after the socialist revolution in 1969.

62. An important aspect of dance performances is the ambiguity dance entails between metaphor and reality. Certainly, breaking the matricentred incest avoidance rules underpinning the *chidede* dance greatly influenced my informant's life, perhaps as much as if she had practically committed incest.

63. One of the most interesting dances related to secret societies is called the *Anyago manyassa*. It includes dances with masks which are sometimes very similar to those one can observe in the African Great Lake region. It is one of the most widespread dances and some levels of affiliation — which do not include the most secret performances — can be acquired without belonging to a local matri-kin unit.

64. This is an important point. During initiation rituals, an authority function is exerted by the elders and a sense of guilt towards the ancestors is created among the young initiates (Marie-Cecile Ortigues and Edmond Ortigues, *Oedipe Africaine* [Paris: Librarie Plan, 1966]) as a result of separation from mothers and other relatives who have taken care of them before adolescence. This characterizes the construction of kinship criteria and binds a strict allegiance to a particular kin grouping.

65. Cerulli, *Somalia* I, p.194; Hersi, "The Arab Factor," pp.116,194; Lewis, "Sufism in Somaliland I," p.592.

66. Amina H. Adan, personal communication, 1992; Declich, "Feminine Muslim Rituals."

67. *Wadaad* and *sheekhs* are very religious Muslim men knowledgeable more than others in the words of the Koran.

68. Lewis, "Sufism in Somaliland II," pp.206, 216.

69. Archival evidence reports that the *mundungo* dance was performed by ex-slaves. I could not trace this dance during my fieldwork in the Gosha area. However, Hassan Osman Ahmed, my colleague at the Istituto Universitario Orientale of Naples and lecturer of history at the Somali National University, suggests the written reports of *mundungo* may be an actual mistransliteration of *maa hurdo* which means "not to sleep" in the Somali language and probably refers to staying up all night for dancing. Hassan was told about a dance referred as *maa hurdo* which was performed annually during three days and nights at the *siyaaro* for Au Osman in Merka town. Au Osman died on the day of his marriage in 1560 A.D. (967 H.), the date written on his grave. An anachronistic legend reports his mother was Bimaal and his father Arab, although the Bimaal were not yet in the area at the time.

70. One of the spirit-possession rituals people remember is called *jin pepo*, although this does not confirm any necessary relation between that and the one existing at the beginning of the century.

71. One of the most widespread spirit-possession rituals in Somalia is named *Numbi* or *Lunbi*, depending on the informant's accent.

72. Alpers, "Dance and Society," pp.135-136.

73. Chiesi, *La colonizzazione europea*, pp.364-365.

74. I am obviously simplifying events in order to highlight the frequency with which the idiom of dance is reported in the historical narrative.

75. All three moral impositions relate to gender-specific behavior. It is also notable that inter-gender relationships are represented through dance.

76. Chiesi, *La colonizzazione europea*, pp.636-638.

77. ASMAE, Relazione mensile dal Basso Giuba, 1937.

78. Actually, some of the dhikri belonging to the Husseinia group (which unites the followers of the Ethiopian *Sheekh* Hussein Bale) entail circles of both men and women swinging together. This is, however, not very common in the villages I visited along the Jubba River.

79. This is epitomized in the Somali proverb, *"Cayaar habeen maxaa loo tumaa haddi wax kujirin"* ("Why should one play dances at night if there is nothing beyond?"), which refers to the possibility of sexual encounters.

80. Parkin, op. cit. (see n.29).

81. Lewis, *Democrazia pastorale*, p.65.

82. T.O. Ranger, *Dance and Society in Eastern Africa, 1890–1970: The Beni Ngoma* (Oxford: Clarendon Press, 1975), p.165.
83. M. Stroebel, *Muslim Women in Mombassa, Kenya, 1890–1973* (London & New Haven: Yale University Press, 1975).

ON CRITIQUES OF THE
INVENTION OF SOMALIA

∞

Edward A. Alpers

Three of the papers on which I will comment focus on a different aspect of the invention of Somalia. Mohamed Haji Mukhtar examines the place of Islam in Somali history; Catherine Besteman discusses the categorization of the so-called "Gosha" of the riverine areas of the south; Christine Choi Ahmed analyzes the way in which Somali women have been characterized in the scholarly literature. Each writer both provides a critique of the received perspectives and offers suggestions for an historically more accurate appreciation of these important topics. A fourth essay by M. Kassim provides an implicit corrective to the notion of invention by drawing the reader's attention to the neglected cultural history of the Banadir coast.

Let us begin by addressing the broader notion of the invention of Somalia that serves as the organizing theme for this volume. First, the collapse of the Somali state and the disintegration of Somali society after the overthrow of the military dictatorship of Mohamed Siad Barre in 1991 has, among its many effects, prompted Somali intellectuals and others to question seriously the very existence of the state and society over which the political struggle had been waged these past two decades and more. To be sure, there had been various straws in the wind during this period, but the concentrated questioning of the cultural and historical assumptions upon which Somalia seemed to rest dates only from the collapse of the state itself. Thus, the volatility, both political and intellectual, of the circumstances in which this reassessment is occurring cannot be overemphasized.

Second, the concept of "the invention of Somalia" also requires some probing, since it raises the question of who has done the inventing and what it is they have invented. The roots of this kind of analysis are found in Hobsbawm and Ranger's seminal volume on *The Invention of Tradition*, which stakes out an entire intellectual agenda for reexamining what Hobsbawm calls "invented tradition."[1] More immediately relevant to this discussion is Hobsbawm's identification of a critical element that links all aspects of "invented traditions":

> They are highly relevant to that comparatively recent historical innovation, the 'nation', with its associated phenomena: nationalism, the nation-state, national symbols, histories and the rest. All these rest on exercises in social engineering which are often deliberate and always innovative, if only because historical novelty implies innovation. . . . Standard national languages, [for example,] to be learned in schools and written, let alone spoken, by more than a smallish elite, are large constructs of varying, but often brief, age.

Continuing this train of thought, Hobsbawm comments (originally with reference to France, but equally relevant for Somalia):

> We should not be misled by a curious, but understandable, paradox: modern nations and all their impedimenta generally claim to be the opposite of constructed, namely human communities so 'natural' as to require no definition other than self assertion. Whatever the historic or other continuities embedded in the modern concept of 'France' and 'the French'— and which nobody would seek to deny — these very concepts themselves must include a constructed or 'invented' component. And just because so much of what subjectively makes up the mod-

ern 'nation' consists of such constructs and is associated
with appropriate and, in general, fairly recent symbols or
suitably tailored discourse (such as 'national history'), the
national phenomenon cannot be adequately investigated
without careful attention to the 'invention of tradition.'[2]

Accordingly, the chapters by Mukhtar, Besteman, Ahmed and
Kassim need to be situated in these political and intellectual
contexts.

Mohamed Mukhtar's passionate analysis of "Islam in Somali
History: Fact and Fiction" presents a compelling critique of
prevailing myths that inhibit our full understanding of the religion that has become virtually synonymous with Somali identity. (See pp. 1–27 of these proceedings) Acknowledging his
debt to the pioneering work of Ali Abdirahman Hersi,[3]
Mukhtar draws upon an impressive range of sources to support
his contention that the alleged northern roots of Islam in
Somali society are misleading and overstated in the scholarly
literature. His focus on Islamicization, as opposed to
Arabization, is an important contribution to the debate on the
Islamic factor in Somali history, as is his declared purpose to
address "not how Islam arrived but rather what factors led to
the advent of Islam in Somalia." His assumption that the northern Somali claim of descent from Arab ancestors "is a cultural
invention developed recently to gain political ascendancy" also
resonates effectively with the broader theme of this volume
while echoing the implications of Hersi's research. Indeed,
Mukhtar's more general broadside, against the propensity of
the modern Somali state to reinterpret Somali culture as "the
custodian of the invented Somali tradition, which glorified the
nomadic tradition, but also ignored and degraded other
Somali traditions," is borne out by my own limited foray into
the area of Somali cultural history.[4]

This said, if Mukhtar is correct in identifying a northern,
pastoral bias in previous reconstructions of Somali history
and culture, especially as these relate to Islam, what he offers
up as an alternative interpretation can only be referred to as
an australocentric perspective that by virtue of its numerous

assumptions raises as many questions as it provides fascinating possibilities. For example, in his discussion of the early history of the southern Somali coast, which rests partly on his reading of Schoff's dated (1912) translation of *The Periplus of the Erhythraen Sea*,[5] one would like to see more of Mukhtar's evidence for the possible connections of the Hawiya with the ancient kingdom of Punt. Similarly, he concludes that "the bulk of Muslim migrants found safe haven" in "ancient towns and markets along the Jubba and Shabelle valleys," the evidence for which dates only to 19th-century accounts of the existence of these places. His assertion is not without its interpretive attractions, but it simply cannot be substantiated on the basis of available evidence. Similarly, Mukhtar's willingness to embrace the self-identification of the Geledi clan of the lower Shabelle region with the 'Umani Julanda tribe (which he does not document) seems no different from the northern claims of clan descent from two early Arab migrants (which he very reasonably questions). Finally, I am concerned that in rejecting the northern and nomadic bias that has dominated the paradigm of Somali studies unchallenged for at least a generation, Mukhtar runs the risk of inventing a southern and agropastoral paradigm that is as least as freighted with regional ethnocentrism as that which it seeks to replace.

Catherine Besteman takes a more restricted but no less significant topic in her careful analysis of "The Invention of Gosha: Slavery, Colonialism, and Stigma in Somali History." See pp. 43–62 of these proceedings.) Focusing her analysis on "the creation of 'The Gosha' as a social category by colonial governments through official discourse and political practices, and by Somalis through ideologically constructed perceptions of difference and hierarchy," Besteman begins by examining the historical roots of the Gosha (the term refers to the forested banks of the lower Jubba River) in the 19th and early 20th centuries, emphasizing the slave origins of these communities and Somali clan affiliation "as an important force in shaping village identity."[6] She then proceeds to discuss some of the perceived characteristics of the people of the Gosha as she encountered them in the field in 1987–1988. These perceptions focus on physical appearance and magical powers. The former serves to distinguish the Gosha from indigenous Somali — a term I prefer to Besteman's utilization of "pure" Somali, which strikes me as being value-laden despite her disclaimers — and reflects the kind of universal representation of the Other with which every society is familiar. While she provides a very stimulating reconstruction of how the lower status of the people of the Gosha evolved, it seems to me that, by separating her analysis of Somali components of this ethnic description and the colonial contributions to its formulation, Besteman may have underestimated the dialectical relationship between the two. For example, in her discussion of the refusal of the Somalis of Kismayu District to be categorized as Africans, she does not really consider that the severity of Somali reactions may have been driven as much by their perception of the racial hierarchy of the British colonial regime as by their own sense of racial superiority. Here I think her analysis would have benefited from insertion into the broader context of other historical studies of the creation of tribes in colonial Africa.[7]

Finally, Besteman explores the formation of Gosha self-identity, drawing upon her fieldwork to provide insights to the internal dynamics of these communities that corraborate the work of others. I would have liked, however, to have seen her address Cassanelli's more historical reading of "the emergence of a Gosha-wide culture" in the 19th century.[8] In this context, too, Besteman's neglect to follow up on her identification of indigenous Somali perceptions of the reputed magical powers of the Gosha is regrettable, since Cassanelli identifies mystical knowledge as an important element in the integration of the Gosha communities before the imposition of colonial rule. Indeed, juxtaposing Cassanelli's reading of the social history of the Gosha with Besteman's reinforces my suspicion that the present-day stigmatization of the Gosha derives primarily from the impact of colonialism on the Jubba region. Nevertheless, Besteman's careful delineation of the way in which the Gosha came to represent the Other in southern Somali society helps to explain at least partly the vehemence with which they were attacked during the civil war that devastated Somalia in 1992-1993. I wish, however, that I could share her hope that "perhaps taking a nationalistic perspective and referring to riverine farmers as minorities is the best approach" to securing for the Gosha "a place of representation and participation in national politics". But as Basil Davidson has so eloquently argued recently, nationalistic perspectives have not served Africa well.[9]

Christine Ahmed's paper, "Finely Etched Chattel: The Invention of a Somali Woman," (see pp. 57–189 of these proceedings) raises important questions about the legacy of androcentric scholarship for Somali studies and on the need for an entirely new research agenda to uncover the reality of the historical experience of Somali women. Although her bold attack on prevailing interpretations of Somali women may strike some readers as overstated or too strident, her careful analysis merits serious attention from all students of Somali society. From her opening dissection of Richard Burton's observations about Somali women, Ahmed contends that their image as chattel has roots in 19th-century English literature and has been perpetuated more recently by an ahistorical anthropology which she associates with one of the doyens of Somali Studies, I.M. Lewis. Ahmed is especially critical of the recent work of Bernhard Helander, which focuses on gender. Whether or not one agrees with her every point about his interpretations, she raises fundamental doubts about the validity of Helander's perspective. Ahmed does not limit her critique to Victorian travelers and modern anthropologists, but points out that even some of the most important historical research on Somali society has either ignored or omitted women. Indeed, where Somali women are the object of scholarly attention, she concludes, the focus is overwhelmingly on those aspects of women's experience that emphasize their subservient position and exotic role in society: e.g., circumcision/infibulation and spirit possession.

After shaking up our perspectives, Ahmed issues some intriguing challenges to scholars who would understand the social history of women and of gender relations in Somali society, principally by focusing on specific feminist theoretical perspectives in anthropology and to different sources of evidence for reconstructing that past. Citing the stimulating work of Karen Sacks,[10] she invites us to explore more carefully, and with a different set of lenses than previously, the complicated web of gender and kinship relations that lies at the center of Somali economic, social, and cultural relations. She makes a strong case, too, for the potential of historical linguistics for opening up the deep past to questions of gender, as it has already to other aspects of African economic and social history. Above all, she urges researchers to talk to women, to listen to their experiences, and to record their versions of the past. Poetry, songs, and aphorisms have for many years been a major focus of Somali studies, so there is a rich literature on which to draw. Ahmed demonstrates how this can be accomplished by probing beyond current readings of some of this material in her discussion of Arraweelo, a legendary Somali queen. Ahmed's readers may not embrace her suggestion that there may have been a more matrifocal period in Somali history, but her willingness to view such possibilities in a serious light obliges us to consider no less seriously the meaning of the myth of Arraweelo, and similar issues, in the context of Somali history. Finally, if Ahmed assumes a somewhat polemical stance in challenging her readers to reconsider the received image we have of Somali women, her conclusion is judiciously temperate in reminding us that before leaping to new answers we need to ask many new questions of the existing evidence and to expand the fund of evidence available for constructing new interpretations of the past on the basis of these questions.

In his refreshing discussion of "Aspects of the Banadir Cultural History: The case of the Bravan Ulama," M. Kassim provides a constructive corrective to both Somali and Swahili historiography that will be appreciated by students of both. (See pp. 29–42 of these proceedings.) His analysis emphasizes the characteristic cosmopolitan inclusiveness of town Islam and places his approach squarely in the mainstream of historians who study the coast. By reminding us of the central significance of this stretch of the coast of eastern Africa, Kassim also provides both an excellent short overview of Banadir history and opens up new prospects for research. For example, one hopes that more of the poetry produced by the five *Ulama* whom he discusses will become accessible to a wider audience, since it clearly provides a unique perspective on Banadir society, as Kassim suggests in his essay. Exemplifying the kind of awareness that Ahmed calls for, Kassim also draws our attention to the singular life of the well born Dada Masiti, an important woman *alim,* poet, and saint. Her kidnapping at Brava and decade-long separation from her family at Zanzibar remind us once again of the vulnerability of female children during the 19th century. At the same time, her retrieval by relatives and return to Brava highlights the interconnectedness of the coast and, especially, of its elite families. Finally, his emphasis on the importance of and open access to education in these towns, while it helps to explain, also raises the question of how we are to explain the emergence of the Banadir to a position of cultural centrality for the coast as a whole.

Kassim's section on the charisma of Sheikh Uways focuses on an incident in the history of Mogadishu that involves a religious conflict over a popular and profane dance called *manyas.* Although his analysis of this episode emphasizes its resolution by the intervention of Sheikh Uways on the side of the faithful and the adoption of an equally popular Uwaysiya *dhikr,* he neglects to mention the obvious point that from a popular cultural perspective, what we have here is the replacement of one form of communal dance by another. It is as neat an illustration in Africa of the conflict between profane and sacred as one is likely to find. Because of Kassim's attention to issues of Banadir culture, I hope that in future publications he will investigate other aspects of this rich history and, especially, that he will seek to situate the towns of the Banadir in the context of the coastal hinterland, as well as in that of the coast.

So where do Somali Studies go from here? Do we simply invent a new Somalia, now that the old is discredited? I think not. For one thing, the Hegelian process of scholarly progress does not hold out much promise since there is so much evidence that the models by which we view the Somali past, in particular, are seriously flawed. For another, with the Somali state in disarray and no clear future yet in sight, we are momentarily unburdened of the influence of a Somali nation-state that has dominated and distorted our collective perspective for the past generation. Let me make it clear that this is not to say that the contributions of those upon whose shoulders we stand are either negligible or without merit. Indeed, without their pioneering work we would all be the poorer. But the responsibility for reinterpreting their work and for developing a more complex, nuanced understanding of the Somali past needs to be disentangled both from the burden of the past and from the political struggles of the moment. And that is our responsibility. If we have been misled by the invention of a Somalia that never, in fact, existed, let us not reinvent a counterfactual one that would be equally divorced from the reality of the past.

Notes

1. Eric Hobsbawm and Terence Ranger, eds., *The Invention of Tradition* (Cambridge: Cambridge University Press–Past and Present Publications, 1983), 1.
2. *Ibid.*, 13-14.
3. Ali Abdirahman Hersi, "The Arab Factor in Somali History: The origins and development of Arab enterprise and cultural influence in the Somali Peninsula," Ph.D. dissertation, University of California, Los Angeles, 1977.
4. Edward A. Alpers, "Dance and Society in Nineteenth-Century Muqdisho," in Thomas Labahn (ed.), *Proceedings of the Second International Congress of Somali Studies, 2: Archaeology and History* (Hamburg: University of Hamburg, 1984), 127-144.
5. Cf. Lionel Casson, ed., *The Periplus Maris Erythraei* (Princeton: Princeton University Press, 1989); G.W.B. Huntingford, ed., *The Periplus of the Erythraen Sea* (London: The Hakluyt Society, 2nd series, no. 151, 1989).
6. Examples of the geographical naming of peoples abound throughout Africa. An especially relevant one for comparison to the Gosha situation may be that of the Mijikenda, who inhabit the hinterland of the Kenya coast and who were known during the

colonial era by the etic name of WaNyika, from *nyika* (KiSwahili), "open, bare, treeless wilderness, open forest with high grass, a barren, desolate region" (*A Standard Swahili -English Dictionary*).

7. See, e.g., John Iliffe, *A Modern History of Tanganyika* (Cambridge: Cambridge University Press, 1979); Leroy Vail, ed., *The Creation of Tribalism in Southern Africa* (Berkeley and Los Angeles: University of California Press, 1991).

8. Lee V. Cassanelli, "Social Construction on the Somali Frontier: Bantu Former Slave Communities in the Nineteenth Century," in Igor Kopytoff, ed., *The African Frontier-The Reproduction of Traditional African Societies* (Bloomington and Indianapolis: Indiana University Press, 1989), 216-238.

9. Basil Davidson, *The Black Man's Burden: Africa and the Curse of the Nation-State* (New York: Times Books, 1992).

10. Karen Sacks, *Sisters and Wives: The past and future of sexual equality* (Westport, Connecticut: Greenwood Press, 1979).

THE EASTERN HORN OF AFRICA, 1000 B.C. TO 1400 A.D.:

THE HISTORICAL ROOTS

∽

Christopher Ehret

The Eastern Horn of Africa — the collection of regions lying east of the Ethiopian rift valley and extending from the Gulf of Aden on the north to far northern Kenya at the south — has been home to a great variety of societies and cultures over the past 3,000 years, and it remains culturally and socially diverse even today. We might wish to begin our story back in the millennia before 1000 B.C., for which archeology is the primary tool, but that field of knowledge has barely begun to uncover the material remains of earlier human history in the Eastern Horn. With the resources available to us so far, principally those of language, we can, however, trace the history of this geographically diverse slice of Africa, with some confidence and in some detail, back into the last millennium B.C.[1]

The Eastern Horn in the Earlier First Millennium B.C.

During the centuries between the 10th and the 3rd or 2nd century B.C., six different ethnic groupings of communities, following broadly three different kinds of economies, occupied the greater portion of the Eastern Horn (see Map 1).

At the far north, in the areas extending from the Danakil depression nearly to Cape Gwardafuy, lived peoples of the North-Lowland subgroup of the Eastern Cushites. The initial settlement of North-Lowland communities in those parts of the Eastern Horn may date from as early as 3000 B.C.[2] Two North-Lowland languages, Afar and Saho, are still spoken today by societies residing to the west of northern Somalia. However, the North-Lowland peoples who inhabited the countries stretching from the Harar-Hargeysa area eastward toward Cape Gwardafuy during the last millennium B.C. did not speak an early form of Afar or Saho, but rather a different, although closely related, North-Lowland language of their own. The name "Ahmar-Dharoor" peoples can be proposed for them, descriptive of the probable extent of their lands, from the Ahmar Mountains near Harar to the Dharoor Tog, the annual stream *(tog)* which empties into the sea near Cape Gwardafuy.

The Ahmar-Dharoor communities raised cattle wherever they could do so, probably even in some northeastern areas of the Horn where today few or no cattle are kept; and they surely raised sheep and goats in larger numbers than cattle. Their favored areas of settlement, because of their cattle-keeping emphasis, are likely to have lain especially in the higher grazing areas, such as between Harar and Hargeysa and around modern-day Ceerigaabo. But they would just as likely have settled in more scattered fashion wherever reliable year-round wells or surface water for supplying their cattle could be found, such as in upper parts of the Dharoor and Nugaal watersheds of the farther northeast. Their territories, by the close of the last millennium B.C., had come to extend also southward from the Harar-Hargeysa region into grazing lands along and to the north of the middle and upper middle Shabelle River. The Fafen Tog, which courses southward from Jigjiga toward the middle Shabelle, would have been among the likely points of attraction for their settlements.

In the higher areas of the northwest, and perhaps also in favored locations elsewhere, the Ahmar-Dharoor peoples would have cultivated grains. The evidence from slightly later times, in the first millennium A.D., tells us that some of the more westerly communities, inhabiting the cooler highlands from Harar to the Hargeysa region, were able to grow wheat, probably along with other crops of similar climatic requirements, and used the plow as a major farming implement.[3] How much farther back in time this kind of agricultural practice was in place in those areas is not yet known.

A second region of early established agriculture lay farther south, in the riverine areas of modern-day southern Somalia and along and inland from the coasts between the Jubba and Tana rivers. Here the dominant farming communities of the early last millennium B.C. spoke a language apparently belonging to the Dahaloan branch of Southern Cushitic. They raised cattle, sheep, and goats, and, living in a hot lowland climate, cultivated crops such as sorghum, African groundnuts, and black-eyed peas. Just how much earlier these Southern Cushites had settled in the lower Jubba and Shabelle river regions is as yet unclear, but their presence there surely antedated 1000 B.C. and could date from as early as 3000 B.C.[4]

The riverine region poses a variety of challenges to food-producing societies. Some areas, especially along the rivers or near old, former river channels, as around Diinsoor, have relatively rich alluvial soils. Interspersed elsewhere through the region are soils of good fertility but dependent on seasonal rain for cultivation, as around Baydhawo; of alkaline soils unsuited to cultivation and problematic for grazing; and of infertile sandy soils especially in the immediate coastal hinterland and in the Doy areas. We suspect that the Dahaloans tended particularly to exploit the areas of good soil fertility where seasonal rainfall was essential to cultivation, and that they tended to avoid the areas right along the rivers, where the tsetse fly would have been a serious threat in those times to their cattle herds.

A third important set of farming and herding communities, the Eastern Omo-Tana, inhabited the grasslands of the far southeast edges of the Ethiopian highlands. (The proto-Eastern Omo-Tana language was previously given the interim name, "proto-Soomaali-I" or simply "proto-Soomaali"; see note 5). From their language derive all the several distinct modern languages — Bayso, Jiiddu, Rendille, Tunni, Garre, Maay, and Maxay Soomaali — considered to form the extended Soomaali subgroup of the South-Lowland East Cushitic languages. Bayso and Jiiddu together form the Genale branch of Eastern Omo-Tana; the remainder of the languages comprise the Dawo ("Soomaali-II" or "Sam") branch.[5]

Residing in parts of the far upper Jubba watershed, the proto-Eastern Omo-Tana began to diverge early in the last millennium B.C. into two separate societies. The territories of the more northerly of these two societies, the proto-Genale, extended probably from the Ethiopian Rift Valley, just east of Lake Abaya, eastward through the lands that lie immediately to the south of the highlands of modern-day Arusi and Bali. Their country is likely to have centered around the upper watershed of the Genale River, a major tributary of the Jubba — hence the name given to them here. The second Eastern Omo-Tana people of the early last millennium B.C. occupied areas slightly farther south, centering probably on the watershed of the Dawo River; this people we can thus call the proto-Dawo.

Both the Eastern Omo-Tana societies of the early last millennium B.C. appear to have strongly emphasized livestock-raising in their economy. The proto-Genale certainly cultivated grain crops, notably sorghum and probably barley (see note 6), along with their herding of cattle, sheep, and goats. The proto-Dawo, whose lands lay at a somewhat lower altitude and were thus hotter and drier than those of the proto-Genale, may in contrast have specialized in cattle-raising while also keeping numerous sheep and goats. Their only grain crop may have been sorghum.[6]

A strikingly different economic strategy from those of the North-Lowland East Cushites, the Dahaloans, and the Eastern Omo-Tana peoples was pursued by the rest of the societies who lived in the Eastern Horn during the last millennium B.C. Subsisting on hunting and gathering, these peoples especially inhabited the areas least attractive, by reason of poor soils or low rainfall, to their food-producing neighbors.

The various food-collecting peoples belonged to as many as three distinct historical traditions. Nothing certain is presently known about the languages of any of these culturally varied communities.[7]

Hunter-gatherers of the Berdaale archeological tradition predominated, it appears, in such areas as those near Buurhakaba and Buurheybe,[8] and also to the north and east of the Shabelle River, in the Muddug and Hawd regions. The Eyle may be their modern-day cultural and economic heirs.

Other gatherer-hunters, of possibly a different cultural background from the Berdaale peoples, lived scattered here and there among Dahaloan farmers and herders in southern parts of the riverine region of southern Somalia and also to the south of the Jubba River. Unfortunately, we know next to nothing archeologically as yet about the food-collectors of those regions. The Aweer, who today speak dialects of the Garre language, are their probable descendants. The Aweer during the first millennium A.D. spoke a Dahaloan tongue themselves, as the Dahaloan loanwords in their Garre dialect show. Their forebears of still earlier times may have spoken Khoisan languages,[9] but that possibility remains to be explored.

Finally, scattered all along the coasts of the Eastern Horn lived small communities specializing in fishing, presumably the cultural forebears of modern-day Reer Maanyo people. Here some archeological information is available; but serious, detailed study and reinvestigation of this information has yet to be undertaken.

The longer-term trends of change, as well as narrower regional developments, in the Eastern Horn over the last millennium B.C. are as yet little understood. Indeed, in the northern and central parts of the Eastern Horn, major changes may have been few. The spread of the North-Lowland East Cushites into areas along the north side of the middle Shabelle River possibly dates to some time in that millennium. Considering the marginality of the western Ogaden to cultivation, this settlement might thus reflect an increasing shift toward dependence on livestock among some of the North-Lowland communities during that period. Slow population growth among the Dahaloan farming and herding populations in the interriverine zones probably also took place.

The use of iron in place of stone in tool-making began as well during the last millennium B.C. in northeastern Africa. In the Eastern Horn, this technological changeover most likely commenced to take hold first among North-Lowland peoples and then diffused southward, via the Ethiopian Rift Valley region, to the Eastern Omo-Tana communities before the end of the millennium. By the last couple of centuries B.C., iron goods probably also began to be acquired from time to time by people in the southern coastal and riverine regions. Such acquisitions would have come principally through irregular trade at the coast with passing merchants, who traveled south from the Red Sea to the East African port of Rhapta, in what is today Tanzania.

Cultural Transformations in the Riverine Regions, 100 B.C. to A.D. 500

Then, toward the very end of the millennium, a new set of factors began to impinge on developments in the Eastern Horn, and in the southern regions, almost abruptly, the pace of social and economic change quickened. New food-producing economies took shape in areas between and along the Shabelle and Jubba rivers, even in areas where hunting and gathering had predominated before. New ethnic divisions and a new complexity of subsistence specializations emerged. The prime movers in these transformations were three groups of communities new to the riverine region (see Map 2).

From the south, following routes that passed through the immediate hinterland of the Kenya coast, came small Bantu-speaking communities, probably as early as the first century A.D. These Pwani people, as we can call them, formed a northern offshoot of the much wider expansions of Mashariki Bantu ("Eastern Bantu") underway in East Africa at the turn of the era. Skilled in an agriculture adapted to moist, wooded country and accustomed to clearing back forest for their fields, they were first and foremost attracted to the then forested bottomlands of the Jubba and Shabelle rivers. Such areas, avoided as they had been by the earlier Dahaloan herders and farmers, lay open to immediate, unimpeded agricultural settlement. The Pwani brought with them the vigorous styles of dance and the drum-based percussive styles of music that came widely to be adopted by later interriverine communities.

At about the same time, two other movements, both involving Eastern Omo-Tana peoples, pressed into the riverine region from the west. In each instance the immigrant communities apparently passed across the dry, hot belt of land lying between the Ethiopian highlands and Luuq, moving from the upper Jubba watershed, with its adequate rains, eastward into the areas of similar rainfall, although higher temperatures, between the lower Jubba and Shabelle rivers. One set of communities spoke the dialect of the proto-Genale language that was to develop into the present-day Jiiddu tongue. The other new settlers spoke a dialect of the Dawo language for which we may propose the name proto-Doy (previously "Soomaali-II), after the local modern word for kind of inferior soils *(doy)* on which their animals may initially have been grazed. The two groupings of Eastern Omo-Tana peoples, it can thus be argued, took up settlement in quite differing environments.

The proto-Jiiddu, the society ancestral to the latter-day Jiiddu communities, moved into lands inland from the coast, extending probably from the Baydhawo area to the far lower Shabelle river. Excellent grazing for cattle as well as areas of good soils for cultivation characterize the districts where proto-Jiiddu settlement seems principally to have gone. The evidence of language indicates that they may particularly have established themselves in areas in which Dahaloan Southern Cushites had been prominent before.

The proto-Jiiddu seem soon to have grown into the most important society of the western half of the interriverine region, and their territories by mid-first millennium A.D. would have covered a much wider portion of that region than do those of the Jiiddu today. This former importance of the Jiiddu is apparent in the numerous Jiiddu loanwords found in the neighboring Tunni language and in the Maay language, dialects of which today are spoken across so many of the interriverine areas.[10]

The proto-Doy communities, in contrast, would seem to have moved into a variety of areas in and around those taken up by the proto-Jiiddu. In their day-to-day economic pursuits focusing on the raising of cattle and other livestock and little given to cultivation, the proto-Doy probably expanded across a scatter of less favored localities, stretching from the Luuq and Diinsoor areas toward present-day Buur Hakaba and Afgooye.

By about the 3rd or 4th century A.D., this scattered-out pattern of settlement had increasingly led to the divergence of the proto-Doy into three local groupings of communities. At the east, near the Jubba River and probably somewhere in the Baardheere region, there emerged the proto-Jubba society. This society in turn gave rise after about 1100 to the Tunni people. Two other groupings of Doy communities, the proto-Garre and the proto-Maay-Maxay (formerly "Banaadir-Northern Soomaali"), can probably best be located in central and southeastern parts of the lands between the two rivers.

By the 4th century A.D, then, a new economic and social arrangement of the cultural landscape had taken shape in the lands that make up modern southern Somalia. Several clusters of Pwani Bantu communities had become established along different stretches of the Shabelle River itself and probably along the far lower Jubba. The Dahaloan Southern Cushites had become a factor of decreasing importance in the historical configuration of the region, probably for the most part having been assimilated into the evolving and growing proto-Jiiddu society. Between the rivers the proto-Jiiddu formed a considerable set of communities, concentrated particularly in the southwestern and central parts of that zone. All around them, to the northwest and to the east, different proto-Doy communities had made a place for themselves, probably by utilizing those areas especially characterized by *doy* soils, adequate for grazing but poor for cultivation. Little used in earlier millennia except by hunter-gatherers, these lands would have been especially easily occupied by pastoralists like the proto-Doy communities, who were willing and able to use the land in ways that did not immediately, at least, impinge on the livelihood of the hunter-gatherers already established there (see Map 3).

New Developments in the North, 300 B.C. to A.D. 500

In the northern parts of the Eastern Horn, change of much less sweeping sorts characterized the end of the last millennium B.C. and the first five centuries A.D.

The most notable external impact came through the growth of seagoing trade in the Red Sea. At the turn of the era, several significant trading emporia existed along the southern shores of the Gulf of Aden, the most significant of these being at Malao (present-day Berbera). Other commercial sites included Mundu (modern Heys) and Mosyllon (probably near modern Boosaaso). A goodly variety of commodities were imported at these locations, such as clothing, drinking vessels, iron wares, and Roman coins. A lesser range of goods passed into the outward bound trade — mainly raw materials, in particular myrrh from Malao and frankincense from Mundu and Mosyllon. Tortoise shell also was a valued product of those coasts.[11] The Ahmar-Dharoor peoples probably locally took the lead in this commerce, although the hunter-gatherers of the far northeastern Horn may also have played a part in the actual collecting of the commodities of the trade.

Inland, around the Chercher highlands to the west of Harar, a new population element may possibly have begun to make its presence felt as early as the 3rd to 5th century A.D. Speaking a language belonging to the Ethiopic subgroup of Semitic, these proto-South Ethiopic people, as we call them, probably at first traveled from the Red Sea coast up the Awash River during the last three centuries B.C., seeking to tap the trade resources of the central Ethiopian highlands. Of recent northern Ethiopian extraction, they could have used their northern connections to act as the inland middlemen of the Red Sea commerce. But within a few generations they had begun to settle permanently in the upper drainage basin of the Awash River, marrying locally, assimilating large numbers of people from the local Cushitic communities, and becoming the nucleus of a new set of interior societies.[12]

Trade seems soon to have faded out as the basis of their livelihood, and their descendants, far more Cushitic than Semitic in their actual genetic ancestry, developed into an indigenous agricultural people. By the 5th century, an easterly outlier of these South Ethiopic societies — speaking a language ancestral to the present-day Harari tongue — had moved into parts of the Chercher highland and become the western neighbors of the Ahmar-Dharoor peoples.

One other factor, the coming of camels to the Danakil lowlands, probably also belongs among the developments of the era from about 200 B.C. to A.D. 500. Camel raising, of immense long-term significance for history in the Eastern Horn, was until as late as 500 probably little known farther east than the Danakil depression. In the Danakil it had great importance for the transformation of the Western North-Lowland society, from whom the modern Afar derive, into a people able effectively to exploit the desert resources. But the intervening highlands to the east of the Danakil, too wet for the camel, seem to have held up its full adoption in the Eastern Horn proper until after mid-first millennium.[13]

Camels, Commerce, and other New Developments, 500-900 A.D.

Between 500 and 900, an unusually diverse array of new historical factors and of older factors redeployed began to shape the course of events in the Eastern Horn of Africa. In both culture and economy major new configurations emerged (see Map 4).

In the riverine regions the ongoing expansion and differentiation of the descendant societies of the proto-Doy people entered a new stage by probably no later than about the

8th century. The prelude to these new directions of social change lay in about the 6th and the 7th centuries, when a number of the proto-Maay-Maxay groups resettled with their herds through a string of localities extending from the Banaadir coast northward along the Shabelle River, possibly as far inland as Buuloburti. Out of this new settlement arose the proto-Maxay ("Banaadir-Northern Soomaali") society, whose language was directly ancestral to the numerous modern Maxay dialects. Those Maxay-Maay communities who remained inland of the lower Shabelle River evolved into the proto-Maay, whose descendants remain so prominent in the interriverine region today.

The timing of these events may be in large part an unintended consequence of the previous several centuries of cultivating activities among Pwani Bantu communities. The Pwani peoples, in clearing the once heavily wooded, tsetse fly harboring lands along the lower and middle Shabelle, would have converted such areas into much more inviting places for pastoral settlement by the proto-Maxay communities. Once the Maxay — and in some areas such as around Afgooye, the Maay — began strongly to establish their presence all around these Bantu communities, the Pwani dialects apparently soon began to drop from use, leaving only a few traces behind in the modern vocabularies of the Maxay and Maay dialects of those areas. But other features of Pwani life, such as the musical and dance traditions, remained strong among the descendants of the Pwani peoples and have been adopted by many of the modern Maay communities of the region.

From the lands along the lower and middle Shabelle, the Maxay expansions progressed gradually northward, reaching as far as the highlands of the Harar and Hargeysa areas by probably the 9th to 11th centuries. The Northern Maxay ("Shabelle-Northern Soomaali") communities, whose movements carried the expansions forward into those regions, came as a consequence into increasingly intimate contact with the Ahmar-Dharoor peoples who had long resided there — a contact revealed in a growing adoption of North-Lowland loanwords into the Maxay dialects. The earliest stage of interaction appears to date from the very beginning of the rise of a distinct Northern Maxay society, located somewhere between Buuloburti and Jowhar at probably around the 8th century A.D.

Among the Northern Maxay groups who pressed northward up the river in the next two or three centuries, the North-Lowland East Cushitic influences grew still more strongly marked, with numerous North-Lowland loanwords entering the Maxay vocabularies, even in some cases penetrating basic vocabulary. The word *casaan,* displacing earlier *guduud* as the word for "red," is a notable such item.[14]

Clearly, the Ahmar-Dharoor communities must in those centuries have lived not only in the Harar-Hargeysa highland zones, but also as far south along the Shabelle River as the stretches near Buuloburti. The kind of borrowings apparent especially as the Maxay language frontier progressed northward show that these North-Lowland peoples were gradually absorbed into the expanding Northern Maxay society. Ahmar-Dharoor people may sometimes have formed the majority element in the localities along the middle Shabelle, when the first stages of the Northern Maxay expansions pressed into those areas around the 8th and 9th centuries. In the highlands from Harar to Hargeysa, erstwhile Ahmar-Dharoor people nearly everywhere would have comprised the majority in the emerging new Maxay-speaking communities of the 10th and 11th centuries.

If the Ahmar-Dharoor farmers and herders were already well established, why then should Maxay ethnicity have eventually prevailed? The answer to this question may be tied to another major development of the centuries between 500 and 900, the appearance in the Eastern Horn of the first large-scale camel-raising. Emerging first to the north of the Eastern Horn, among the Beja and Western North-Lowland peoples living in the Danakil depression of the Northern Horn of Africa, camel-keeping seems, from the economic vocabularies of the Doy and Jiiddu languages, to have spread from the Danakil to the riverine region no earlier than between about 500 and 800. Only around the 8th or 9th century can it be said to have become a solidly established set of breeding practices in the latter region.[15]

Camel-raising transformed the scope and reach of food-producing ways of life in the Eastern Horn. For the first time it would have become possible to utilize the poorest of the sandy soils of southern Somalia, where surface water was lacking entirely and grass was scattered and sparse. For the first time also the very dry lands lying to the north and east of the Shabelle River, and the even hotter and drier lowlands of the far northeast as well, would have become exploitable by pastoral people in a systematic and regular fashion. Similarly, too, the long north-south belt of very dry country lying inland along the eastern foot of the Ethiopian highlands, and passed over by the earlier proto-Doy and proto-Jiiddu settlements, would finally have become regularly exploitable by livestock-raisers.

What the overall evidence suggests, then, is that camel-raising indeed diffused from North-Lowland–speaking peoples to the Maxay of the middle and lower Shabelle in the third quarter of the first millennium A.D., but not from the cultivation-oriented Ahmar-Dharoor communities who lived in the Harar-Hargeysa highlands or even from their cattle-raising relatives along the Shabelle River. Rather, camels came probably directly from a different set of North-Lowland communities, resident in the Danakil depression and ancestral to the modern Afar, passing via the dry lands of the middle Shabelle into the hands of an already strongly pastoral and perhaps already expanding Maxay society.

Adapting more rapidly to the raising of camels than their North-Lowland neighbors, the North Maxay gained a strong new impetus for expansion. Now requiring added grazing for camels, they can be expected to have spread more rapidly than before and to have begun to settle in lands often well away from reliable water supplies of the Shabelle River or the Fafen Tog. In the Harar-Hargeysa highland areas, their raising of both cattle and camels would have allowed them to filter in and all around the farmable areas, taking up the extensive variety of drier or more rugged environmental niches that had been little used previously, and in time encroaching on the good farming areas as well. Their presence would even more strongly have been felt farther east, in the especially dry and rugged northeastern parts of the Eastern Horn, where cattle-raising North-Lowland communities would previously have been restricted to a few favored locales.

If this scenario is correct, the arrival of Northern Maxay people in the region would have begun to break down the contiguity of the Ahmar-Dharoor settlement areas and gradually to undermine the North-Lowland dominance of the cultural and economic landscape. The adoption of new social linkages, connecting the local Ahmar-Dharoor communities to Maxay clans and lineages, seems the probable mechanism by which accommodation between the competing ethnicities most often came about. Northern Maxay dialects gradually became the language of the land, and the new, imported kin ties usually replaced the old. By these processes the potentially disruptive pressures of Maxay settlement could be domesticated, while in most essentials the local peoples and often their older ways of subsistence could remain in place.

Oral tradition provides us another line of sight into this era of ethnic and language shift. From the distribution of relict clan affiliations among the modern-day Maxay-speaking groups, it seems evident that the original Maxay society of the 6th or 7th century A.D. was comprised principally of people of the Dir clan-family. Dir affiliation is retained today by only a few scattered groups at the extremes of the distribution of Maxay dialects, notably the Biyimaal of the coast south of Muqdishu and the Cisa of the Diredawa-Zaylac region in the north. In addition, the major later-arising clan-families of the north, the Isaaq and the Darood, both have in fact a Dir ancestry, although they mask it for cultural-historical reasons as a maternal descent connection.

A second clan-family, the Hawiye, in time became the predominant affiliation among the Maxay communities who live about the lower middle Shabelle. Hawiye tradition claims collateral descent with the Dir from a common ancestor, Irrir. But the narrowly contiguous distribution of most of the

Hawiya today favors an alternative solution — that their clan-family emerged at a significantly later stage as an offshoot rather than a collateral relative of the Dir. That conclusion also conforms to the view in most oral tradition that the Dir are the "oldest" of the Maxay Soomaali.[16]

In any case, it was the Dir clan-family that carried the Northern Maxay expansion into the Harar-Hargeysa highlands. The adoption of Dir kin affiliations by local, previously Ahmar-Dharoor speaking communities often then accompanied the ethnic and language shifts that turned those regions into Northern Maxay lands.

As might be expected, not all of the Ahmar-Dharoor peoples were fully integrated into the clan system of the emerging new social dispensation. The Gadabursi of the Borama area to the northwest of Hargeysa are the most prominent example. Though today a Northern Maxay-speaking people, their claimed connection to the Dir clan-family is apparently a tenuous and ambiguous one.[17]

Economy, Religion, and Kin: New Factors, New Directions, 900-1400 A.D.

For the five centuries after 900, three major historical themes stand out. The first in importance, because of its wide repercussions, was the rise anew of seagoing trade along the coasts of the Eastern Horn. The second, almost equally significant development, was the emergence of pastoral nomadism as a distinctive economic and social adaptation. With this development can be associated the spread of the new Darood and Isaaq clan-families. The third theme was the fuller and wider establishment of camel pastoralism, with or without nomadism, through the Eastern Horn. Note the necessity here of drawing a distinction between nomadism and pastoralism. Although the nomads were consistently pastoral, many other groups remained strongly pastoral without becoming fully nomadic in their residence patterns.

In the centuries right around the turn of the era, commerce first began to reach the coasts of the Horn in regular, yearly fashion. A number of ports, as we have seen, were in operation along the northern shores of the Eastern Horn. Along the Indian Ocean seaboard, the major trading focus of 2,000 years ago lay much farther south, probably in Tanzania, at the town of Rhapta, although merchants could find lesser stopping-off points for food and water along the modern Banaadir coast. By the 6th or 7th century this early commerce seems probably to have declined into insignificance, at least to the south of Cape Gwardafuy.

In the 9th and 10th centuries, however, a new era of sea going commerce commenced. In its volume and its consequences for the hinterlands of the coast, the new commerce soon far surpassed that of earlier times. The chief product coming from the Eastern Horn of Africa was ivory. Items of lesser importance included tortoise shell, rhinoceros horn, and ambergris, while along the coast of the Gulf of Aden frankincense and myrrh may still have retained some significance in the trade. Slaves may have been an early export farther to the west, from the Northern Horn, but did not become a significant item in the trade of the eastern coasts.

The major movers in the new commercial era along the Indian Ocean coasts were the Swahili, a Bantu-speaking people whose earlier origins lay in small coastal village settlements in Kenya. The Swahili derived from a subgroup of the Mashariki Bantu, the Sabaki, distinct from the earlier Pwani settlers along the Shabelle River. Already by the 10th century at least two Swahili cities, Shanga and Manda, had grown up on different islands in the Lamu archipelago; and numerous smaller towns had been founded all along the eastern African coasts by Swahili merchants, who travelled as far south as Chibueni on modern-day southern Mozambique seeking the commodities of their trade. Along the Banaadir coast, too, the Swahili came to trade, there founding, notably, the city of Baraawe and probably contributing also to the establishing of Muqdishu, one major old section of which has the name Shangaani, showing by its phonetic shape its Bantu origin (but as yet of uncertain meaning).

Originally stimulated by commercial demand from the Middle East, the new trading era, whether along the northern or the Indian Ocean coasts, established material links between the Eastern Horn and the early Islamic societies. These links in turn helped over the longer term to spread knowledge of the Islamic religion into the Horn. Already in Swahili towns of the 9th century there were some Muslims, and other Muslims would have lived as well in the ports of the Gulf of Aden, such as Zaylac. All along the Indian Ocean coast, however, the full establishment of Islam as the religion of the towns seems to have taken place in about the 12th and 13th centuries. For it is in those centuries that the major period of mosque-building and the wide use of other signs of Islam, such as Muslim burial monuments, began.[18]

Between 1000 and 1400, Islam commenced to be taken inland beyond its initial points of entry via trade, spreading from the coastlands into the interior of the Eastern Horn. There it competed with the indigenous Cushitic religion, a monotheistic system of belief in which God was called *Waaq* and associated symbolically with the heavens. The hereditary chiefs of clans and clan-families, such as the *rooble* of the northern Dir groups or the *waber* of some Hawiya groups, clearly originated as religiously-based clan heads, whose influence and authority came from their community ritual roles and the numinous associations of such roles in the old Cushitic religion. The name *rooble* specifically evokes the image of a chief with the powers of rain-making (it derives from the old Soomaali word **roob* ="rain"). Even today, this religion has left deep influences on the local forms of Islam in the Eastern Horn.

As for the economies of the interior of the Eastern Horn, it seems entirely possible that true nomadism took shape there only between about the 9th and 14th centuries. Nomadism is not, it should be pointed out, one and the same thing as pastoralism. People who emphasized pastoral pursuits to almost the exclusion of cultivation are actors of old in the drama of Eastern Horn history. This kind of emphasis dates surely as early as the proto-Doy communities who arrived in the inter-riverine region by early in the first millennium A.D., and it may have begun even earlier with the Dahaloan Southern Cushites.

But all these communities, although probably sometimes seasonally mobile, can be expected to have built lasting houses in which they lived the greater part of the time.

True pastoral nomadism, where the herding communities from time to time during the year pick up all their belongings, pack them on their animals, and move off to new locations, is probably a relatively late feature everywhere in world history. The earliest such nomadism in northeastern Africa likely took shape in the Red Sea hills and the Danakil depression of the Northern Horn. In the Danakil region, at least, nomadism probably depended on the coming of camels; there a fully nomadic style of life would have emerged during the first millennium A.D., if not somewhat earlier. And while camels began to be adopted widely in the Eastern Horn by the period 500–900, it is not at all certain that the nomadic herding of those animals had fully developed until after 900.

When and where, then, did a pastoral, fully nomadic way of life first appear in the Eastern Horn? The question cannot be answered for all time until we have much better archeological evidence than is presently available. But a reasonable conjecture as to the timing and locus of its appearance may nevertheless be made by inference from other kinds of evidence.

This conjecture proposes that the rise of pastoral nomadism was signalled in the far northeastern parts of the Eastern Horn by a particular set of social developments — the creation of two new clan-families, the Darood and the Isaaq, out of the Dir clan-family at around the 13th and 14th centuries. These two new clan-families became the strongest propagators of the idea that pastoral nomadism is somehow especially noble. Their areas of origin, both in oral tradition and by inference from the distribution of their primary branchings today, lay in exceedingly dry areas — areas often both rugged and rocky, as well — where the camel-keeping and nomadic habits together would have greatly enhanced subsistence productivity.

This proposed conjunction of events would have had one other accompanying element — the adoption of Islam. In intangible culture, the emergence of the Darood and the Isaaq seems quite clearly to have gone along with a shift in religious belief. The Darood and Isaaq differentiated themselves from their historical Dir ancestry by each claiming an Arab father and a Dir mother as the couple from which they all sprang, and tracing their genesis to that founding pair. The Arab fathers, who continue today to be revered Muslim saints, in both instances represent the claim of a particular new cultural ancestry; the Dir mothers represent the actually indigenous historical roots of the clan-families. The saints themselves were surely real men, despite their now legendarized status; their true historical roles, which made them so worth claiming as ancestors, presumably would have been those of the crucial proselytizers of the new religion, Islam.[19]

What made the era so powerful a time in the historical imagination that entire new clan-families should have emerged out of the old? Perhaps it was not one set of events alone, but the conjunction of the two developments that together transformed a people's sense of self-worth. Nomadic pastoralism converted them from economically marginal communities, able to raise a few animals with great difficulty in the driest and most rugged locations of the Eastern Horn, into people with an enhanced capacity to use their old environment and a practiced ability at moving that allowed them to seek out better areas elsewhere. At the same time, taking up Islam gave them a non-material claim to the prestige and worth of belonging to a world religion.

The practical consequence of the establishment of pastoral nomadism for the Darood and the Isaaq was their spread by the 15th century over wide portions of the lands north and east of the Shabelle River. In many cases, their early expansions may have proceeded into areas little used before by herders and not at all by cultivators. They may, in other words, have spread effective pastoral pursuits into some areas inland from Raas Xaafun and in the Hawd and Ogaden that in the 12th century may still largely have been hunter-gatherer country.

The ideas of pastoral nomadism may have been taking

hold rather more widely during the period than just among the Darood and Isaaq. A number of the Hawiya groups living near the lower and lower middle Shabelle River can be suggested to have been early adopters of this way of life. Perhaps, similarly to what can be proposed for the Darood, the emergence of the Hawiya as a distinct clan-family was in some manner tied to the economic changeover involved in nomadism.

Another area of probably fairly early spread of nomadism was the dry north-to-south belt of interior lands lying just east of the Ethiopian highlands. And a portion of Maay-speaking cattle-raisers living between the Shabelle and Jubba also took to nomadism at some less certain point in the past. But on the whole, the southern half of the Eastern Horn was a region of much better rainfall than the farther northeast, and in most southern areas fully nomadic existence may have had to wait until the Darood expansions of the last three centuries.

Even without full nomadism, the keeping of camels became an increasingly well established fact of economic life between 900 and 1400. In several interriverine areas of poorer soils or lower rainfall, the camel was adopted as an adjunct to the already well established raising of cattle.

The most notable step in the spread of camels came with the immense expansions of the Garre, a set of developments beginning most probably in about the 9th or 10th century. The Garre, a descendant society of the proto-Doy people, kept large numbers of cattle as well as camels, it appears from the linguistic evidence. Whether the adoption of camels, suggested to date to around the 6th to 8th centuries in the interriverine region[20], helped to trigger off the Garre expansions is not certain. The close sequential ordering of the two sets of events makes this possibility an interesting one, though. The directions of the Garre population movements, from some as yet undetermined part of the interriverine region, into the drier lands to the west and into the similarly drier interior of northeastern Kenya, suggest that camels, so well adapted to dry conditions, may have something to do with the Garre expansions.

South and west of the Jubba River, the Garre moved into

country where the local communities, both the hunter-gatherers and those with herding economies, still spoke Dahaloan Southern Cushitic languages. The pastoral Dahaloans were apparently fairly quickly assimilated into the newly dominant Garre communities. The hunter-gatherers, known today as the Aweer, remained economically distinct, although in time they too gave up their Dahaloan tongue in favor of the Garre language.

From the 11th down the 15th century, the Garre appeared to have faced little challenge to their control of the territories between the lower Tana River and the middle Jubba River. The Jiiddu and one Doy people, the Tunni, appear from oral traditions of the coastal Swahili towns to have raised cattle and crops to the south of the Jubba, in the immediate hinterlands of the coast. But the Garre continued to be the major people through most of the trans-Jubba interior until the coming of the Oromo into the region in the 16th century (see Map 5).

Looking Ahead: the Period from 1400 to 1900

By the 15th century the Eastern Horn encompassed almost as great a variety of languages and peoples as it had 2500 years before. One Bantu language, a dialect of Swahili, was spoken in Baraawe, even though other Bantu languages once used along the Shabelle had been displaced by the languages of the expanding Maxay of the period 700–900. Five or more distinct Eastern Omo-Tana languages, including Jiiddu, Tunni, Garre, Maay, and Maxay, could be found in different parts of the Eastern Horn. The hunter-gatherers had become a very small proportion of the overall population and, where they did persevere, now spoke Eastern Omo-Tana languages. But a new range of economic variety had come into being, from specialist cultivators to cattle-raising farmers to cattle nomads to camel nomads to merchants and townspeople.

Developments since 1400, better served in the historical literature than the eras we have been considering, have tended more often than not toward expanding the commonalities of historical experience among the peoples of the Eastern Horn. Islam already had become the most common religion nearly everywhere by the 15th century. In the southern regions, the Ajuraan imamate of the 15th and 16th centuries brought large areas under a single, loose rule. At the same time, commerce spread increasingly inland, strengthening the ties between different southern regions and between the coastal towns and the interior.

A different basis of cooperation took form after the fall of the Ajuraan state, in the emergence of the Rahanweyn confederacy of Maay-speaking communities in the interriverine interior. Then in the 18th and 19th centuries, a still different development, the spread of Darood communities southward via the river region and the dry western interior into the lands south of the Jubba, enforced another, often less welcome kind of common experience on many of the peoples of the Eastern Horn.

Over the long term, an increasingly complex interpenetration of different peoples with different kin connections and, in the south, often speaking quite different, even if related, Eastern Omo-Tana languages, took shape. Swahili in its Baraawe and Bajuni dialects continued to be important along the southern coasts; and in the 19th century, the slave trade coming from East Africa brought even an additional component of Bantu-speaking people into the mix, most significantly represented today by the Zigula-speaking Gosha of the lower Jubba river. That complex heritage is still in place today.

Notes

1. This article draws heavily on the historical research of the writer during the late 1970s and early 1980s in Somalia, on the evidence and findings in Christopher Ehret and Mohamed Nuuh Ali, "Soomaali Classification," in Thomas Labahn, ed., *Proceedings of the Second International Congress of Somali Studies* (Hamburg: Buske, 1984), and on the work of Mohamed Nuuh Ali, "*History in the Horn of Africa, 1000 B.C.-1500 A.D.: Aspects of Social and Economic Change between the Rift Valley and the Indian Ocean*" (University of California, doctoral dissertation, 1985). A Fulbright-Hays research award provided essential support for the writer's major fieldwork

in 1982, while other helpful funding came from U.C.L.A. faculty senate grants.

2. C. Ehret, "Cushitic Prehistory," in M. L. Bender, *The Non-Semitic Languages of Ethiopia* (Ann Arbor: University of Michigan, 1976).

3. This kind of livelihood is evidenced by a number of North Lowland Eastern Cushitic loanwords found in Maxay Soomaali, e.g., *irfi* ("plowshare") and *sareen* ("wheat").

4. Because the Dahalo language forms by itself one of the three primary branches of Southern Cushitic, its split from the rest of the group dates to the end of the proto-Southern Cushitic era, approximately in the second half of the 4th millennium B.C. If the earliest Dahaloans moved shortly thereafter to the coastal areas, their arrival there could well date as early as 3000 B.C.

5. See appendix to this article. The name "Sam" was used for the Dawo subbranch in B. Heine, "Some Cultural Evidence on the Early Sam-speaking People of Eastern Africa," *Sprache und Geschichte in Afrika* 3 (1981): 169–200.

6. Just two terms for a grain species, **mesengo* and **hadhuur* (Northern Maxay *hadhuudh*) are known to have been preserved from proto-Eastern Omo-Tana in the proto-Dawo language. The first of these only and always referred to sorghum. The second term apparently originally meant "barley," as it still does today in the Bayso language of the Genale subgroup. It was retained in proto-Dawo but shifted in meaning to "sorghum."

7. See note 9.

8. Personal communication, Professor Steven Brandt, April 1994.

9. The evidence both from Dahalo and from proto-Southern Cushitic support the conclusion that the pre-Dahalo food-collectors of the regions between the Jubba and Tana Rivers spoke a language or languages of the Khoisan family; see C. Ehret, *The Historical Reconstruction of proto-Southern Cushitic Phonology and Vocabulary* (Berlin: Reimer, 1980), chap. 2, and C. Ehret, *Ethiopians and East Africans*, especially pp. 10, 11, and 33.

10. Numerous examples appear underlined in the vocabularies listed in Ali, *History in the Horn of Africa*, Appendix II.

11. Lionel Casson, *The Periplus Maris Erythraei* (Princeton, N.J., Princeton University Press, 1989).

12. C. Ehret, "Linguistic Clues to Social History in the Northern Horn, 500 B.C. to 500 A.D.," in Taddese Beyene, *Proceedings of the Eighth International Congress of Ethiopian Studies*, vol. I (Addis Ababa, 1986).

13. These conclusions are consistently indicated by all the various kinds of lexical evidence for the use of camels found in the Doy languages and in Jiiddu; see Ali, *History in the Horn*, especially Chapter IV.

14. Ali, *History in the Horn,* Chapter V, cites a considerable number of such loanwords and shows how these words became progressively more numerous in the farther northern Maxay ("Northern Soomaali") dialects.
15. See note 13.
16. See mapping of Soomaali clan-families in I. M. Lewis, *The Peoples of the Horn of Africa* (London: International African Institute, 1955), fold-out map at end.
17. The sources on this point of interpretation are cited in I. M. Lewis, *Peoples of the Horn,* pp. 15–17.
18. Randall Pouwels, *Horn and Crescent* (Cambridge: Cambridge University Press, 1987), pp. 22–24.
19. These proposals derive from a carefully even-handed application of the usual interpretative techniques employed by historians elsewhere in Africa and the world for the analysis of the content and meaning of oral traditions.
20. See note 13.

Appendix 1
Relationships of Eastern Omo-Tana
(Soomaali) Languages

The Omo-Tana subgroup of Lowland Eastern Cushitic has the following divisions, as shown in Ehret and Ali, Soomaali Classification (earlier, interim names for the divisions are shown parenthetically within quotation marks):

I. Western Omo-Tana
    A. Dasenech
    B. Arbore, Elmolo
II. Eastern Omo-Tana ("Soomaali-I")
    A. Genale ("Bayso-Jiiddu")
        1. Bayso
        2. Jiiddu
    B. Dawo ("Soomaali-II"; "Sam")
        1. Rendille
        2. Doy ("Soomaali-III")
            a. Jubba (Tunni, Geeliidle)
            b. Garree
            c. Maay-Maxay ("Soomaali-IV")
                (1) Maay [dialects: Gelede, Afgooye, Diinsoor, Baydhawo, Bay, Xudur, etc.]
                (2) Maxay ("Banaadir-Northern Soomaali") [four dialect-groups:
                    (a) Banaadir: Xamar, Merka, Biyimaal, etc.;
                    (b) Baraawe;
                    (c) Jowhar; and
                    (d) Northern Maxay ("Shebelle-Northern Soomaali"), including all dialects spoken along middle Shabelle River and to the north and east of the river, also Baali, Digoodiye, and Darood dialects spoken south of Jubba)]

Appendix 2

Map 1. Eastern Horn of Africa, c. 500 B.C.

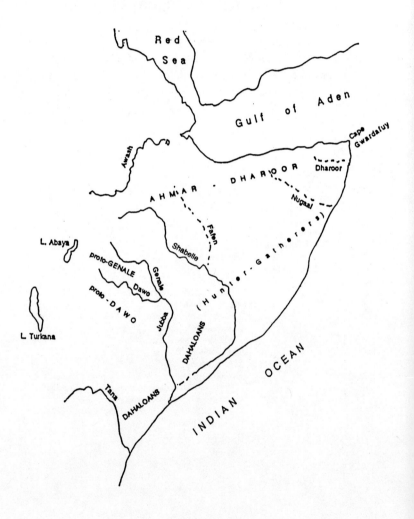

Map 2. Eastern Horn, c. second century A.D.

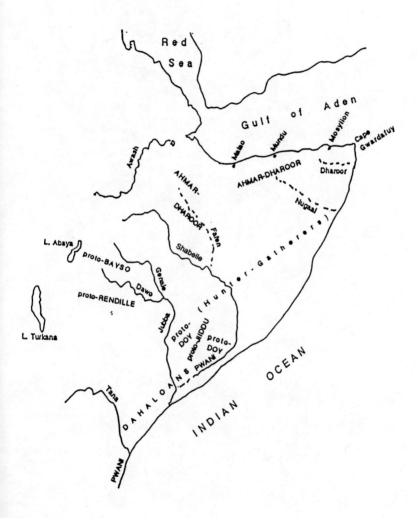

Map 3. Eastern Horn, c. fifth century A.D.

Map 4. Eastern Horn, c. eighth century A.D.

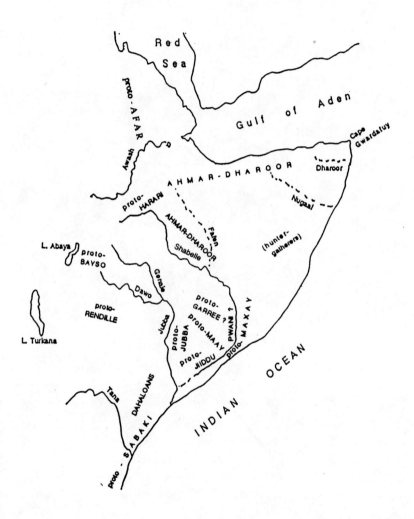

Map 5. Eastern Horn, c. fourteenth century A.D.

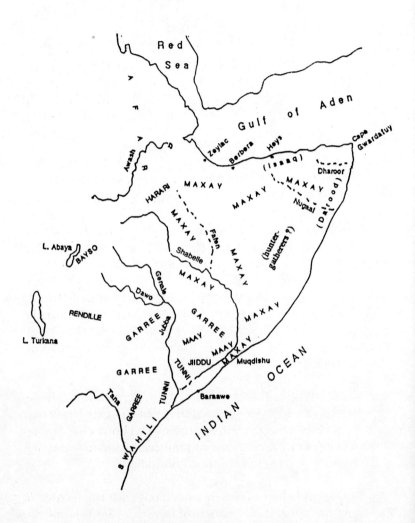

Contributors

Christine Choi Ahmed is a Ph. D. candidate in African History at the University of California, Los Angeles. She is a recipient of a Fulbright-Hayes Dissertation Fellowship, a Social Research Grant, and a Woodrow Wilson Dissertation Fellowship in Women's Studies.

Ahmed Qassim Ali was born in Hoddur, Somalia. As a hydrauli engineer he worked in the design and execution of several irrigation and civil engineering projects in Somalia. He opposed the military dictatorship and actively participated in its ouster. He is cofounder and editor of the Mogadishu weekly *Jamhuuriyadda*. Since 1992 he has been in the U.S. where he teaches and writes about Somalia.

Edward A. Alpers is Professor of History and Dean of Honors and Undergraduate Programs at the University of California, Los Angeles. In 1980 he was a Senior Fulbright Scholar in Somalia, where he taught at the College of Education, Lafoole, of the Somalia National University.

Catherine Besteman teaches Anthropology at Colby College. She has also taught at Queens College of the City University of New York and has published articles and book chapters on Jubba Valley land tenure, social identity, historical memory, and the current crisis in southern Somalia.

Francesca Declich is currently associated with the Center of African Studies at the University of London (SAOS) and carries out research among matrilineal groups in Northeastern Tanzania. Among other issues her present research focuses on the dynamics of adaptation to forced migrations. She was educated at the London School of Economics and the Istituto Universitario Orientale and afterwards has been Visiting

Research Fellow at the University of Oxford. The chapter contained in the book is based on fieldwork which was carried out along the Jubba River (Jilib and Jamame Districts) in Somalia between 1985 and 1988 and constitutes the main body of field data for her doctoral thesis.

Christopher Ehret, Professor of history at the University of California, Los Angeles, is author of scores of books on early African history and also a leading expert on Historical Linguistics in Africa.

Mohamed M. Kassim has a B.Sc. degree in Computer Engineering and is currently working as a senior programmer/analyst in Toronto, Canada. Mr. Kassim is a native of Brava, Somalia, and has been actively involved in researching the cultural history of the Banadir coast.

Abdi M. Kusow received a bachelor's degree in Sociology from Michigan State University in 1990 and a Masters of Urban Planning from the University of Michigan in 1992. He is currently working on his doctoral degree in Sociology at Wayne State University. His main interest in reference to Somalia is in the mythical concepts about the origin of the Somali people. He is also interested in the social structure/organization of southern Somalia.

Abdalla Omar Mansur, a former deputy Dean of the Faculty of Languages and Professor of Cushitic History and Languages at the Somali National University, is now affiliated with Dip. di Linguistica III Universita di Roma.

Irving Leonard Markovitz, professor of Political Science at Queens College and the Graduate Center of the City University of New York, received his Ph. D. from the University of California, Berkeley. He is author of numerous articles, books, and translations related to African politics and society. His *Power and Class in Africa* is in its sixth edition. In addition to his many professional activities, he has directed seven National Endowment for the Humanities summer institutes for college teachers.

Mohamed Haji Mukhtar, Ph. D. al-Azhar University (Cairo, Egypt), is associate Professor of African and Middle Eastern History, Department of Social and Behavioral Sciences, Savannah State College, Savannah, Georgia. Among his many studies are "The Emergence and Role of Political Parties in the Inter-river Region of Somalia from 1947 to 1960 (Independence)," *Ufahamu* 17, no. 2 (1989); *Somalia, World Bibliographical Series,* co-authored with Mark W. Delancey (Clio Press, 1988); and "Arabic Sources on Somalia," *History in Africa,* 14, (1987).